The Women's Directory

Women are now, and will continue to be, taking a much fuller part in the decisions which affect their lives. This book is a guide to the issues which concern women individually and collectively, and a directory of organizations, groups and resources. It covers areas such as job training, child care, money, the menopause, trade unions, rape, films, contraception, the Sex Discrimination Act, pregnancy, stress, equal pay, literature – and these are just some of the vast number of subjects discussed. It is a directory not only for those who already know of the changing possibilities for women but also for those who are just aware of these changes and would like to know more about them. It lists names, addresses, telephone numbers of the enormous number of organizations, of all kinds, of interest and use to women. With its discussions of the issues, resources list, bibliography and comprehensive index, the directory brings together fragmented information never before available in book form. It will be a standard reference book for all women and all those who want to know what women are thinking and doing.

VIRAGO is a feminist publishing imprint: 'It is only when women start to organize in large numbers that we become a political force, and begin to move towards the possibility of a truly democratic society in which every human being can be brave, responsible, thinking and diligent in the struggle to live at once freely and unselfishly.'

SHEILA ROWBOTHAM, *Women, Resistance and Revolution*

The Women's Directory

Carolyn Faulder,
Christine Jackson,
Mary Lewis

VIRAGO
in association with
Quartet Books London

First published by Virago Limited
in association with Quartet Books Limited 1976
A member of the Namara Group
27 Goodge Street, London W1P 1FD

ISBN 0 704 33805 X

Typeset by Bedford Typesetters Limited

Printed in Great Britain by litho by The Anchor Press Ltd
and bound by Wm Brendon & Son Ltd
both of Tiptree, Essex

Contents

Women's History:

some events that have affected women and some of the things women have done.

1792   Mary Wollstonecraft writes *A Vindication of the Rights of Women*, the first manifesto of the British women's movement

1812   bread riots throughout the country, often initiated by women

1832   First Reform Act passed, specifically excluding women from the franchise

1837   first Chartist petition prepared by London Working Men's Association includes female suffrage, but this clause dropped on publication

1838   first Custody of Infants Act allows the rights of access of a mother to her child, the result of a campaign led by Caroline Norton

1842   Coal Mines Act excludes women and girls from underground work

1845   during Highland clearances, women resist eviction while men run away and watch

1847   first Factory Act restricts women to a 10-hour working day

1849   one of the earliest strikes of women in industry (bookbinders) failed

1850   beginning of national agitation for female suffrage and women's property rights

1850s   first colleges for higher education for women formed

1857   first Divorce Act makes it possible to obtain legal separation or divorce through the law courts

1867   John Stuart Mill moves amendment to second Reform Act that 'man' should be replaced by 'person', and fails

1868   first public meeting of Suffrage Movement held in Manchester

1869   Municipal Franchise Bill passed giving women ratepayers the vote in local elections

1870   women elected to the newly created School Boards

1874	Emma Paterson organizes the Women's Protective and Provident League – the beginning of women's trade unions
1875	Emma Paterson and Edith Simcox first women delegates to the TUC; make a plea for equal pay
1875	first women poor law guardians
1877	Annie Besant tried for publishing a birth-control pamphlet
1878	Matrimonial Causes Act allows a wife to get a separation order and maintenance and custody of her children if her husband is convicted of assault on her
1878	further Factory and Workshop Acts regulate women's hours of work
1878	women admitted to London University
1882	Married Women's Property Act makes all the property of a married woman her separate property to deal with as she pleases
1885	W. T. Stead campaign on white slave traffic in young virgins to continent, followed by Criminal Law Amendment Act which raises age of consent from 13 to 16 and imposes penalties for procurement of minors
1886	repeal of Contagious Diseases Act after campaign led by Josephine Butler: the act allowed any woman thought to be a prostitute to be forcibly examined and imprisoned
1886	Guardianship of Infants Act gives mothers certain rights over their children: deserted wives can sue husbands for maintenance
1888	famous strike of match girls led by Annie Besant, successful
1888	first resolutions passed by TUC for equal pay
1891	courts decide a husband has no right forcibly to detain his wife in order to obtain restitution of conjugal rights
1891	first demonstration of working women in Hyde Park (laundresses demanding to be included in Factory Acts)
1898	Women's Trade Union League affiliated to TUC
1903	Women's Social and Political Union formed, at the home of the Pankhursts in Manchester
1905	first militant action of new suffrage movement: Christabel Pankhurst imprisoned

1906   National Federation of Women Workers founded by
Mary Macarthur and Gertrude Tuckwell

1906   first mass imprisonment of suffragettes following
demonstrations

1907   split in suffragette movement: Theresa Billington-Greig
and Charlotte Despard form Women's Freedom League

1908   Edith New and Olivia Smith chain themselves to the
railings of 10 Downing Street

1909   suffragette campaign turns to stone throwing and arson.
First forced feeding of imprisoned suffragettes begins

1910   Black Friday mass lobby of Parliament by suffragettes.
119 arrested, several seriously injured, 2 later die

1911   the Bermondsey rising of women factory workers wins
concessions on wages and trade union rights

1912   suffragette campaign of window breaking leads to
charges of conspiracy against Emmeline and Frederick
Pethick-Lawrence and Emmeline Pankhurst

1913   suffragette movement goes underground following police
harassment

1913   the 'Prairie fire in the Midlands' (thousands of female
operatives in engineering factories strike for higher wages)

1914   marches of the East London Federation of Working Women
for the vote led by Sylvia Pankhurst

1915   First World War brings suffragette activities to an end as
they demand the 'right to serve'

1915   half a million women go to work in munitions industry

1917   Women's Peace Crusade launched by Charlotte Despard
and Ethel Snowden to campaign against the war and
conscription

1918   women over 30 given the vote

1918   women employed during the war on munitions dismissed.
Mary Macarthur organizes a campaign for unemployment
pay

1918   female transport workers all over the country strike for the
same pay increases as men

1919   first woman elected to Parliament, Constance de Markiewicz for Sinn Fein; does not take her seat

1919 Sex Disqualification Removal Act declares that no one should be disqualified from holding public office or civil or judicial posts by their sex or the fact of their marriage

1919 enactment of Maternity and Child Welfare Bill which provides for advice, treatment and social assistance for pregnant women

1928 women get the vote on the same basis as men

1931 home service of civil service opened to women, but they must resign on marriage

1936 Abortion Law Reform Association founded

1937 Matrimonial Cause Act extends grounds for divorce to cruelty, desertion and insanity

1945 women again lose their jobs after working during Second World War

1967 Abortion Act passed, allows abortion in certain circumstances

1968 Strike of women machinists stops production at Fords

1970 first national conference of the Women's Liberation Movement in Britain

1970 Equal Pay Act passed, to become law in 1975

1971 first national women's liberation demonstration for equal pay, equal education and job opportunities, 24-hour nurseries, free contraception and abortion on demand

1972 campaign for rights by night cleaners, with support of members of women's liberation

1974 British women married to foreigners given the same right as men for their spouses to live in Britain

1974 contraceptive advice and supplies made available free on the National Health Service

1975 Sex Discrimination Act becomes law, making illegal discrimination on grounds of sex in employment, advertising and the provision of goods, facilities and services.

Introduction and Acknowledgements

This book is a guide to many of the issues which concern women, individually and collectively, and a directory of organizations, groups and resources. It discusses and gives practical information on subjects such as job training, the menopause, wages for housework, nursery provisions, contraception, trade unions, battered wives, the Sex Discrimination Act – and many others. There is information on novelists, films by and about women, groups to join, conferences, women's studies, organizations which help, and so on. It is a directory not only for those who already know of the changing possibilities for women, but also for those who are just aware of these changes and would like to know more about them.

There is a growing number of books and articles about women and we have tried to bring together some of the main ideas and concerns of these into one volume. Coverage of some issues is brief: we have been limited by space. But we've included sections on what we feel are the main aspects of women's role in Britain in the 1970s, at the same time guiding readers to further sources and resources. The bibliography and resources sections are very full and include details of help and self-help groups: and we have cross-referenced throughout the book. We haven't been able to give the price of all the publications mentioned: but wherever possible we have recommended pamphlets and cheaper books.

Some things had to be left out altogether. In particular we regret that we haven't discussed the special problems of women who belong to national minority groups in the country. We have deliberately avoided duplicating the material in *Women's Rights: A Practical Guide* by Anna Coote and Tess Gill (p.224), a mine of information about the laws and regulations which affect women and the means by which women can defend and extend their rights.

Chapters of the book have been written by different authors. We have sometimes argued and disagreed on the opinions expressed, but our collaboration throughout has been so close and stimulating that we decided to present the book as the product of joint authorship. The section Celebrations was prepared by others, and we want to thank the following for their contributions: Verina Glaessner on film, Cathy Itzin on theatre, Alison Weir on literature, Meredith

Oakes on music, members of the Women's Free Arts Alliance on the visual arts. Our grateful thanks go to Liz Mackie and the National Council for Civil Liberties for permission to reproduce the cartoons on pp. 88, 116, 120, 134, to Jeanette Sutton, Liz Mackie and *Spare Rib* for permission to reproduce those on pp. 3, 27, 137, to the Science for the People collective for permission to reproduce those on pp. 32, 62, 69, 77, 79, and to *Women's Report* for permission to reproduce those on pp. 104, 108, 114, 155. Our greatest debt is to Ursula Owen, of Virago, who was present at all our meetings, and should really be included among our number.

By the time of publication there will inevitably be some inaccuracies and exclusions: this will be particularly true of some of the women's organizations. Groups change, ideas change and individuals move; this fluidity and flexibility is an important creative part of the women's movement. Wherever possible we have given the address of more permanent contacts as well as details of individual group convenors.

Finally we would like to say that we have all been involved in the women's movement for a number of years. We have written this book partly to share our experiences with others and partly to celebrate the existence and positive achievements of the movement.

We hope to produce further editions, and ask our readers to help by sending information about groups and activities, and any other information which might be useful in this directory.

Carolyn Faulder, Christine Jackson, Mary Lewis, 1976

How to use this directory

The directory is divided into sections, which are listed on the contents page. These sections contain information and discussion of issues, with names and addresses for contacts and further information, and references for further reading. In addition, you will often be referred to the resources and bibliography sections at the back, both of which are divided into the same sections as the body of the book. There is also a comprehensive index.

For instance, if you want to find out about grants for retraining, you look in the index under 'grants' or 'retraining', which will refer you to the section After School. There you will find information and discussion on the issue, some contact addresses, cross-references to the resources section After School for further information, and references to the bibliography section After School for further reading.

Our bodies
Our minds

Trying to understand how we live in our skins is an important development in women's lives. Now that victories are beginning to be scored on the traditional battleground of equal rights, women have come to realize that liberation must include the right to assume responsibility for their bodies, especially in areas connected with sexuality and child-bearing.

But you can't be responsible for something you don't understand, the functions of which you are not very sure about, perhaps don't want to know too much about, because you feel scared or guilty or disgusted by what goes on – especially 'down there'. Why don't we love our cunts the way we love our faces? Why do we so often feel ashamed to 'let go' in our lovemaking? Why do we sometimes take such a sneaky, sniggering interest in other people's sex lives? And why has most sexual slang become such an awful mixture of prurience and vicious contempt? 'Screwing' and 'banging' hardly conjure up visions of ecstatic tenderness and we use words like 'prick' and 'cunt' to describe someone really unpleasant.

These attitudes are fostered in ignorance and prejudice. For centuries penis power has reigned supreme. Human weaknesses have been credited to the womb, human strengths to the penis. Sex has been seen as meant mainly for procreation, and only incidentally for pleasure (men only) and the view that anatomy is destiny has been used by some as a weapon to keep women down, placating them with the consoling thought that only by bearing children can they experience true fulfilment, become real women.

This is not the place to embark on a full-scale study of the female body and human sexuality. What we can do is give you some guidelines to modern theories, particularly as they affect women, many of them now being put forward for the first time by women. Suggestions for follow-up reading are in the bibliography (p. 224).

Nor is this a mini-manual on sex techniques. There are enough of those around already.

As women learn more about their own bodies and their own responses, they are also learning that their sexuality is part of everything they do, think and feel, the images they have of themselves, their attitudes towards other women, their love for men and women. The physical act of intercourse is only one expression of an almost infinite number of possibilities in our sexual range. Sex is in our heads, in our hearts and in our genitals, and at different moments in our lives we want to play different themes. For some women fulfilment has meant working towards more honest sexual relationships with the men they live with or sleep with; for some, living a while without intense sexual relationships, possibly total celibacy; for others an acceptance, affirmation or discovery of sexual feelings towards other women.

Whatever direction we choose, there is no one way which is intrinsically superior to the others. Sex becomes miserable, secretive and destructive when there are no choices and little or no knowledge. So this chapter starts with the basic physiological facts about women's sexual and reproductive organs, links this knowledge to a woman's right to control her own fertility, then looks at some of the ways in which women can express their sexuality, discusses the nature of orgasm, and finally considers some of the mental problems women encounter. All the groups, organizations, clinics and books referred to are indexed in the appropriate sections at the end of the book.

A woman's right to know

Facts about menstruation

The *menarche* describes the beginning of *menstruation*, a monthly bleeding from the vagina, caused by the womb (*uterus*) shedding its inner lining (the *endometrium*) after the unfertilized egg (*ovum*) has failed to implant itself in the wall of the womb. *Menarche* can happen quite normally at any age between 9 and 17, but 13 is about average in Britain. It marks the middle stage of *puberty*, the transitional period of development from childhood to maturity, and signals the fact that the girl is now entering upon the reproductive phase of her life, which will continue until she is aged between 45 and 55.

Puberty usually starts some two years earlier, with developing breasts and the growth of pubic hair (covering the *mons veneris*) and axillary hair (in the armpits). A girl at this age frequently shoots up to her full height, whereas boys often continue growing taller into their early 20s.

The *menstrual cycle* is the time from the first day of menstruation to the first day of the next menstruation and on average lasts 28 days. However, longer and shorter cycles for the same woman within a year are perfectly normal, and many normal women never have a cycle which lasts longer than 21 days or less than 30 days. It's sensible always to make a note of the first day of menstruation so that you can establish the pattern of your menstrual cycle; then you won't be taken by surprise when your next period starts, and you'll also know immediately when it's overdue.

A *period* is the time of the menstrual flow, which varies with individual women from 2 to 8 days. The amount of blood loss also varies from woman to woman and at different times in her life. During the first year or so of menstruation a girl's periods are often irregular and painless, which may mean that she's not ovulating (*annovulatory*).

Ovulation is the release of a mature egg from one or other of the ovaries and is sometimes felt as a sharp pain known as *mittelschmerz* (literally, middle pain) on either the left or right side of the lower abdomen. Occasionally it's also marked by slight spotting of blood.

This is what happens during the menstrual cycle

A series of hormonal actions are controlled by a 'menstrual clock' situated in the hypothalamus gland at the base of the brain. This gland works like a computer, receiving certain information from the central nervous system *via* the cerebral cortex and relaying 'instructions' to the pituitary gland, also sited in the brain, to release the appropriate hormones at the appropriate time of the month. The first hormone released into the bloodstream at the beginning of menstruation goes straight to one of the ovaries to ripen an egg, usually only 1 a month. A girl baby is born with literally hundreds of thousands of immature eggs in her ovaries, of which only some 300–400 will mature during her reproductive life. The rest wither away. At the same time as the pituitary hormone is ripening the egg, the ovary is sending out its own hormone, *oestrogen*, which, also travelling *via* the blood-

FEMALE REPRODUCTIVE ORGANS (SIDE VIEW)

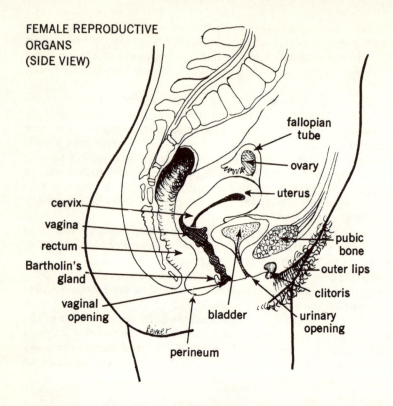

stream, goes ahead to prepare the *endometrium* for receiving the mature egg. At ovulation, about 14 days after the start of menstruation, the ripened egg bursts out of its follicle (a sac) to start its 6½-day journey down the *fallopian tube* to the waiting womb. Meanwhile, a second ovarian hormone called *progesterone* is being produced in the empty follicle, also a result of pituitary activity, which then races ahead in the bloodstream to make the *endometrium* the perfect reception centre for the egg, by now hopefully fertilized. If it is, as a result of union with the male seed (*sperm*), the egg implants itself in the moist, spongy *endometrium*, and new hormones to support the pregnancy are produced by the pituitary gland; if they aren't, the unwanted lining disintegrates and is washed out by the menstrual blood, together with the unfertilized egg. The whole process then starts all over again.

With so much split-second timing dependent on such a delicate, intricately-related mechanism, it's hardly surprising that most women suffer from menstrual discomfort at some time in their lives. *Amenorrhoea* is the absence of menstrual periods. It's 'primary' if a girl hasn't begun menstruating by the age of 18, and 'secondary' if her periods cease at any time in her life. Pregnancy is an obvious natural cause if she's been having sexual intercourse. Otherwise it may be due to hormonal imbalance, stress, disease or a congenital defect. If it happens to you, get medical advice.

Dysmenorrhoea is menstrual pain and there are two types, *congestive* and *spasmodic*. Both can be cured by hormonal therapy. *Spasmodic dysmenorrhoea* describes the sharp cramps, most often suffered by adolescent girls and young women, which begin on the first day of the period and can be very acute; but they wear off after a while and can be helped to disappear faster with a pain-killer, a hot-water bottle or gentle exercise. (Sex and orgasm is a sovereign remedy.) The pain is restricted to the lower back and stomach, areas of the body which are controlled by the uterine and ovarian nerves, whereas *congestive dysmenorrhoea* is general unlocalized pain and can affect any part of the body, often up to a week before the period is due. Typical symptoms include nausea, a dull dragging pain in the lower abdomen, a swollen stomach, puffy wrists and ankles (caused by retaining water), headache, backache, tender breasts and constipation. These physical symptoms are often worsened by feelings of lethargy, depression or acute irritation, collectively known as *premenstrual tension*, which is relieved only when the menstrual flow is fully established.

In spite of the obviously physical nature of both these types of pain, women are often told to take no notice and to pull themselves together, or are dismissed as neurotic by their doctor. Upbringing and social religious attitudes do have some effect on the way a woman reacts to this monthly manifestation of her femininity, but Dr Katharina Dalton has written a helpful book (p. 227) in which she says that mothers are more likely to pass on their physical tendencies to their daughters, rather than their mental attitudes. Doctors are only just beginning to understand the underlying factors in *premenstrual syndrome* (an accumulation of symptoms occurring in the few days before menstruation), but this much is clear: what was so often contemptuously dismissed as psychosomatic or neurotic

17

distress is far more likely to be due to a hormonal imbalance result-ing from the pituitary gland producing either too much or too little of the ovarian hormones in relation to one another or to the rest of the body.

Spasmodic dysmenorrhoea is due to too much *progesterone*, therefore *oestrogen* therapy is required, and for women who don't want to get pregnant, the contraceptive pill is an ideal solution. *Congestive pain* is due to a build-up of *oestrogen* and can be relieved by administering *progesterone*, a natural hormone, which is different from the *progestogen*, a synthetic substance, contained in the pill. Many doctors don't appreciate this difference between *progestogen* and *progesterone* and go on prescribing the pill to women whose symptoms then get worse because *progestogen* actually reduces the level of *progesterone*.

From earliest times men have regarded the monthly gush of blood with a mixture of awe and revulsion.

Many myths and superstitions about the menstruating woman have existed in all civilizations, usually to her detriment. She's been thought unclean, untouchable, a source of evil and, even today, in some corners of the world she'll be blamed for turning the milk sour or for making the meat go off.

In our own more sophisticated, but not all that much better-informed society, women are often dismissed as incompetent and incapable of holding down responsible jobs because of menstruation or the meno-pause. It's all too easy to blame a woman's mistakes or moods or plain inefficiency on 'that time of the month', but women don't have a monopoly on irrationality or mood fluctuation or hypochondria or neurosis or any other failing. Men aren't so obviously influenced by their hormones because their bodies aren't subject to the same regular cyclic patterns. But they are no less prone to disabling physi-cal and personality disorders, often due to a poorly functioning body chemistry, and no one suggests that this should prevent them from getting good jobs. There's indeed a good argument for saying that women are often better fitted for jobs needing a stable, responsible character because they've learnt to take monthly inconvenience, even pain, in their stride.

Facts about the menopause

This is the ending of menstruation and means that a woman has reached the end of her reproductive life. She stops ovulating and her *oestrogen* level drops dramatically. It may happen suddenly: from one month to the next she has no more periods. More often it takes anything from 2 to 5 years or even longer. Her periods become irregular and scanty. She may suffer from headaches, dizziness, nausea, painful intercourse (because her vagina is no longer lubricating) or any of about 20 different symptoms. Hot flushes and night sweats, sometimes bad enough to drench the sheets, usually come in the later stages of menopause after the ovaries have stopped functioning. Because of the long-drawn-out nature of this process, it's unwise to stop taking contraceptive measures until at least a year after the final period.

The average age for the menopause is in the late 40s, but many women have a natural menopause as early as their mid-30s or as late as 60. If a woman's ovaries are removed because of disease or as part of a total *hysterectomy* (operation to remove uterus, fallopian tubes and ovaries), the menopause will set in.

About 15% of women go through the menopause with no trouble at all. The rest are likely to have some problems, emotional if not physical, because the physiological process often coincides with a time for general stock-taking.

In our youth-orientated sex-dazed culture this can be devastating for the woman who suddenly realizes that she can no longer rely solely on her looks to be attractive; her children are leaving home, and maybe both she and her husband are feeling that they've not made enough of their life together and be looking elsewhere for a different life. The woman who hasn't had children, whether voluntarily or involuntarily, may regret this final seal on her infertility. Thoughts about death are inescapable and sometimes overwhelming.

Many women, however, find that the menopause brings in a new, more vigorous and enjoyable life.

They have time at last for all sorts of interests and activities which their previous domestic responsibilities didn't allow them and, finally released from the fear of pregnancy, they can really enjoy sex. Many women have orgasms for the first time in their 50s.

Hormone replacement therapy is treatment to replace the *oestrogen* deficiency which occurs when the ovaries stop functioning. It has many good effects, including restoring vaginal elasticity and lubrica-

19

tion, and getting rid of hot flushes and depression. In the long term it reduces the development of brittle bones, a particular hazard for elderly women, and enthusiasts claim many other advantages for it. In the United States it has been widely used for 20 years, but British doctors have been much more cautious about it and until recently it was almost impossible to get on the National Health Service. If you want to know more about it, first consult your GP, but if he's indifferent or hostile to the matter it's worth getting advice from your nearest NHS MENOPAUSE CLINIC (p. 199). Some women's centres are now also running menopause clinics. Alternatively, consult WOMEN'S HEALTH CARE, 7 Coniston Court, Carlton Drive, London SW15 2BZ, who can advise you where to find specialists and further information. It's very important that the treatment is given by a doctor who knows what he's doing because each woman needs an individually monitored dosage.

Another issue on which WOMEN'S HEALTH CARE can advise you is if you are worried or unhappy about your doctor's recommendation that you should have a *hysterectomy* (p. 19). Sometimes, not always, such an operation is suggested, particularly to older women not wanting any more children, for no good medical reason but simply because it's more convenient, in an over-burdened health service, for doctors to remove a problem by surgical means rather than by prolonged medical treatment. The after-effects of an unnecessarily induced menopause may be anything but convenient to the woman herself.

Recommended reading: *No Change* by Wendy Cooper (p. 227).

Women together: self-help and health groups

Men can look at their genitals, handle them, examine them, play with them and compare them with others because they hang down outside the body, while women's sexual organs are relatively hidden and inaccessible, except by touch. Perhaps you remember lying on a bed as a girl, in front of a mirror, parting your outer vaginal lips (*labia*) with your fingers and anxiously trying to peer up that dark hole; if you did you will also remember you couldn't see very much. You had to rely on your friends then and later your doctor, using a cold, steely instrument and a strong light to tell you what s/he saw. Many women have their first internal examination, as this is called, when they are pregnant, and it can come as quite a shock. Girls who use tampons and follow the diagrams telling them how to insert them are likely to know a little more about the position and shape of their sexual organs, but feeling is not the same as seeing. All this has changed since women have taught themselves the simple art of self-examination.

About 6 years ago a group of women in Los Angeles who were meeting regularly for consciousness-raising sessions realized that it didn't matter how varied their sexual experience might be; if they were fundamentally ignorant about their bodies, as they were, they were not only vulnerable to exploiting doctors, but they were limiting themselves as full human beings. In addition, they didn't have the advantages of a National Health Service.

So was born the truly revolutionary idea of self-help through self-knowledge. At last the mystique of doctor-as-god, with exclusive knowledge, was being challenged. SELF-HELP CLINIC ONE was established and gave guidance to other groups wanting to do the same. Carol Downer and others toured the United States and Europe, giving talks, slide shows and practical demonstrations of how a woman can examine her own vagina.

Since then, self-help groups, health centres and, in some places, women's clinics have flourished and are an important part of the women's movement. Some never progress much beyond the self-examination stage, but that in itself, for any woman who has experienced it among a group of women, some of whom she may already be close to, while others she hardly knows, is a unique expression of solidarity.

To overcome your inhibitions, to look, learn and be learned from, and then to share the same experience with each woman in the group is to make you understand what your own womanhood means to you.

What happens in a self-help group

Women learn to use a speculum, an instrument looking rather like a duck's bill which is used to open the vaginal cavity to allow examination of the vaginal walls and the cervix. With the use of a lamp (or torch) and a mirror, women learn to examine themselves for changes on the cervix which indicate other changes in the body. For instance pregnancy can be spotted very early on because the cervix changes colour from pink to a deep red or even blue. They learn to recognize the difference between the cervix of a woman who has had children and one who hasn't; they can spot yeast infections and also gonorrhoeal ones long before a woman might ordinarily suspect that anything was wrong with her. This means that she can get medical help in good time, instead of only when serious damage has already happened. Women also learn to recognize what a well woman looks like and that there are many variations of normality.

THINGS WOMEN LEARN

IN A BASIC SELF-HELP COURSE

How to use a speculum
Cervical examination
Pelvic examinations (feeling the position of the uterus)
Breast examinations (p. 47)
Pregnancy tests

To get the group going, you need an experienced woman to demonstrate these skills. It may take up to 3 weeks before all the women in the group feel at ease with their speculums, which they will be using at home between meetings as well as keeping a chart of the changes they notice. Some stop at that point. Others will decide they want to learn advanced self-help procedures including *menstrual extraction*. This is a simple, painless, safe method of extracting the menses on or about the first day of the period month, using a kit called the Del-'Em, which was invented by Lorraine Rothman (one of the founding sisters of the first American self-help group). *Menstrual extraction* is a 5-minute procedure which eliminates a 5-day nuisance, but it's not the same as the early abortion method called *menstrual regulation* or *interception* or *endometrial aspiration* (p. 42).

Other groups use their new knowledge about their bodies to campaign for better health facilities and information for all women, including a uniform abortion service, better ante-natal care and treatment during childbirth. Others are researching into methods of contraception and their side-effects (often played down by doctors); learning about diet and nutrition, herbalism, massage and other alternatives to conventional medicine.

> **Self-help doesn't encourage women to be their own doctors. It does aim to take the mystery out of medicine and to put control of women's bodies back where it belongs, in the hands of women themselves. Doctors are technicians, not gods, and their main duty is to put their expertise at the disposal of their patients.**

An informed woman knows how to ask the right questions about herself, understands why a certain treatment is being prescribed and is in a stronger position to take decisions, such as where she will have her baby (at home or in hospital), or what method of contraception to use.

Our Bodies Ourselves, written by the BOSTON WOMEN'S HEALTH COLLECTIVE (p. 226) at about the same time as SELF-HELP CLINIC ONE was being set up, is a marvellous manual on all aspects of women's emotional and bodily well-being. As well as providing clear, comprehensive information about everything women need to know about themselves, it includes women's own experiences (some of them very moving) and also gives an extensive bibliography for further reading. Penguin are bringing out a British edition soon.

A Women's Health Handbook (p. 227) is by Nancy Mackeith, who trained at SELF-HELP CLINIC ONE in Los Angeles and now spends much of her time travelling round the United Kingdom advising women and helping them to start their own self-help groups. This is a comprehensive guide to the work of these groups and their relationship to other aspects of the women's movement.

Plastic speculums (better than metal, being cheaper and not so cold) can be bought from medical supplies shops or obtained direct from Nancy Mackeith, c/o Feminist Books, PO Box HP5, Leeds. They are cheaper bought in quantity, so it's worth deciding first whether you intend to expand your group or link up with others.

A report of the Sheffield Women and Health Conference (the first of its kind to be held in Britain, in October 1974) is available from 8 Burngreave Bank, Sheffield 4, 15p plus postage. It contains reports from workshops and shared views and experiences.

For a list of established self-help groups see p. 197.

A woman's right to choose

There is a tendency to think that once we've got free, reliable, safe and easily available contraception for everyone – and we're still a long way from attaining that ideal – women's problems will be solved. The pill is often promoted as a solution to all discontents, but even were it to be 100% satisfactory for all women (which it's not), birth control, important though it is, is only one aspect of a woman's sexual life. For example, if something goes wrong and she becomes pregnant unwillingly, she doesn't have the right to abortion on request. That is directly denying a woman the right to control her own fertility. Some doctors will refuse to give a woman an abortion unless she also agrees to sterilization, and although they have no legal right to insist on this, the combined effect of her desperation and their 'moral' pressure usually makes it impossible for her to refuse.

Women are denied not only the right to choose; there are often inadequate choices in the first place. A woman may want to keep her child, but in present conditions a woman making this decision has to be very determined and brave. Lack of housing, nursery facilities or suitable job opportunities for a single woman with a baby drive her into isolation and extreme poverty – hardly ideal conditions for bringing up a child. A woman who discovers that she likes sleeping with other women meets prejudice and hostility in every quarter, even though lesbianism, unlike male homosexuality, has never been treated as a punishable offence. If such a woman is a teacher or social worker it's more than her job is worth to reveal her lesbianism. If she's a wife and mother, her husband will meet with extreme sympathy in the divorce courts, and she may well lose the custody of her children.

Girls are still being brought up to believe that marriage and children are the ultimate goals for their happiness and fulfilment, despite the visible experience of their mothers and all evidence to the contrary. One in four of all marriages in Britain now ends in divorce, and one-third of teenage marriages break up.

Unless women are fully informed about all the choices open to them, without moral or financial pressures, they aren't able to choose.

The right to choose motherhood

In the past women had no choice at all. They simply had as many children as their health allowed them and were usually dead by the age of 40. Today, those women living in the more developed countries can and do choose the number of children they will have, but very few consider the much more fundamental question: do they want children at all? Single or married, this decision is personal and individual, because although it affects and involves the father, it should ultimately depend on what the woman herself wants and knows to be best for her. Children shouldn't be conceived to prop up a failing marriage, or to boost a declining population or to make a woman feel 'truly a woman'. Becoming a parent changes your life drastically and for a woman particularly can be mentally and physically exhausting.

Yet what usually happens? A couple marry, sometimes without even discussing whether or not they want children. They simply assume that in due course they'll behave like everyone else and produce a family. Deprived grandparents drop hints, friends who are already busy producing demand to know why they don't join the club and many other people, often complete strangers, have only to realize that they are talking to a childless woman to launch immediately into a diatribe about selfishness, missed opportunities, a lonely old age and so on.

Not all women are natural mothers and some never learn to be mothers. The myth of the maternal instinct is a dangerous one. Women are taught to believe that they are born with it and consequently can be very distressed to discover that after all the effort they feel quite numb about this scrap of humanity that they've produced. Mother love is a fragile, growing perception of a new relationship. It takes time and peace and loving support to help a woman through the first days and weeks of caring for her child, yet so much is done to disrupt this initial process of learning, and through learning, loving.

Childbirth

Although often painful, childbirth should be a shared and joyful experience. In cold reality, it's often mechanical and de-humanized. In this section we briefly describe the stages of pregnancy and childbirth and look at some of the choices women should know about. For detailed information about what happens to a woman's body during and after pregnancy we recommend *Our Bodies Ourselves* (p. 226) and also suggest that you look at some of the other books mentioned in the same section of the bibliography.

Signs of pregnancy

The first obvious one is an overdue period. It's important to find out as soon as possible whether you are pregnant, which is done by testing an early-morning urine sample put in a *clean* bottle. Many WOMEN'S CENTRES (p. 173ff) offer free, on-the-spot pregnancy testing, as does the BRITISH PREGNANCY ADVISORY SERVICE (BPAS) (p. 198), which also runs a postal service. The PREGNANCY ADVISORY SERVICE (PAS) (p. 198) charges £1. Family doctors also do pregnancy testing, but usually for a fee, and it may take a week to get the results if they send the sample to the local hospital. Alternatively you can go to your local FAMILY PLANNING ASSOCIATION (FPA) or BROOK ADVISORY CENTRE (address in telephone book), both of which charge a small fee.

OTHER SIGNS INCLUDE

— **morning sickness (can be quite unpleasant but usually wears off after 3 months)**
— **swelling breasts due to milk glands preparing for lactation**
— **a need to pee frequently due to uterus expanding and pressing on bladder**

Ante-natal care

The moment a woman knows she is pregnant she should go to her doctor. S/he'll give her an internal examination and work out the date of birth, 40 weeks from the first day of her last period (but of course, babies seldom arrive on the exact day). Some GPs specialize in obstetrics (childbirth), and if you're lucky enough to have such a doctor s/he's probably the best person to see you through your pregnancy because you'll have personal, continuing attention from one person, whereas often in hospital ante-natal care a woman may never see the same doctor twice. Providing your blood test and urine sample are satisfactory and you show no signs of developing complications, you'll need only monthly check-ups for the first 6–7 months. The baby moves (quickens) at about 4½ months. It's important to look after yourself during pregnancy, which means eating well, eating the right foods, trying to avoid smoking or drinking or taking drugs of any sort (even aspirin is inadvisable) and resting as much as possible. This may be difficult if you're working and impossible if you already have one or two small children, but perhaps you can get a friend or neighbour to take them occasionally, or can organize a baby-sitting rota through your women's centre.

In theory everybody agrees that they're a good thing; in reality, they're patchy in quality, thinly spread over the country as a whole, and in some places (particularly in the North) they hardly exist at all. Sometimes they're run by the hospital, sometimes by the local authority and, depending on who is willing and available, they may be taught by a midwife, a physiotherapist or a health visitor, each of whom will have very different attitudes. There seem to be no evening classes or evening clinics for the working future mother in the National Health Service.

THE NATIONAL CHILDBIRTH TRUST (p. 199) runs natural childbirth ante-natal classes in most parts of the country. These are taught by women who are themselves mothers and have been trained to do the breathing exercises which will help you when you're in labour. Obviously they can't guarantee you a painless childbirth, but will teach you how to control your contractions and so take part much more closely in the birth of your child without being befuddled by drugs. They also involve fathers, so that the couple prepare together for childbirth. Over the years the Trust has won increasing respect from the medical profession, which is now much more ready to let women practise their methods in labour. But there are pockets of conservatism everywhere, and many women have been dismayed by the hostility they've met from doctors and nurses in hospital.

If there are no ante-natal classes in your area, it's worth getting Sylvia Close's record, *Practising for Childbirth* (£1.35 including postage) from the NATIONAL CHILDBIRTH TRUST (p. 199).

Where to have the baby – Home or Hospital?

Although Britain has one of the best domiciliary midwife services (for home births) in the world, doctors are now trying to achieve 100% hospital confinements, saying it's safer, more efficient and cuts down the risk of last-minute emergency dashes. A woman having either her first or fourth baby will find it very difficult to insist on having her baby at home because of the medical risks attached to either an untried uterus or a much-used one. Plainly, if you suffer from some chronic condition like diabetes or have any problems with your pregnancy, then it's essential to have your baby in hospital. However, if you want to have your baby at home and there are no good reasons against doing so, but your doctor won't agree, then contact the SOCIETY TO SUPPORT HOME CONFINEMENTS (p. 199), which is campaigning to help women in this respect and which has a countrywide list of doctors and midwives who are in agreement with its aims.

What happens at birth

There are 3 stages of labour. The first starts with pains in the lower back and with contractions, initially separated by long intervals, but the gaps gradually shorten and the contractions become more intense. When they have reduced to about 10-minute intervals, the time has come to call the midwife or to leave for the hospital. Women who have already had a baby may find that the whole process speeds up at this stage. A shave of pubic hair and an enema (to clear the bowels) are inescapable parts of the hospital routine, and then it's bed in the labour ward. This is the time when women badly need comfort and support and are too often left alone. Loneliness at this stage can be a cruel and frightening experience. Hospitals plead staff shortages, and only a few of them are sensible enough to allow husbands or friends to sit with women in labour. Women who've had a baby at home remember gratefully the comfort of a loving person rubbing their backs, talking to them between contractions, helping them with their breathing and hearing the soothing murmur of ordinary life going on around. Usually during this stage, but sometimes earlier or later, the bag of waters (*amniotic sac*) which has held the baby in warm floating suspension will burst.

The second stage of labour starts after a few very sharp, hard contractions, during which time the *cervix* dilates to its full extent (about 10 cm) to allow the baby's head (sometimes it may be some other part of the body) to come through. This is called crowning and is accompanied by very strong bearing-down contractions to expel the baby from its mother's body. Properly managed, this needn't be painful, as the birth canal (*vagina*) is an elastic, nerveless organ and the baby can slip through quite easily. After the baby has been delivered and the blood drained from the *umbilical cord*, this will be clipped and the baby slapped to cry (to expand its lungs) if this hasn't already happened during birth. S/he will then be weighed, washed and wrapped in a blanket.

The third stage of labour comes about 20 minutes after birth, when the afterbirth (*placenta*) is pushed out with a few contractions. This is the spongy, heavily-veined organ which has fed and oxygenated the baby during the 9 months of pregnancy. If the doctor had to make a cut to widen the exit for the baby the woman will now be stitched. This is called an *episiotomy* and is sometimes left to a medical student to do, which is wrong, because bad sewing can result in painful healing and may occasionally affect sexual intercourse.

The right to choose between natural or induced childbirth

The above describes the normal way of delivering a full-term baby. In fact many women are now experiencing a much more speeded-up, 'managed' labour in which the contractions are artificially induced.

With *induction*, the following usually occurs; the woman comes into hospital on a pre-arranged date, the evening before delivery is scheduled. The usual preparations are made (bath, enema, shave). Then at 9 next morning she is put on an *oxytocin drip* (a synthetic hormone to replace the natural labour-inducing hormones), which hastens and intensifies the contractions. This can be much more painful than if the uterus is left to get on with the job in its own time, so she will get more *pethidine* or other pain-killing drugs; yet it's well known that too many drugs during birth will affect the baby. It becomes quite literally doped up, often has to go into intensive care and has a poor sucking reflex. Sometime in mid-afternoon, or earlier if the drip has been effective, she may be given an injection into the spine (*epidural*). This anaesthetizes her from the waist down to give her a painless delivery, but also reduces the final-stage contractions, which means that about half of these induced babies are delivered with forceps.

Sometimes an induction is necessary, and if there are good medical reasons which are explained to the woman, she's probably wise to accept this: for instance, if the baby is very late or, alternatively, if there are indications that it should be born earlier than the due date because it doesn't seem to be getting enough nourishment from the placenta. However, it's quite clear that more and more inductions are being done for social reasons. Doctors don't want to be called out of bed in the middle of the night, night staff are difficult to get; making childbirth a 9 to 5 routine is so much more 'efficient'. Jean making childbirth a 9–5 routine is so much more 'efficient'. Jean Robinson, chairman of THE PATIENTS' ASSOCIATION, 335 Gray's Inn Road, London, WC1, and Sheila Kitzinger of THE NATIONAL CHILD-BIRTH TRUST (p. 199), have made separate surveys of induction based on reports from the women themselves and are seriously worried about several aspects of induction.

The lack of choice. **Women are just told to come in and induction is often not explained to them. If they dare to object, preferring to wait until the baby starts 'naturally', they are thought of as neurotic or troublemakers.**
The lack of emotional support. **Wired up to machinery, filled with injections and subject to all sorts of medical interference; husbands and friends are often shooed away, and nurses are too busy to give the encouragement a woman needs at this time.**
The loss of bonding. **It's known that the time after birth when a woman can quietly cuddle and examine her baby is important for establishing a relationship.**

Compare this with the *Leboyer* method of natural childbirth. Frederick Leboyer is a French obstretician who believes that we do terrible violence to new-born babies by hauling them out into a bright noisy world, holding them up by their feet like chickens, slapping them, dumping them on cold scales, wrapping them tightly in clothing and whisking them away from their mothers who may not see them again for several hours. He suggests that babies delivered in this manner are in hell, which explains the screwed-up eyes, the terrified yelling, the quick retreat into the foetal position and sometimes the reluctance to suck.

This is the way he delivers babies.

'After birth in a dark, hushed room, the baby is placed straight on to
its mother's belly where s/he starts quietly breathing. The skin to
skin contact is vital and the mother has a chance to stroke and rub
her baby. Together they recover from the battle fatigues of birth.
Then, when the umbilical cord has stopped beating, never before,
it's cut. The baby is gently lowered into a warm (body temperature)
bath and allowed to stretch its limbs. Often it smiles at this stage.
Then it's lifted out, wrapped in loose, warm soft clothing and left
alone for the first time but, unlike conventionally delivered babies
who usually start screaming at this point, the Leboyer baby is likely
just to shut its eyes and sleep.'

He has written a remarkable book called *Birth Without Violence*
(p. 227) describing his methods and has also made a film. Kate Russell (p. 199) is a midwife who delivers babies both at home and in
hospital, with a GP, by the Leboyer method. She can only help
women living in her area, but says that it's very important for
women who would like their babies to be born this way to talk it
over with their own district midwife or the doctor looking after them
at the ante-natal clinic.

For a personal description read Nancy Mackeith's account in *A Women's Health
Handbook* (p. 227).

The right to choose between breastfeeding and the bottle

Although doctors and nurses pay lip-service to the value of breastfeeding – it protects the baby from infections, particularly gastro-
enteritis – women are not always given enough encouragement.
The baby is often thrust at them by a busy nurse, who might take
it back again if it doesn't immediately clamp on to the nipple. The
nipples themselves are often tender and painful to begin with and
mothers worry that their baby isn't getting enough milk. However,
it's really worth persisting if you can and want to, because once
you are back in your own familiar surroundings and freed from the
rigid hospital time-table, you and your baby will be able to adjust
to each other.

It's wise always to empty one breast at each feed, as this promotes
lactation and the more you breastfeed the more milk will come.

Breastfeeding is cheap, safe, convenient, and can be a deeply satisfying experience. It does away with all the business of sterilizing bottles, making up feeds and worrying if you're over-feeding the baby, especially if you feed on demand (when the baby wants to) instead of according to the 4-hour clock. As the baby gets a bit older you'll be able to skip a feed every so often and give him/her a bottle. If you do this, or if you bottlefeed from the beginning, this allows you some freedom and a chance for other members of the family to share in caring for the baby. If you're lucky enough to have friends who have produced babies at the same time, you could even share out the breastfeeding between you, like 3 women we've heard of who breastfeed each other's babies when one or other of them needs a few hours away.

THE NATIONAL CHILDBIRTH TRUST (p. 199) has produced some excellent leaflets for women who want to breastfeed, which you should get before you have the baby, as they tell how to prepare your breasts during pregnancy. The Trust also has 250 breast counsellors all over the country who will give you immediate help if you're having problems. Contact the Trust for the name and telephone number of the one nearest to you.

If you can't or don't want to breastfeed, don't feel threatened by that either. Working mothers have a particular problem, because there are few crèches at their place of work, maternity leave is short, if they get it at all, and there are inadequate facilities in public places for breastfeeding. Most dried milk for babies can be bought at reduced prices in health clinics, but recently some of the cheapest brands, including National Dried, were withdrawn because they were too unlike human milk and were suspected of causing some cot deaths. It's very important to follow the instructions carefully. *Never* give more or less than is stated. Check anyway, with your health visitor or at the clinic, that the brand you're using is okay.

Another pressure group concerned with all aspects of childbirth, the WOMEN'S CHILDBIRTH PROJECT (p. 199), is campaigning for a woman's right to choose if, when, where and in what manner she will give birth. These rights include: free contraception and abortion on request; no compulsory hospitalization, social induction or other unnecessary medical interference in the process of birth; and better ante-natal facilities, particularly in more deprived areas.

The right to choose not to conceive

This is part of a woman's overall right to control her own fertility, but she can't use this right properly unless she knows about all the birth control methods available and can make an informed decision to choose the one which suits her best. Women have been legally entitled to free contraception since April 1974.

Many local authorities and hospitals run their own family planning clinics. The FAMILY PLANNING ASSOCIATION (p. 198) and the BROOK ADVISORY CENTRE (p. 198) have clinics all over the country and are now part of the National Health Service. In some of the more remote areas, local authorities run a domiciliary service where the woman can be advised in her own home by a health visitor or community nurse. Many women are either frightened by or embarrassed to go to a clinic. The HEALTH EDUCATION COUNCIL (p. 197) runs educational programmes and advertising campaigns and supplies leaflets on request. An increasing number of women's centres and health groups offer advice and information, particularly about side-effects which too often are glossed over by doctors.

However, there's still a great need for much more open discussion about contraception and much better sex education, including clear practical information about the various methods of birth control, starting at least as early as the third form in a secondary school.

Of the 120,000 unwanted babies born every year, the Health Education Council estimates that most are due to the couple using no form of contraception.

The FAMILY PLANNING ASSOCIATION still finds great difficulty in getting its advertisements accepted, and although they can now be shown in cinemas, they are banned from television.

While it's important to acknowledge the social effect of large families, population control, when imposed as a matter of government policy, can manipulate people. THE WOMEN'S ABORTION AND CONTRACEPTION CAMPAIGN and FERTILITY RIGHTS (p. 198) are pressure groups within the women's movement which criticize population control from a feminist point of view.

The following chart briefly describes various currently acceptable methods of contraception; their advantages, disadvantages and where to get them. However, there is no simple foolproof method which suits all women, and the continuing new evidence about the effects of the pill and the IUD on some women shows that we should all be cautious about using these methods.

'Regular hormone treatment (either for contraceptive purposes or for the suppression of menopausal symptoms) causes a multitude of biochemical changes in the body. The long-term effects of those changes has yet to be measured, and indeed cannot be assessed finally until the present generation of women have completed their natural life cycle.'

The Times Science Report 26 January 1976 commenting on article in *New England Journal of Medicine* (22 January 1976) about link between the pill and gallstones.

We've included on this chart only *recommended* methods of contraception. Other methods like *coitus interruptus*, which involves the man withdrawing his penis before coming (*ejaculation*), and the safe period (*rhythm method*), where the couple avoid intercourse during those days in the middle of the month when the woman is ovulating, are too unreliable and unsatisfactory to be worth considering. Douching the vagina is ineffective and can cause infection. Breastfeeding or the woman holding back from orgasm are no protection against conception. If you're using any of these methods, it would be wise to change to one of the recommended methods.

Methods of Contraception

Name	What It Is	How It Works	Advantages	Disadvantages	Where to Get It
INTER-UTERINE DEVICE IUD (Coil or Loop)	–Several types of small flexible device (plastic or metal) inserted into the woman's uterus through the cervix	–No-one quite knows but favourite theory is that it stops fertilized monthly egg from implanting	–Doesn't interfere with intercourse –No worry about forgetting –Reliable – only about 2% failure rate	–Can be expelled without the woman being aware of it – about 25% are rejected in the first 6 months –Can cause heavy periods & cramps –Increased risk of infection, pelvic inflammatory disease and ectopic pregnancies –Occasionally perforates the wall of the uterus	–Doctor or FAMILY PLANNING CLINIC –Important that person inserting IUD has been trained –Annual check-up essential
CAP (Diaphragm) Must be used with spermicide jelly, cream or foam	–Rubber cap (various types) which fits over neck of womb (cervix)	–Acts as physical barrier preventing sperm from entering the womb	–No side effects –Doesn't interfere with intercourse	–Messy –Takes a bit of time learning how to insert – must be inserted no more than 2 hours before intercourse and left in for about 8 hours after	–Must be fitted by doctor (GP or FAMILY PLANNING CLINIC) –Cap has life of 18 months to 2 years but should be checked every 6 to 12 months

Name	What It Is	How It Works	Advantages	Disadvantages	Where to Get It
CAP (cont)				—Must be washed and checked for faults after use —2.4% failure rate, if used properly	
SPERMICIDES (Chemical contraceptives) in cream, jelly, foam or pessary form	—Chemical barrier	—Immobilize or kill sperm in the vagina	—Easy to get —No need for prescription	—Can't be used on their own —Messy —Can cause allergies	Chemists or FAMILY PLANNING CLINIC
STERILIZATION (female)	—Surgical operation —2 types 1 *Laparotomy* – cutting, tying or removing the fallopian tubes 2 *Laparoscopy* – tiny incisions in the abdomen to burn (cauterize) tubes	—Makes it impossible to egg to travel from ovary to uterus	—Almost 100% reliable (there are very occasional cases of a woman becoming pregnant after sterilization) —Doesn't interfere with sex life —Permanent	—Irreversible so you can't change your mind about having more children —Occasional side-effects in menstruation	—Hospital after talking to your GP —OR FAMILY PLANNING CLINIC
CONDOM (French Letter)	—Thin rubber sheath which is slipped over erect penis just before intercourse	—Sperm are prevented from entering uterus	—Easy to buy —Easy to use —Offers some protection against VD —No side effects	—Has been known to slip off —Can be perforated by finger nail or if bought from old stock may be perished —8 to 10% failure rate	—Chemists, barbers and some men's lavatories or from your local FAMILY PLANNING CLINIC

Name	What It Is	How It Works	Advantages	Disadvantages	Where to Get It
VASECTOMY (male sterilization)	– Minor surgical procedure to cut and tie *vas deferens* which carry semen from testes – Can be done under local anaesthetic	– Prevents sperm from reaching penis	– Very simple and easy to have done – No side effects – 100% reliable providing you follow the doctors' instructions & don't have intercourse without another contraceptive for the first 6 weeks – Doesn't interfere with sex life	– Irreversible in in most cases so you can't change your mind about having children	– Either at your FAMILY PLANNING CLINIC or in hospital
PILL	– Pills containing *oestrogen* and/or *progestiogen* – 2 types 1 *Combination* Contains maximum 0.05 *oestrogen* and up to 4 mg *progestiogen*	– Taken once a day for first 21 days of menstrual cycle – *Oestrogen* prevents ovulation – *Progestiogen* thickens cervical mucuous and the uterus lining from preparing for egg implantation	– almost 100% reliable – Doesn't interfere with intercourse – Some women feel very well on the pill and have increased sexual desire (*libido*)	– Easy to forget – Can have unpleasant side effects: loss of libido, headaches, depression, nausea, weight gain, thrush – More serious (occasional) effects: thrombosis, liver tumours, hypertension, gallstones	– Only on prescription – The doctor should take a full medical history, blood pressure should be checked regularly during the first year of use, and you must have annual medical check-ups more often if you suffer from

Name	What It Is	How It Works	Advantages	Disadvantages	Where to Get It
PILL (cont)				–Women who *must not* take the pill are those who have had or are suffering from: thrombosis, cancer, hormonal disorders, heart condition, stroke, liver disease or cystic fibrosis –Inadvisable for women over 40 or young girls with irregular periods without careful medical consultation	migraine, diabetes, asthma, epilepsy, varicose veins or are over 35
	2 *Mini-pill* *Progestogen* only	–Taken every day thickens cervical mucuous and changes lining of uterus, BUT inhibits ovulation in only about 40% of women	–Doesn't interfere with intercourse –Very few side effects	–Far less reliable than combination pill	–Same as above

The right to choose never to have children

This is obviously a quite different decision from that taken by the woman who feels she has completed her family and wants to remove entirely the risk of getting pregnant. A woman who doesn't want to be a mother and is convinced that she's never likely to develop maternal feelings, should be sterilized if she wishes. However, if she's under 25 she'll find it very difficult to get a doctor to agree to the operation. If she's married, the doctor will almost certainly insist on the husband's signed agreement, although legally there's no obligation under English or Scottish law to obtain it. All the same, a married woman, with or without children, would be unwise to have herself sterilized without first talking about it fully with her husband. A man or woman asking for sterilization should assume the operation is irreversible, although there are exceptional cases where doctors have been able to reverse the operation.

For further information about clinics and centres offering contraceptive advice, p. 198. Recommended reading: *Textbook of Contraceptive Practice* by John Peel and Malcolm Potts (p. 227).

The right to choose not to have an unwanted child

This is as important for a woman as the right to choose whether or not she wants to conceive. A woman's right to abortion on request is one of the main platforms of the women's movement (p. 171), and is a right for which many other women have been asking.

Under the 1967 Abortion Act there are 4 conditions allowing a woman to have an abortion with the agreement of 2 doctors who must sign the 'green form'.

- **The continuance of the pregnancy would involve risk to the life of the pregnant woman greater than if the pregnancy were terminated.**
- **The continuance of the pregnancy would involve risk of injury to the physical or mental health of the pregnant woman greater than if the pregnancy were terminated.**
- **The continuance of the pregnancy would involve risk of injury to the physical or mental health of the existing child(ren) of the family of the pregnant woman greater than if the pregnancy were terminated.**
- **There is a substantial risk that if the child were born it would suffer from such physical or mental abnormalities as to be seriously handicapped.**

Clauses 2 and 3 are significant because they allow doctors to consider a woman's situation and, if they think it necessary, give her an abortion on social grounds. Examples might be a woman with 5 children, living in sub-standard housing with a husband earning a low wage, or a 16-year-old schoolgirl, physically perfectly capable of bearing a child, but whose future would be ruined if she were to have a child at this stage in her life.

However, one of the major failings of the Act has been the uneven provision of National Health Service facilities; this is far more serious than the profiteering which has been going on in private clinics, due mostly to these gaps. This has happened partly because the National Health Service was given no extra money to cope with the demand and partly because of the conscience clause in the Act which allows a doctor or anybody else with a 'conscientious objection' to abortion to refuse to 'participate in any treatment authorized by this Act'. So it is that there are well-known black spots in the country like Birmingham and Leeds and Sheffield where it's almost impossible for women to get abortions on the National Health Service. This means that either they're forced to go through with the pregnancy or they are driven into the private sector where some unscrupulous doctors have been charging huge fees.

The BRITISH PREGNANCY ADVISORY SERVICE and the PREGNANCY ADVISORY SERVICE (p. 198) were set up as non-profit-making charities in order to offer women safe and relatively cheap abortions. They offer a very good, caring service which includes abortion and birth control counselling, with the aim of informing the woman about all her options so that she's in a position to make up her own mind.

They now also offer day-care abortions done by the vacuum aspiration method (pp. 43 and 198) to women who are less than 12 weeks pregnant and who fulfil certain other conditions. If it's difficult for a woman to raise the £65 (approximate cost depending on type of abortion), they will help with an interest-free loan.

About three-quarters of all doctors want to keep the 1967 Abortion Act as it is, while having certain abuses cleared up like the unscrupulous commercial pregnancy advisory services which send women off to expensive clinics. Hundreds of thousands of women who have had abortions, and many more who know how vital it is for them to have this fail-safe if contraception lets them down, are resisting the frightening anti-abortion backlash which erupted in 1975 with James White's Abortion (Amendment) Bill. Among the restrictive measures it proposed, the 2 most serious were:

– A woman wouldn't be given an abortion unless it could be shown that continuing with the pregnancy would either involve *grave* risk to her life or a risk of *serious* injury to the physical or mental health of either herself or her children.

– The burden of responsibility for doing an abortion and for proving that it was necessary was to be shifted to the doctor.

If the first condition were to become law, far fewer women would be entitled to an abortion, with only one result – they would be driven into the back streets, and all the horrors and dangers of illegal abortion would be with us again. The second condition, made law, would mean that if a woman were to bring criminal proceedings against a doctor for performing an abortion on her, the doctor would have to prove her or his innocence, which, as the Haldane Society of lawyers points out, 'breaks the fundamental principle that it is for the prosecution to prove the defendant guilty rather than for a defendant to prove his or her innocence'.

On 21 June 1975 more than 20,000 people marched in protest through London against the James White Bill.

THE ABORTION LAW REFORM ASSOCIATION (ALRA), a powerful fact-finding pressure group since the '30s, reconstituted itself and is now known as A WOMAN'S RIGHT TO CHOOSE (p. 198). It publishes an action guide for pro-abortion campaigning and also keeps an up-to-date list of publications on abortion. THE NATIONAL ABORTION CAMPAIGN (NAC) was formed to fight the James White Bill and has local branches all over the country. Contact addresses and practical campaign information are available from headquarters (p. 197), which also sends out a regular news-sheet on both local and national activities. The WOMEN'S ABORTION AND CONTRACEPTION CAMPAIGN (p. 197) arose directly out of the women's movement several years ago and has been campaigning ever since for freely available abortion, evenly distributed throughout the country. Their other activities include publicizing the harmful side-effects of commonly used contraceptives, such as the pill and the IUD, and opposing any population policies which ignore individual desires and relationships. They say that women alone should be in control of their fertility (p. 39).

Although most women in the movement see abortion on request as their right, they respect and sympathize with those women who, for religious or other reasons, would not themselves choose to have an abortion.

- The number of deaths from abortion decreases every year. In 1972, 10 women out of 157,000 died as a result of a legal abortion.
- It's now safer to have an abortion (the mortality rate is 6 per 100,000) than to give birth. In the same year the rate for maternal deaths was 15 per 100,000.
- Early abortion is even safer. In 1971 the rate was 3.5 per 100,000.
- One in 3 pregnancies throughout the world are ended by abortion.
- The number of annual abortions in this country is beginning to drop dramatically. In 1974 there were 163,117 in England and Wales. In 1975 there were 140,521, representing a decline of 14%, which is only partly accounted for by the diminishing numbers of foreign women coming to this country as the abortion laws in their own countries are reformed.
- in 1976 the number of abortions decreased still further, including those for girls under 16.

WHAT TO DO IF YOU WANT AN ABORTION

- Have a pregnancy test as quickly as possible (p. 26).
- Consult your doctor, but if you think s/he'll be unsympathetic or find that s/he's reluctant to help you, go to one of the centres listed on p. 173ff.
- If you can afford it and don't want to risk any delay, go to one of the non-profit-making registered charities listed on p. 198. You'll be able to talk about it all.

Methods of abortion vary according to the stage of pregnancy. The earlier you have one, preferably in the first 12 weeks, the better and the safer it will be for you.

First 3 days – Morning-after pill is a high-dosage *oestrogen* pill with unpleasant side-effects (vomiting) and should be taken only once or twice in a lifetime after unprotected intercourse (say rape) at a time when a woman knows she was ovulating.

First 14 days – Interception, sometimes called *menstrual regulation* or *endometrial aspiration* is done by *vacuum aspiration* (described below). Using the same suction technique but with only a 4 mm flexible tube (*cannula*), which means the cervix need not be dilated at all, the contents of the uterus are gently extracted. A few women may require local anaesthetic, but it is about as painful as having an IUD inserted and needs the same amount of skill from a doctor. Midwives and nurses could also be trained in this method. In America, it's widely used for day-time abortions, but in this country, apart from a trial run on 200 women under the auspices of the Department of Health and Social Security (the results of which haven't been publicized), it isn't practised.

Up to 12 weeks – Vacuum aspiration. A flexible plastic tube (*cannula*) is inserted into the uterus through the cervix and the other end is attached to a machine which draws out foetal and placental material. Depending on the stage of pregnancy, a 5–6 mm or larger *cannula* is used, but it doesn't involve dilating the cervix to the degree that is necessary with the more traditional D and C.

Up to 14 weeks, sometimes later – Dilation and Curettage (D and C). This is a minor operation requiring a general anaesthetic. The cervix is dilated and the contents of the uterus scraped (*curetted*). Often done for other reasons like infertility or minor fibroids. More traumatic to the uterus.

After 16 weeks – Saline induction and prostaglandins are different ways of inducing an abortion by contractions. Can be fairly painful and has the highest rate of complications. It's really a mini-labour.

18 to 24 weeks – Hysterotomy, a major operation which involves cutting through the wall of the uterus; leaves a scar.

These are the approximate best time-scales for the different methods, but it depends very much on the individual doctor's attitudes. If s/he's pro-abortion, s/he'll try to use the most painless and suitable method for the stage of pregnancy; if s/he's old-fashioned, s/he'll use the D & C always in preference to vacuum aspiration; and if s/he's basically anti-abortion, s/he might even give the woman a hard time 'to teach her a lesson'. Some women are having hysterotomies at 9 weeks or less, and are probably sterilized at the same time. Others are having vacuum aspirations after 12 weeks, which can be dangerous. Inappropriate abortion techniques are probably the main reason for complications, which include infection, haemorrhaging and an 'incompetent cervix', i.e., the muscle is permanently weakened after dilation (probably because it was done roughly) and may cause the woman to miscarry when later she does want to become pregnant. The best abortions are done by skilled, practised doctors who do them frequently and who are not disturbed by conscientious objections.

Ideally, all early abortions (before 12 weeks) should be done in out-patient abortion units. This would avoid painful encounters in the gynaecological wards between those women longing to have a child and others who are just as desperate not to have one. Unfortunately, so far there are only a few of these units attached to NHS hospitals and they can take only women in their area. They are also available through the two private charities (p. 198).

What to do when things go wrong

Infertility

One in 10 marriages is infertile, and if a couple desperately want a child it's no good consoling them with the thought that they're doing their bit for population control. Until quite recently, it was always presumed to be the woman's 'fault' if she couldn't conceive. Women felt guilty and miserable at not being able to 'give' their husband a child. To be a barren woman has been the ultimate disgrace throughout the centuries and in most cultures. Today, however, it has been shown that a third of infertile marriages are due to the woman, a third to the husband and the remainder to a combination of causes common to them both. Yet the false ideas of 'fault', or confusing a man's virility with his fertility, still linger on.

If you've been trying hard to start a baby, don't be put off by the doctor saying 'give it time' or 'relax' or 'take a holiday'. If after 6 months nothing happens, get expert advice. Many FAMILY PLANNING CLINICS and hospitals have fertility clinics. The most common causes of infertility in a woman are blocked fallopian tubes, non-ovulation and obstruction of some kind of the passage of the sperm through the cervix. A man may be producing few or no fertile sperm. Some of these difficulties are more easily cured than others. For instance, the non-ovulating woman may respond to one or other of the fertility drugs, hormones which work by stimulating the ovarian follicles to ripen and to shed their eggs (p. 15 for detailed description of what happens during menstrual cycle).

Vaginal infections

The normal healthy vagina is moist, produces a thin, whitish mucus and has its own bacteria to keep it acid and to ward off infection. Women are sometimes needlessly worried about the appearance and smell of natural discharge, a fact that has been monstrously exploited by companies selling vaginal deodorants. These deodorants are unnecessary, expensive, irritating and potentially harmful. If the bacterial balance in the vagina is upset for any reason, it may be invaded by organisms which cause inflammation of the vaginal and surrounding tissue, an abnormal, thick, yellowish, unpleasant-smelling discharge and acute irritation.

THRUSH (Candida) is one of the commonest. It's a yeast infection and may be caused by the contraceptive pill, diabetes or a course of antibiotics for some other condition which kills off the protective vaginal bacteria. A drug called Nystatin, applied in the form of a pessary which is put in high up the vagina, is the usual medical treatment, but self-help methods may cure you faster.

1. Don't wear nylon pants or tight trousers which prevent the air circulating and drying off excess moisture.
2. Don't soak in hot baths, but take extra care to keep your vulva and bottom clean, using a boiled flannel 3 times a day.
3. Eating yogurt if you're taking antibiotic pills often helps and some women find relief by putting yogurt into the vagina.

NON-SPECIFIC VAGINITIS. If the infection persists or presents other symptoms such as pain in the lower back or swollen glands in the abdomen, see a doctor as it may be due to some other cause and need different treatment.

TRICHOMONAL VAGINITIS (Trich) is caused by a one-celled parasite usually found in the vagina, but men may have it too in the urethra or the prostate. It's usually caught through having sex with someone who's got the infection, but it can also be passed on by using someone else's wet towel, flannel, bathing suit or pants. It can be cleared up quite quickly with a drug called Nimorazole (brand names Nascogin and Nulogyl). Many women don't know they have it, but others have symptoms as for vaginitis and a burning sensation when they pee which may make them think they have cystitis.

CYSTITIS is an inflammation of the bladder. Familiar symptoms are wanting to pee every few minutes, blood passed in the urine and a tremendous burning sensation. It's important to drink a lot of fluid; water and fruit juice are best. Get medical treatment, but if you find the condition keeps coming back, it's worth getting Angela Kilmartin's book *Understanding Cystitis* which is excellent, especially on explaining self-help methods. Don't be put off by some of the more lurid case-histories she describes (p. 227). She founded the U & I CLUB (urinary infection in your home, p. 199) and lectures and advises on the subject all over the country. She has also produced a leaflet, *Self-Help in Cystitis*, which is full of useful tips for the treatment of both cystitis and thrush (available free from the same address).

Veneral diseases (VD)

Passed on by having sex with someone who's infected and *always* require medical treatment. VD clinics are attached to major hospitals all over the country. They may be called by another name like

'Special Clinic' or a person's name to disguise their real function. Unfortunately, many of them still have a very gloomy and forbidding atmosphere. Try not to be put off by this or by the occasional moralizing doctor, as it's essential to be cured as fast as possible. If you are nervous or embarrassed you can take a friend with you to the clinic. Considerably less than half of the people who go to VD clinics in fact don't have VD, but if you have any suspicious symptoms or think you've had sex with someone who may have VD, perhaps someone you don't know very well, it's wise to have a check up. Women are particularly vulnerable because quite often they don't have visible symptoms. The two major diseases are *syphilis* and *gonorrhoea*. Both can be cured by penicillin.

SYPHILIS is caused by a coil-shaped organism called *treponema pallidum* and in its early stages is acutely infectious. It can survive only in moist areas like the genitals, anus and mouth and can be passed on only by intimate sexual contact, hence the appearance of the first sore or chancre, usually on a man's penis or on a woman's cervix, which she's unlikely to know about, as it's painless and eventually disappears. If not treated at this first stage the treponemes multiply rapidly through the blood and the *second stage* symptoms include headaches, sore throat, mild fever and aching bones which may come and go for about 4 years and not be recognized for what they are. The *third stage* is latent and may go on for anything from 5 to 50 years, during which time the person becomes considerably less infectious to others. In the final *fourth stage*, if the disease has been untreated, it may attack one or other of the body's systems, usually the heart or the central nervous system with very unpleasant and eventually fatal results.
It's difficult to diagnose syphilis as the chancre will disappear spontaneously, and blood tests are effective only in the second and third stages and have to be done repeatedly.

Pregnant women are always tested for syphilis as it can be passed on to the baby and if not treated before the fourth month may kill or deform it. Blood donors are always tested for syphilis. Treatment is simple and effective. A series of penicillin injections with follow-up tests cures most patients, even in the latent stage.

GONORRHOEA is passed on only through sexual intercourse and affects only the genito-urinary organs. Symptoms appear within 2 days to 3 weeks of infection, and in men are very visible with a pus discharge and a painful, inflamed penis. Unfortunately 70% of women don't know they have gonorrhoea because they have no obvious symptoms like vaginal discharge or pain when peeing. Untreated gonorrhoea in women can cause serious complications including swollen glands in the groin, cystitis and worst of all, *salpingitis*, inflammation and scarring of the fallopian tubes, which may become blocked, causing permanent sterility. The gonococci live in the cervical mucus and lining of the urethra and the best way of testing for the disease is microscopic examination of the discharge. Pregnant women who remain untreated can infect their baby as it passes through the birth canal in childbirth, making it blind. Ideally, women should be screened for gonorrhoea routinely, perhaps at the same time as they have a smear test.

Treatment is simple and effective with penicillin, although some strains have shown themselves resistant and the dosage has had to be stepped up.

Other minor, sexually passed-on conditions

GENITAL WARTS clear up usually with local treatment. A similar virus is

GENITAL HERPES which are cold sores in the genital area and are much more difficult to cure.

SCABIES is a tiny mite which penetrates the skin of finger webs, wrists, ankles or penis and causes intense itchiness, but is easily cured.

CRABS are pubic lice and are easily got rid of.

Cancer

The most common form of cancer in women is *breast cancer*. About 1 woman in 17 develops the disease, and more than 11,000 women in the United Kingdom die from it every year. Early detection is very important; most experts believe that this gives a woman an 80% survival chance, but there's no way at present for a woman to be screened on the National Health Service if she has no symptoms and no history of breast cancer, but just wants to take precautions. It's therefore very important that every woman should learn to self-examine herself once a month, preferably just after her period. Feeling your breasts carefully with soapy hands in the bath is also a good method.

WARNING SIGNS TO LOOK OUT FOR
- **An unusual lump or thickening**
- **Discharge from the nipple**
- **An alteration in the shape of the breast**
- **Any pain or discomfort not felt before**
- **Any distortion in the shape of the nipple**

Visit your GP immediately if you have any of these symptoms and insist that s/he refers you immediately for National Health Service screening where, apart from careful manual examination you will be given either a *thermography* or a *mammography* (infra-red and X-ray techniques). Only 1 in 5 of the women who are referred to a specialist turn out to have breast cancer; the rest have cysts (easily treated either by cutting them out or extracting the fluid) or other benign conditions. Many women have 'lumpy' breasts, particularly after the age of 35, due to changes in their glands and hormonal functions, but this doesn't mean that they should be any the less careful about self-examination. The most vulnerable age for developing the disease is between 45 and 55.

Treatment depends on the nature of the lump (they vary in degree of malignancy) and also whether the disease has spread to other tissue, particularly to the lymph nodes under the armpits. A surgical operation of some sort is usually necessary; first there is a *biopsy* which means cutting out a piece of suspect tissue under general anaesthetic to examine it for malignancy. If the disease is confirmed then the doctor must decide whether to take away the whole breast (radical mastectomy) or just to remove the lump. These are alternatives you must discuss with her/him before the operation.

Breast cancer and the fear of losing a breast and becoming sexually mutilated haunts most women, but it's terribly important to face up to the possibility. Betty Westgate, who had a mastectomy several years ago and knows just how important it is for women to talk and to be helped *after* the operation, has formed the MASTECTOMY ASSOCIATION (p. 200).

If you can afford it, BUPA (p. 200) provide a total gynaecological and health screening service and run a mobile breast cancet screening unit which spends about a month in each town. It's available to any woman, referred by her GP, with or without symptoms, at a cost of £18. It's expensive, but so far there are very few NHS units. BUPA has also published a booklet, *Breast Cancer Self-Examination*, an aid to early detection, which can be bought at W. H. Smith bookshops or from their headquarters (40p including p&p).

Cervical cancer kills about 2,500 women every year, but it can nearly always be cured providing that it's discovered early enough, because the pre-cancerous cells may appear up to 15 years before the disease itself. Almost entirely due to the persistent campaigning of the WOMEN'S NATIONAL CANCER CONTROL CAMPAIGN (p. 200), all women over the age of 25 are now entitled to an annual smear test (*cytotest*) either in hospitals, local authority clinics, health clinics or in one of the campaign's 4 mobile clinics. FAMILY PLANNING ASSOCIATION (FPA) clinics and the BROOK ADVISORY CENTRES also always do a smear test as part of their routine check-up. It's very important that when you have this test you also ask the doctor to examine your breasts. The *cytotest* is very simple and painless: the doctor takes a sample of mucus from the cervix and sends it to a laboratory where a cytologist examines the cell structures for abnormalities. It's a useful test, not only for cancer, but for other unsuspected conditions like meningitis.

These are the two most common forms of cancer peculiar to women, but they can also get cancer of the uterus, ovaries and vagina, quite apart from cancers common to both sexes. Breakthrough bleeding, unusual discharge, or pain in the lower abdomen are all warning signals which should take you to your doctor, but remember that more often than not they will indicate a relatively minor condition.

Women alone, women and men, women and women

It's often assumed that because today everyone talks so much and so openly about sex we must all understand everything there is to know about our sexuality. In fact, we're only at the beginning of recognizing our true sexual natures and needs. Women, especially, have been the victims of a long history of cultural and religious ideas which have taught that woman's sexuality is there to satisfy man's needs and that she can find her pleasure only in giving him pleasure. This has, on the one hand, stifled the expression of women's true sexuality and, on the other, created the notion that if women don't enjoy being the passive recipients of male sexual needs, they are, somehow, inadequate women. In fact, many women at various times in their life may experience celibacy. Sometimes that state may be forced on them, but it can also be a positive and satisfying choice. Sex can be a great pleasure, but it is not a necessary aspect of living for everyone, or at all times, and the social pressures to enter into sexual relations with men may sometimes be unpleasant for some women.

Freud developed psychoanalysis as a method of treating people's mental disorders by making them talk about anything and everything that came into their minds (called *free association*), especially their subconscious past. He drew back the curtain on many dark areas of human understanding, particularly through his revelations about the importance of our childish sexual experiences on our adult lives. At that time it was considered deeply shocking to suggest that innocent little children were capable of behaving sexually, which just shows how good human beings are at forgetting things they don't want to remember. He introduced concepts such as the 'oedipus complex' to explain a boy's sexual attachment to his mother and corresponding jealousy of his father, resulting in guilt-stricken emotional conflict and 'penis envy', the emotion every little girl is supposed to feel when she realizes she doesn't have the marvellous male organ. Some of his insights have been immensely productive, even when they have been disputed or disproved by later theorists, if only because they have made us think in new directions about our psycho-sexual natures. But in one area Freud's influence has been disastrous.

He believed that there were two distinct kinds of female orgasm, the 'clitoral' one, which derives from the *clitoris*, the small hooded knob above the entrance to the vagina (p. 50), and the 'vaginal' one, which a woman can experience only when she is penetrated by a man's penis. Not only are they different physiologically, according to Freud, but they are also innately different psychologically, the later vaginal one being immensely superior to the early clitoral experiences of young girls masturbating and experimenting erotically. The mark of a woman's sexual maturity was when she could cast off her clitoral longings and engage herself only in vaginal orgasm. This distinction is not based on any concrete facts, and has caused many women to feel sexually inadequate, unnecessarily.

Most of us have been brought up to think that sex is something you keep to yourself, and even if we don't actually think it's dirty,

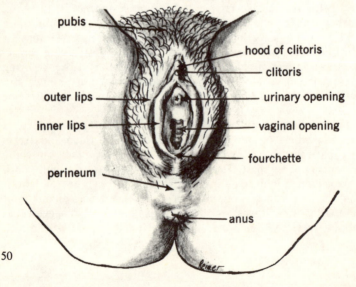

50

women don't easily tell each other what it feels like to make love and be loved. They may talk about what happens, mothers may tell their daughters what to expect, but they don't describe their own pleasures or disappointments. Perhaps it's too difficult for women to cross generations (children are often appalled by the realization that their parents still make love, and parents whose own married life may have been very unsatisfying can feel acutely jealous imagining their children in sexual situations), but it should be possible to talk to your women friends and learn from sharing experiences.

Very often our first experiences of sex are very disappointing, and after it's over we may wonder what all the fuss is about. Other times we find that we are able to have a wildly exciting sexual relationship with someone with whom in other respects we don't have much in common. We may continue to love someone long after we have stopped wanting to sleep with them. Sometimes we feel randy for days on end; at other times sex is just uninteresting. What turns us on and off sex varies with our moods, our circumstances, the people we are with and how we feel about ourselves.

It's impossible to expand here on the variety of sexual experience and the reasons why people have such different expectations and needs. Thousands of books have been written on the physiology, the psychology, the how-to-do-it 'ology and all the other imaginable 'ologies of sex. The best of these are included in our bibliography, but we would like to give a special mention to *Our Bodies Our Minds* (p. 226), because this describes better than any other book we know how *good* it feels to be a woman and how rich can be the range of sexual expression.

As we said at the beginning of this chapter our sexuality is in the whole of us, not just our genitals. Often sex goes wrong because people worry too much about 'making it', so they work at sex as if it were an endurance test, giving themselves 10 out of 10 if they manage to 'come' together. In fact, simultaneous orgasms are probably much more rare than people imagine and they are certainly not necessary for satisfying sex. Anyway, you can over-emphasize the need to have an orgasm every time and there are many forms of sexual and sensual pleasure which don't necessarily involve having one. Men, especially, are victims of this performance ethic, which is understandable because if they don't have an erection they aren't going to achieve penetration, but penis into vagina isn't the only way to enjoy sexuality. Women who fake orgasm in order not to shake their man's confidence and secretly worry that they are incurably frigid are just as much victims of the wrong outlook, imposed on them by expectations and roles which make it difficult for them to be honest emotionally.

Masturbation, for instance, is one of the ways we can love ourselves or love our lover. More often it's a pleasure we reserve for ourselves, for the times when we are on our own and maybe want to indulge ourselves with a fantasy. Many people retain a puritan hangover about masturbation, thinking of it as something dirty and shameful, when in reality it is a marvellous way for a woman to learn about her body. By caressing, exploring, loving herself all over, she learns to please herself, and this will give her confidence to ask her lover really to love her in a variety of ways. Women can masturbate themselves in all sorts of ways, with their fingers, crossing their legs and rubbing rhythmically, doing exercises, using an electric vibrator.

A good book to help you understand and develop your body's potential is *Getting Clear: Body Work for Women* (p. 227). Some women find it helps to talk to others about their experiences and to share their secret fears and hopes. In America they've taken this a step further, to help women who find it difficult to have an orgasm or maybe have never had one, by running what they call pre-orgasmic therapy classes. Women are encouraged to talk about their difficulties; they examine their own and each other's bodies, look at films showing how women masturbate, learn to do exercises and spend at least an hour each day doing 'homework'. It may sound dauntingly professional or a bit cold-blooded, but women who have done it say it is a warm and loving experience and that they go back to their lovers refreshed, renewed and no longer afraid to do and to ask for what pleases them.

One of the benefits of exploring our sexuality and coming to terms with it (more than that, enjoying it) is that women are at last throwing off the guilt and the deep-seated sense of inferiority they have been taught to accept about themselves. The idea of strong desires and lust in a woman is becoming acceptable, and the myth that women don't want to take sexual initiatives is being exploded. Sexual confidence for women can only be a good thing for sexual relationships, and experiencing one's lover as an equal is an important part of developing the confidence to express sexuality, and all that that implies, openly. In the past women were afraid to admit that they were lesbians. We know that Queen Victoria refused to recognize that lesbianism could exist and it was, therefore, not made a criminal offence, unlike male homosexuality. Nonetheless, lesbians were made to feel deviant, ridiculous ('what on earth do they do to each other?') 'half-women', and it is only now, with the development of the women's movement that they have been encouraged to 'come out of the closet'. The growing solidarity between women has supported and encouraged those who are gay, both among themselves and in their relationships with other women. It has also allowed women who may not be lesbian or bi-sexual to express their warmth and affection for each other physically.

The only people who can say what it feels like to be a lesbian are lesbians themselves. Look at *Our Bodies Our Minds* for some moving personal accounts of the joys and delights, pleasures and pains that lesbian women find in loving each other. See also p. 226ff for books, novels, etc., written by lesbians. For a list of groups, organizations and publications for lesbians, p. 200.

Mind in a woman's world

More women than men suffer from mental illness. One in 6 ends up in a mental hospital compared with 1 in 9 men. A recent survey of mothers with young children revealed that 42% of them were suffering from clinical depression, which means depression bad enough for treatment, pills or visits to a psychiatrist.

More women are reported as alcoholic than previously, more women are suffering from agoraphobia and post-natal depression, more young girls are getting *anorexia nervosa*, the illness where they starve themselves to get thin until they literally can't eat. Why are these things happening? Is life hard to cope with for women?

Well, yes it is, mainly for reasons that have directly to do with the stereotyped roles that are forced upon them and the demands that are made of them to conform to what is often an unbearable reality. Brought up to behave in a feminine way, the young girl learns that her place is always to be at some man's feet (Daddy's little girl, the nice girl next door, helpmeet to the boss, blushing bride, radiant mother); these are the images which society constantly pushes at her and urges her to accept. And when she tries to live up (or should it be down?) to these standards (often an impossible task for economic as well as psychological reasons) and fails, and tries again, growing more desperate with each lapse from graceful womanhood, she immediately wonders what's wrong with *her*, not what's wrong with the society which creates a reality so different from the dream.

First we must find out who we are. It's a long drawn-out process which starts in childhood when we begin to realize that we are separate different people from our parents. But we may never find ourselves if we aren't encouraged to become genuinely independent people, ready to take responsibility for our own lives and the mistakes we'll inevitably make. Forcing unreal roles upon women, making them see themselves always in relation to someone else (somebody else's wife, mother, general bottlewasher, never *me*, a woman, a person with a distinct, unique character and needs) keeps women eternally vulnerable. Here we are concerned only with what happens when women find they can't live up to society's unnatural expectations of them.

Just as a double standard operates in our sexual morality – women should be passive, accepting, servile; men should be strong, demanding and aggressive – so too we have a double set of standards for what we think is mental health.

A recent American study revealed that the average clinical psychologist included in his definition of a 'mature adult woman' the following characteristics: 'being more submissive, less independent, less adventurous, more easily influenced, less aggressive less competitive, more excitable in minor crises, having their feelings more easily hurt, being more enotional, more conceited about their appearance, less objective.'

Not exactly a desirable catalogue of characteristics and one which suggests that a mature woman is an immature human being. Women who resist these deforming stereotypes are called aggressive and unfeminine; women who escape to the bottle or swallow tranquillizers are branded as neurotic; women who refuse to marry are called frustrated; and mothers who are forced to live in bad housing conditions and then can't cope with their children are labelled inadequate. No wonder some women go mad. (See p. 227 for several interesting studies of the double standards applied in psychological theory and psychotherapy. Particularly recommended are Phyllis Chesler's *Women and Madness*, Juliet Mitchell's *Psychoanalysis and Feminism* and a collection of essays called *Psychoanalysis and Women* edited by Jean Baker Miller.)

It would be taking much too partial a view to suggest that it's only social conditioning and role stereotyping which drives women mad. We are just beginning to understand about the effects of chemical and hormonal interaction on our bodies. As the section on the menstrual cycle showed (p. 15), there is a very fine balance to be maintained if our bodies are to function 'normally', and the criteria for normality vary from person to person. Furthermore some degree of stress is necessary for human survival. Our minds and bodies are programmed (some better than others) to deal with crisis, danger and threats to our well-being. Not every woman who is subjected to intense stress succumbs. Nor could we possible deny that men too are frequently victims of society's unrealistic expectations; the pressures to succeed, to support their families, always to be strong and manly when sometimes they want to break down and cry, admit their weakness – these also can be intolerable strains.

Women, however, are often trapped in a double-bind situation. Family doctors have finally caught up with the idea that possibly as many as 60% of the patients who present themselves in the surgery with sometimes quite trivial complaints (like endless colds or recurring mild pain which has no apparent physical cause) may really be suffering from mental stress of some kind. And if the patient is a woman, to take a typical example, a harassed young mother with more children than she can manage, not enough money and living in sub-standard housing, the doctor knows well enough the cause of her depression, but what can s/he do? Unless the woman's situation is immediately alarming, s/he hasn't got time to do more than prescribe her some tranquillizers, possibly write a note to the social services and send her on her way, knowing that probably half of the people still waiting to see her/him are burdened by similar intractable problems.

Taking pills for a depression which is caused by circumstances beyond the doctor's control is like taking a pain-killer for raging toothache before going to the dentist; both give temporary relief, with the difference that eventually the toothache will be cured whereas the doctor knows that he will see his patient over and over again, unless there is some radical change in her situation.

This is not to say that tranquillizers are without their advantages; they can help in a severe crisis and they do blunt anxiety, but they can't be regarded as a cure. There is also the danger – and here comes the double bind – that they will be prescribed for symptoms which do have a deep-seated physical cause but which the doctor has failed to investigate. Women particularly often find themselves fobbed off with the suggestion that they are being neurotically over-anxious even when they may have something potentially serious to show like a lump in the breast.

It's bad enough to be dismissed as stupid and hysterical by a doctor who imagines s/he's superior because s/he's the possessor of a certain expertise when you are in a reasonably calm state of mind; to the woman who is suffering from a crippling psychological condition like agoraphobia, for instance, which means that she daren't put her head out of doors even for a walk or a ride on a bus, such an attitude can be devastating. It is in reaction to these arrogant medical assumptions that so many self-help groups have been formed in the field of mental illness. We have listed some of them on p. 201ff, and they really are worth contacting, whether or not you are getting help from your doctor, because you will be met with sympathy and help from people who understand what you're talking about because they've been through the same experiences.

Depression is a normal reaction we all have from time to time: when we're going through a difficult period in our lives, when we're very tired, after an illness or sometimes for no particular reason. People often feel they ought to be able to control their depression, but it's difficult to do this, and you shouldn't expect it of yourself. It's usually harder to cope with depression when you're alone in the house, with small children etc. – having to do a day's work outside the home can be a diversion from one's problems. Depression is something we all have to live with at some time or other in our lives, but it can become severe and prolonged. There are warning signals which indicate that something more serious may be wrong and that we need outside help. These include:

unshakable lethargy

dread of getting up and facing the world

**feeling very isolated and unable to do anything about it
like seeing friends or talking to people**

a profound feeling that nothing matters

feelings of guilt and despair

Often a woman suffers this kind of depression after she's had a baby. Some doctors believe that it is caused by drastic changes in hormonal levels, but because no one has told her that it may happen, she feels there is something wrong with her as a person. She thinks she is wicked and unnatural because, instead of loving this baby she has been longing for, and enjoying motherhood, which everyone had told her would be blissful, she is filled with guilt, terror that she may harm the baby in some way, and a crushing sense of responsibility.

What to do if you feel you can't cope with a situation any longer:

Try talking it over with a friend or a sympathetic member of your family.

Contact one of the women and psychiatry groups listed on p. 200ff to see whether they can put you in touch with a local self-help group or give you other advice. Some of the self-help groups teach women how to do *co-counselling*. Basically, this is building up a relationship between 2 people, where each learns in turn to listen supportively and to discharge her own emotional hurts and distress. Really, it's doing what we would like to do for close friends in trouble and what sometimes we expect from them, but because the relationship is monitored by a skilled, sensitive third person known as a 're-evaluation counsellor' the outcome is likely to be more constructive. The support and warmth you will get from a women's group and the realization that you're not alone with your problems may be all that you need. But this therapy is not enough for

someone who is severely disturbed in which case you must

Go and see your doctor. If s/he's better than average s/he'll listen to you and maybe pull you through. Otherwise, s/he may think it necessary to *refer you to a psychiatrist*. Again the treatment you receive is a matter of luck. Some psychiatrists really do their best to listen and help. Others are brusque, too busy to give you more than 5 minutes of their time every 3 months and are occasionally downright unkind.
S/he may think it necessary to *send you to a hospital*. Treatment varies depending on the patient's condition and the particular views of the doctors. Some rely heavily on drugs, others on *electro-convulsive therapy* (ECT) or psychoanalysis. You may be there either voluntarily or compulsorily. For your rights under the Mental Health Act consult *Civil Liberty: The NCCL Guide*, by Anna Coote and Lawrence Grant (p. 229).

If you are worried about the treatment you or a member of your family is getting, contact MIND (NATIONAL ASSOCIATION OF MENTAL HEALTH) (p. 202) who, as well as having a wide network of contacts and information about professional and self-help groups, also run an advisory casework service and a legal rights service. The MENTAL PATIENTS UNION (p. 202) have local groups and also supply literature on request, including a comprehensive directory of drugs and their side-effects. *Mind Out* is a monthly consumer magazine for anyone who's in contact with the mental health services either as a patient or as a professional.

We've only been able to skim over the whole area of mental

health, indicating very briefly the areas of discussion and disagreement. However, we hope you will fill in the gaps by looking up our bibliography or by getting in touch with groups or associations (p. 201) which are doing research and campaigning or are offering support.

Women are to be excluded from the draw for 64 places in the eleventh annual world conker championships, to be held at Ashton, near Oundle, Northamptonshire, in October. Hitherto only men have taken part. Mr Frank Elsom, chairman of the organisers, said: " The event would be ridiculed if it was open to women." — THE TIMES, 1976

Living Together
Living Alone

Most people want to, and have to, live with other people at least some of the time. This chapter is about some aspects of living with other people or living alone.

Most women marry and have children. Most of them have freely chosen their marriage partner and many have borne children because they wanted to; marriage and children may provide them with love, companionship, sexual satisfaction and security. Women who do not marry or who, through death or separation, find themselves without a partner may find fulfilment through their independence. Some women may go on living with their parents, or find satisfactory alternative ways of living for part or all of their lives; sharing a home with a friend or friends of the same or opposite sex, living communally with a group of people or getting a residential job in something like a school or a hospital.

But monogamy and motherhood may mean frustration and unhappiness. Independence may mean isolation and loneliness, and living with other people in different kinds of ways may bring insecurity and impermanence.

There are no final or simple answers to the problems of finding good living arrangements in our present social and economic structure. We live in a society which morally, legally, economically and socially upholds and encourages people to live within the 'nuclear' family: a unit of wife, husband and their children only. Houses and cars are built to fit it. State benefits and tax laws are based on it (p. 134). Advertising, TV, and the media generally assume it is the 'normal' arrangement. Yet the numerous people who are elderly, widowed, single, divorced, separated, homosexuals, those with dependent relatives, don't fit into these patterns.

Marriage

TYPES OF HOUSEHOLD IN GREAT BRITAIN 1971

Married couple with one or more children	7,337,000
Married couple with no children	4,523,000
Married couple with or without children, and with parent or other relative or grandchildren, i.e. couples living within the 'extended' family and three-generation family	933,000
(Total households including a married couple	12,793,000)
One parent with one or more children	1,000,000
One person only	3,320,000
Households of all unrelated persons	344,000
Other combinations	857,000
Total of all households	18,314,000

The table above shows that out of 18 million households in this country, nearly 13 million include a married couple.

Marriage is the norm. People even re-marry at a greater rate than they used to. The average age of marriage of spinsters is now 22.

By the age of 26, more than 80% of women are married, and 90% eventually marry.

Marriage is portrayed as the ideal end of a love relationship. From Jane Austen, writing at the beginning of the 19th century, to the writers of short stories for contemporary women's magazines, heroines are just about to reach the altar and, it is assumed, enjoy marital bliss for the rest of their lives, when the story ends. Romance ending in marriage is the stuff of literature, music, advertising copy and sex education. But of course the story doesn't end there. One in four marriages ends in divorce, and many others pass through periods of unhappiness and bitterness but are maintained for the sake of the children or because the partners have no alternative.

What advantages can there be to marriage or to living permanently with one man? It can provide a sense of emotional security, of mutual trust, and often the reality of economic security for both partners. It can create companionship and allow the ease of intimacy with another person, a compensation for the impersonality and difficulties of the outside world. It can allow the expression of love and affection and the permanent availability of sexual satisfaction. The matching of two complementary personalities may be stimulating and fulfilling. The family may provide a stable environment within which children are brought up. At a more material level, living with another person allows for day-to-day convenience: one set of sheets to be changed, one meal to be cooked.

Yet marriage often isn't really the open choice it might seem. In our society, to marry is to be 'normal', and people often feel a good deal of pressure to conform with social normality. They feel inadequate if they don't, and know too that in some respects unmarried life will be harder. The same is true for having children; social pressure decrees to quite an extent that if you marry you have children, and that it's slightly abnormal, not to say inhuman, *not* to want them. Hence, pressures lead people into marriage, often almost automatically, and from there to parenthood.

It's difficult to make any meaningful generalizations about marriage; it varies for each couple. Yet marriage is also a *social* fact, not just a personal one, and therefore people are under some pressure of convention not only to marry, but also to have a particular kind of marriage.

Marriage may not always turn out to be what it's made out to be. This is one reason marriages 'go wrong'. Another is that people change. Most people get married when they are young; their personalities are always evolving, their needs changing. Given the much greater life expectancy it's hardly surprising that people who get married in their early 20s, or later, find that even after 5 years their situation and emotional needs have so changed that their 'partner in life' becomes a burden. Security may become a condition of dependence. Within a few years of being married, most women, in particular, don't have any real choice about where they sleep and who else sleeps in the same place. Their economic dependence on their husbands and their responsibility for the care of young children effectively decides where they live. Companionship may become stifling. You are a couple. You are expected to like the same things and the same people. It's assumed that two people can fulfil one another's every emotional and sexual need, while for many people this may not be true. Attempts by women (though not by men) to act independently of their husbands is likely to meet with their and other's disapproval. Intimacy creates vulnerability. Arguments may be used to attack your partner's identity. Love may turn into

61

jealousy and possessiveness. Sex may become a ritual. Sharing material goods may create conflict. And finally, marriage does not suit all women, either because they find the married state oppressive or because they married the wrong man.

Obviously some are a success story. But for many women, marriage may mean drudgery, an unsatisfactory sex life, a restriction on job opportunities (because where they live is usually determined by their husband's job), little time to develop their own interests, endless compromises for the sake of harmony, and the irritation of petty squabbles about petty domestic issues which emerge through strain, tiredness or boredom.

If marriage goes wrong, one main difficulty is likely to be communicating with your partner. Many marriages flounder because of the inability and unwillingness of the partners to talk about their grievances and to understand the other's problems. If you can talk to your man without becoming involved in a shouting match, it may be possible to sort out some of your resentment and anger. The difficulty of sitting back and really discussing the reality of your existence together cannot be minimized, but it is worth trying to break down the barrier of unsaid and often unacknowledged problems. The problems may be relatively minor and therefore worth trying to solve without breaking the marriage. If it's a question of sexual incompatibility, get advice (p. 201). If the causes of unhappiness are more general, try consulting your local MARRIAGE

GUIDANCE COUNCIL (p. 201). A better means of sorting yourself out may be through sharing the problem with a friend, particularly with another woman. Some kinds of groups within the women's movement may provide you with at least the experience of discovering that your problem is not unique and the solidarity and understanding you need to cope with it.

A survey of 10,000 women readers of *Woman's Own* showed that 50% of the wives thought their sex life was below average; 25% said they had committed adultery. As previous marriage surveys have indicated, children make marriages worse, and the more children the worse it becomes.

Another solution may be to change the style of the marriage, acknowledging that it cannot provide for all your psychological and emotional needs and that it cannot be an exclusive relationship. George and Nena O'Neill in their book *Open Marriage* describe how marriage can mean two independent people sharing their lives together but allowing for other relationships, which may be sexual, and acknowledging and living out their separate identities. Of course, it's much easier for men within the structure of the nuclear family, as they are usually more mobile, more involved in worlds outside the home, and thus more easily able to form relationships with other people. Women with children are often housebound and therefore socially and geographically isolated. Their circle of contacts is likely to be limited to neighbours, family and shop-keepers.

Because of the social pressure to maintain a monogamous marriage, the partner who has an affair is likely to become involved in a labyrinth of deceit, lies and secrets. Because they find love and sexual excitement with another person, people often feel they should reject their marriage and move into another one. The partner left behind feels jealous and humiliated. Some of these crises could be helped if people could begin to acknowledge that at different periods of our lives each needs different kinds of emotional attachments with both sexes, that one person often cannot provide all we want from people, but that these facts do not necessarily mean that the primary relationship is a mistake or a poor one. Two people who can work that out are likely to enjoy a more open and more honest marriage. But it is difficult to change emotions just by wanting to. Emotions are affected, amongst other things, by economic and social circumstances. Women are very often dependent on men and jealousy and possessiveness may be a reaction to this dependency, a fear that they will lose their security and identity with the loss of their partner.

Divorce

If breakdown of a marriage is very serious, separation and divorce may be necessary. This is not necessarily a failure. Many people tend to feel some guilt, but that will pass. Most marriages break down because the expectations and desires of both partners have not been fulfilled, because they have become different people, because the accumulation of unhappiness becomes overpowering. 100,800 out of 117,017 divorces granted in 1974 were undefended. In other words, 80% of those who sued for divorce went through a meaningless and expensive legal ritual in a situation where there was no dispute. It may be the best thing for the marriage to end. It may mean the end of unrewarding dependence and tyranny for many women. Many more women are now initiating divorce proceedings. It's not an easy decision. You have to face yourself and to think about how you'll live in the future. You have to face your children and worry about how they'll cope if you separate. You have to face relatives and friends who may be torn between disapproval, pity and sympathy. You have to face the outside world in the shape of the law. An inappropriate procedure which costs the state £10 million a year in legal aid fees alone will lurch into action to hear a display of your most intimate problems. And then, perhaps most difficult of all, you have to live day by day as a divorced or separated woman, with all the problems of not fitting into the 'normal' social patterns.

For detailed advice on how to get a divorce, look at:
How to Conduct your own Divorce, by Gil Friedman; *Breaking Up: A Practical Guide to Separation and Divorce and Coping on Your Own*, by Rosemary Simon; *Getting a Divorce*, by Edith Rudinger (Consumers Association); *Women's Rights: A Practical Guide* by Anna Coote and Tess Gill.

Not getting married

You don't have to get married. You can live in a permanent relationship with one man and have children without going through a legal or religious ceremony. There are advantages and disadvantages economically and socially to this arrangement which are set out clearly by Anna Coote and Tess Gill in their book (p. 224). They also reproduce in the appendix a contract which can be drawn up between two people who want to share their life on an equal basis whether they marry or not. The contract is adaptable to your needs. It can cover property rights, responsibility for housework, sexual fidelity, what name you use, financial arrangements and so on. A similar document was reproduced in the May 1973 issue of *Nova*. Such contracts have not yet been tested in the courts but even if they're not legally enforceable, they may serve a useful purpose by forcing you to think, before you enter a relationship which is likely to affect the rest of your life, of how you want it to work and of what problems might emerge. Couples in love seem to spend more time discussing the names of their future children and the chairs they are going to buy than the fundamental questions of how they are actually going to live together.

Lesbian couples

Lesbian couples who establish a permanent relationship are likely to enjoy or to suffer the same kinds of experiences as heterosexual people, with the added problem of coping with often unpleasant and ignorant social disapproval from society and perhaps from their families. They may react by hiding the true nature of their relationship, by isolating themselves within the gay community or by trying to face the consequences of their lesbianism openly. Whatever they do they particularly need the support of other women (p. 172ff).

Living without a partner

There were 3.3 million single-person households in this country in 1971, 2.4 million (72%) of them female. Of the single female households, 78% were aged 60 or over.

Some women choose to live alone. The advantages of their situation can be all the positive side of the disadvantages of marriage: social and sexual freedom and independence, job and residential mobility, solitude, privacy and doing what you want to do when you want to do it. Women with absorbing careers and active lives often find that they can maintain these only if they do not have the responsibility for another person in their domestic world. Some have more or less permenant relationships with one man without sharing the same home. It's easier for younger women to live like this. But women who reject marriage are likely to be subject to endless boring questions from friends, relatives, and strangers, about why they're not married and why they don't settle down, and to be excluded from social occasions designed for couples and families. The stereotype of the woman alone has often been derogatory. They are assumed to be frustrated, hard, unattractive involuntary spinsters. To be a bachelor, on the other hand, appears much more dashing, has much more social acceptance, even approval. Furthermore, the dominant sexual mores allow unattached men to 'sow their wild oats' even if it means paying for it, while a woman who enjoys more than one sexual relationship is likely to be labelled promiscuous.

Of course many women have their solitude forced upon them by separation, divorce or death. There are 1 million single-parent households in the country and more than half are women. There are nearly 3 million widows, compared to 700,000 widowers.

For many widows, being alone, especially if it happens suddenly, is a traumatic and painful experience. Suddenly they yearn for the ordinariness of someone else around, the pleasure of sharing daily life. It's the end of a sexual relationship, the deprivation of a familiar and loved body. Decisions have to be made alone. The lights have to be turned off and the doors locked at night alone. There's no one to share the pleasures and responsibilities of the children, and other families are often self-absorbed in ways which exclude incomplete families or halves of couples. Economic and social support is removed. The situation for a woman whose husband leaves her or who leaves her husband is similar in many ways, but she also has to cope with the humiliation of rejection or the shame of her 'failure' and less immediate sympathy from people around her.

Living in other ways

There are many other ways in which women live, some involuntary, some experimental, some temporary. In particular, in the period between leaving their parent's home and entering a marital home, many women find all kinds of short-term solutions to sharing a home although the number of households made up of people who are not related is very small: 344,000 out of 18 million. And this figure includes homosexual relationships as well as unmarried couples.

But some women (and men) are trying to create more permanent kinds of residential patterns, alternative ways of living with others of the same or opposite sex, without the constraints of living within the nuclear family. These patterns range from the house of 'bed-sitters' where each person or unit (couple, parent or parents and child) has their own independent living space; more communal patterns where a kitchen and leisure space is shared by all the residents; where the preparation of meals, food buying, cleaning, etc., is done as a group and the work shared among the members; to the commune or collective, where a group of people, usually with the same social aims in life, share all aspects of their lives in order to achieve political, emotional and physical closeness and comradeship.

The advantages of communal living are many, however varied the degree of integration or the size of the household. It's cheaper where property is rented or owned and often means that people can enjoy a higher standard of housing than they could alone. It provides companionship which may be particularly valuable for single people and single parents. It may allow for a more flexible balance between individual privacy and solitude, and loneliness. It enables isolated people to come together and through the group provide themselves with some emotional and economic security. Children learn to mix easily with other adults, and parents can be relieved of the pressure of sole responsibility for their children. Communal living can be more flexible and relationships have more chance of being equal. More positively, it is a situation for exploring different ways in which people – adults and children – can live with, work with and care for each other.

One disadvantage can be impermanence; someone may want to move out and thus break the solidarity of the group, though this may be less shattering than the break-up of a couple, which leaves each individual alone. New members demand adjustment by the changed group. Communal living can mean there are 10 people to have arguments with and worry about. And, as with marriage, people change.

Our Children

It's often thought that because many women are demanding 24-hour nurseries and abortion on request (p. 171) this means they're a bunch of heartless females who, if they don't succeed in suppressing children before birth, care nothing for them afterwards and are anxious only to dump them on someone else for as long and as often as possible.

The truth is quite different. These women care deeply about children, their own and others. They care about the way we bring up our children, the attitudes and expectations that are instilled into them, the miserable lack of opportunities so many of them have. They care about the way mothers are expected to cope, often under the most appalling conditions of bad housing, very little money and isolated living, say in a tower block or on a bleak housing estate.

We can touch only briefly on the main areas of concern for women who care about the future and well-being of children, but we hope that by giving addresses and talking about groups who are actively campaigning already, we'll be able to help with particular problems and to suggest areas where change is needed. Mothers especially want to know about other women's experiences and to find ways of pooling resources, because so often they are very isolated in their homes with young children and with no other adults to talk to for many hours each day.

Child schooling

'Give me a child until the age of 7 and he is mine for life', said St Ignatius Loyola, or words to that effect. What you teach children, not just out of books, but in the form of attitudes, assumptions, beliefs, will have a lasting effect. Today's child-care experts agree with him, although most of them would add that the first $2\frac{1}{2}$ years of a child's life are the most important in this respect and that, before the age of 5, s/he is capable of learning and absorbing more than at any time afterwards.

So what do we do with our children? We spend a lot of time making sure they know how to behave like a 'proper boy', a 'typical little girl'. Right from the start, it's blue for a boy, pink for a girl. Girls are often picked up and cuddled more than boys by their mothers, who are afraid to make their sons 'soft'. Fathers like to boast about their flirtatious daughters and to spot the embryonic footballer or mechanical genius in their sons. Kind friends and relatives give soft dolls and furry creatures to girls, whereas boys are given sharp, hard things like toy cars, bricks and pistols. That's just the start of the socializing process, but as they become more aware of the world around them and of the place they have in it, children's impressions are reinforced by the books they look at, where they see that boys do exciting things while girls sit about waiting for someone to take them along, or don't figure at all. Animal stories are no better and, as for the nursery rhymes and classical fairy stories that we've all been brought up on, can you think of one brave, admirable heroine among that sorry band? Downtrodden Cinderella, foolish Red Riding Hood, pathetic Little Miss Muffet; they're all so feeble compared with Georgie Porgie who only has to kiss the girls to make them cry or little Jack Horner sticking his thumb in the pie and declaring 'what a good boy am I' – or the gallant prince on a white charger rescuing Sleeping Beauty from her 100 years' sleep.

These are the stereotypes children imbibe with their milk and rusks, long before they've had a chance to try out alternative roles or test their own feelings. Their first games often reflect their early impressions; girls copy their mothers, behave like miniature house-wives and mothers, whereas boys are more often allowed to play noisily, kick balls around etc. Obviously, there's nothing wrong with the games themselves, but what is wrong is our automatic assumption that they're defined by sex, so that you may hear parents apologizing for their 'deviant' children ('she's such a tomboy', 'he's an awful sissy') and concluding 'but I suppose s/he'll grow out of it'.

Indeed they usually do, although 'grow' is perhaps not the best way to describe the restrictive role-playing into which children are often forced. As they go to school, begin reading, watch television they learn that whereas girls aren't expected to do certain things, like fly aeroplanes, fight in wars or become engineers, boys must be ready to do anything. It's the *flexibility* of boys' choices more than their nature which is important; boys, of course, suffer from their own stereotypes, but they're less restrictive. The yawning gap between their own inclinations and adult expectations becomes clear to children often at quite a young age, and as it's easier to accept than to resist such powerful influences, most of them adapt to the roles offered them.

So first we must look at ourselves and see how our own con-ditioning affects our attitudes towards our children. Sexist textbooks and reading books, and sexist attitudes in the classroom add to the difficulties of giving children more freedom to develop, as do some of the more traditional attitudes in the world they live in or among the friends they make. It's often hard to cope with other children who laugh at the idea of boys learning to sew or girls wanting to play football.

The Sex Discrimination Act makes it illegal for schools to discriminate between boys and girls in the facilities they offer, so now if a girl wants to do woodwork or a technical subject, like mechanical engineering, she can (if the facilities exist in the school), and a boy can opt for sewing, cooking or typing if that's what he wants. It's good as far as it goes, but it takes time for the law to change attitudes. More than that, we need to make a fundamental reappraisal of the *way* we teach children – the books we use and the methods we choose. There are some books available which discuss the sex role stereotyping which goes on in families, schools, work, etc., and how things might be changed (p. 228). There are also people working on the material children are given to read.

Children's books

There are several groups working in this area. THE CAMPAIGN TO IMPEDE SEX STEREOTYPING IN THE YOUNG (CISSY), p. 203, was formed in 1971 by 6 women: teachers, writers and an illustrator. They've worked systematically, by talking to publishers and in schools, to show just how insidiously children's books reflect sexist attitudes. They produced *Good-bye Dolly*, the children's books issue of *Shrew* (p. 192), which analysed reading primers, picture books, elementary science text books, sex education for teenagers and novels about jobs. They've also published a pamphlet, *Cissy Talks to Publishers* (15p plus postage), from 35a Eaton Rise, London W2.

THE CHILDREN'S BOOKS STUDY GROUP (p. 204) is a collective of men and women concentrating on class bias in books and on the way the family is presented to children. They plan to publish a critical pamphlet which will also define criteria for judging children's books.

THE WOMEN'S EDUCATION COLLECTIVE (p. 177) has a sub-group for children's books, which is writing a non-sexist reading scheme aimed at primary school children and secondary school non-readers.

LIBRARIANS FOR SOCIAL CHANGE (p. 208) are generally concerned with what people are reading, but they also have a children's group which liaises with publishers and librarians to encourage the publication of non-sexist books. One issue of their magazine was devoted to children's books (15p), available from 67 Vere Rd, Brighton, Sussex.

Better schooling

Many teachers, parents, social workers and not a few children are unhappy with schools as they are. However, media reports about violence, truancy and illiteracy exaggerate the symptoms of unrest while rarely trying to discover the causes. Schools are complicated places where many of the problems of society in general are magnified – problems of children coming from different backgrounds, problems of sex roles, of authority and how it's used, of the learning process, of expectations of teachers and parents.

Schools vary in the extent to which they allow or welcome parent participation. Some have parent/teacher organizations, and these vary too in the amount of involvement by parents. Others prefer to keep parents at more of a distance, while still others will encourage quite a lot of informal involvement by parents. You have to find out what exists for each individual school. There are several campaigns and organizations, often started by parents to improve educational facilities in their own area. THE ADVISORY CENTRE FOR EDUCATION (ACE) (p. 204) holds a complete register of parent campaigns so that people can learn from each other's experience and find out how to deal with official bodies. Other groups concerned in the same kind of issues are listed on p. 204. There *are* ways in which people can affect attitudes and teaching in their children's schools.

De-schooling

THE CHILDREN'S RIGHTS WORKSHOP (p. 203) is mainly concerned with providing information about alternatives to education acceptable under the 1944 Education Act. They help people starting new projects and publish several pamphlets outlining different alternatives. They also keep a list of Free Schools and other co-operative schemes (15p).

If you want to see how a Free School works and what the atmosphere is like, you can visit the *White Lion Free School* (57 White Lion St, London N1) every Tuesday evening from 7 to 9 without making any prior appointment. For a good account of how to start and run such a school, get *How to Set Up a Free School – alternative education and the law*, by Alison Truefitt (30p) from the White Lion School. David Head has edited a Penguin Educational Special called *Free Way to Learning: educational alternatives in action* (50p), which looks at what is currently happening.

Child care

THE 1944 EDUCATION ACT required Local Education Authorities to see that 'provision is made for pupils who have not attained the age of 5 years by . . . nursery schools or . . . nursery classes'.

IN 1945 THE MINISTRY OF HEALTH CIRCULAR 221/45 stated: 'The proper place for a child under 2 is at home with his mother . . . the right policy to pursue would be positively to discourage mothers of children under 2 from going to work; to make provision for children between 2 and 5 by way of nursery schools and nursery classes; and to regard day nurseries and daily guardians as supplements to meet the special needs (where these exist and cannot be met within the hours, age range and organization of nursery school and nursery classes) of children whose mothers are constrained by individual circumstances to go out to work or whose home conditions are in themselves unsatisfactory from the health point of view, or whose mothers are incapable for some good reason of undertaking the full care of their children.'

IN 1960 THE MINISTRY OF EDUCATION CIRCULAR 8/60 stated that resources could not be spared for an expansion of nursery schools nor could teachers be spared who would otherwise teach children of compulsory school age.

IN 1967 THE PLOWDEN COMMITTEE REPORT recommended that 'part-time attendance at a nursery school is desirable for most children'.

IN 1968 THE MINISTRY OF HEALTH CIRCULAR 37/68 advised that day care facilities should only be provided for children with special needs, i.e. if they were the children of unmarried mothers needing to work or their mothers were unable 'to look after them adequately' or for serious health reasons, like living in overcrowded home conditions or being handicapped. It also advised local authorities to make greater use of facilities provided privately or by voluntarily organizations in other words, facilities which were not dependent on State aid.

ALSO IN 1968 THE URBAN AID PROGRAMME was launched with an initial budget of £3 millions to be spent on nursery schools and classes, day nurseries and children's homes in 'districts which bear the marks of multiple deprivation . . . with deficiencies in the physical environment, overcrowded housing, family sizes above the average; persistent unemployment; a high proportion of children in trouble or in need of care . . . or where there is a substantial degree of immigrant settlement'. (Home Office Circular 225/68)

IN 1972 THE CONSERVATIVE GOVERNMENT'S WHITE PAPER, EDUCATION: A FRAMEWORK FOR EXPANSION, announced a detailed programme for increasing the number of nursery school places with the ultimate aim of offering places to all 3 and 4 year olds whose parents wanted them to attend.

IN 1975 THE LABOUR GOVERNMENT announced that £500 millions would be cut from future spending on the under-fives and that virtually all building projects would be stopped.

IN 1976 many Local Education Authorities are not taking up even their reduced budget allocation for nursery schools. Many more are underspending it. Their miserliness has, however, benefited one authority, the INNER LONDON EDUCATION AUTHORITY (ILEA), which has taken up an informal offer from the Department of Education and Science (DES) of an additional £300,000, enabling it to go ahead with its nursery school expansion programme.

After the end of the Second World War (1949) there were 80,000 day nursery places compared with 20,000 in 1973. Today only 7.7% of children aged 3 and 4 have access to nursery schools in Great Britain compared to 50% in EEC countries including France, Belgium and Italy.

Pre school facilities for under-fives

Type	What They Do	To Whom Responsible	Advantages	Disadvantages
NURSERY SCHOOLS 1974 15,500 full-time places 30,000 part-time places (maintained)	Educate children aged 3½–5, including maintained, direct grant, private schools recognized as efficient, and other private schools	DES (Department of Education and Science) LEA (Local Education Authority)	Help children to develop 1) *socially* by stimulating their natural curiosity, and bringing them into contact with adults and children outside their family circle 2) *educationally* by developing their use of language and skills. Also help in early identification of special difficulties	1) Not enough of them 2) Not always a choice for parents between full and part-time attendance 3) Although maintained schools are *free*, private ones can be very expensive
NURSERY CLASSES 1974 32,500 full-time places 62,000 part-time places (maintained)	Held for children aged 3–5 in a primary school or other school which is not a nursery school	DES LEA	1) Same as above 2) If located in same building as primary school makes transition to compulsory school easier	1) May not be as well equipped or staffed as purpose-built nursery school 2) cost – same as nursery schools
LOCAL AUTHORITY DAY NURSERIES	Cater for children from 6 months to 5 years mainly to relieve family problems and provide care for children of working mothers	Dept. of Health and Social Security (DHSS) Social Services Dept.	1) Most are open from 8 am to 6 pm and all the year round 2) responsible, qualified staff (nursery nurses)	1) Don't provide any education 2) not enough of them, very difficult to get your child in unless s/he qualifies under one of the *special need* categories 3) quite expensive

Type	What They Do	To Whom Responsible	Advantages	Disadvantages
PRIVATE DAY NURSERIES AND DAY CARE CENTRES	Licensed premises where children under 5 are looked after during the day	DHSS Social Services Dept	If it's run as a co-operative or community venture, involves parents and allows for more flexible attitudes towards child care	1) Very dependent on calibre of individual or group running them 2) can be expensive
CRÈCHES	Look after children from 0–3. Often organized by factories and private companies, help attract women workers	DHSS Social Services Dept	1) Safe place to leave your child 2) can visit your child during the day 3) qualified staff	1) Often ties women to boring low-paid jobs. Offering crèche facilities may be used by management to keep down wages
PLAYGROUPS	Organized on voluntary part-time basis for children under 5 by mothers who sometimes employ a full-time, paid supervisor	DHSS Social Services Dept	1) Parents can get more out of bringing up their children by chance to share experience 2) when backed by either PRE-SCHOOL PLAY-GROUPS ASSOCIATION or SAVE THE CHILDREN'S FUND, standards will be high	1) Not suitable for working mothers 2) doesn't attempt to do more than supervise play, which may be frustrating for the older child
CHILD-MINDERS 39,200 registered	Look after one or more children in their own home. Number of children allowed limited for each minder	DHSS Social Services Dept	If person is registered and has experience or a modicum of training, your child will be safe and well cared for	Thousands of illegal child minders: some may be highly responsible, but may take more children than they should, in order to keep costs low; some may be quite unfitted for looking after children (p. 77)

When women are needed to help out the country in its hour of national need, like in times of war, or to promote a booming economy, then little is said about a mother's 'duty' to care for her children, but come a recession with inflation and soaring unemployment, as now, then it's back to the home for mothers and an end to talking about the special importance of giving every opportunity to children under 5 for developing their potential.

What is available

It's important to understand the distinctions between the various types of private as well as maintained child care facilities which do exist. They vary in quality and quantity according to the priority given them by individual LEAs. Some, like pre-school playgroups or the One O'clock Clubs, involve the mothers; others, like state day nurseries or child-minders, cater mainly for working mothers or for mothers who for some reason aren't able to cope with their children full-time. Private nurseries are open to anyone who can afford their fees. The chart below outlines the main points of each.

On page 205 we list the organizations which are campaigning for better and more child care facilities, not only for the under-fives but during school holidays and after school – which can be especially difficult for working mothers. Because of the shortage of statutory facilities, most local authorities welcome people who are prepared to run something efficiently on a voluntary non-profit-making basis.

THE PRE-SCHOOL PLAYGROUPS ASSOCIATION (PPA) (p. 206) got going as a self-help group more than 10 years ago, and now more than a quarter of a million children in England and Wales attend PPA groups, as well as 1 in 8 of Scottish children. They are *always* organized by mothers, usually on a rota basis, and they try to keep the fee as low as possible. In addition to the Penguin handbook, the PPA publishes many useful pamphlets on how to set up and run a playgroup. Colleges of Further Education also often run courses for training supervisors or anyone else interested in playgroups. The best playgroups provide an excellent environment for children to learn through play, but they do vary, depending on the ability of the organizers. And they are not schools, so they don't employ trained teachers, nor do they have to do any more than comply with the regulations laid down by the Social Services

Department, like having enough lavatories and enough people in charge for the number of children.

Child-minders are a much maligned section of the community. Undoubtedly, many abuses do happen and the CHILD MINDING RESEARCH UNIT (p. 205) has disclosed some appalling cases of 'baby farming', where children may be left for hours on end in dirty, unheated rooms, fed badly and never played with or given any stimulus at all. These situations reflect more on the way we, as a society, value the well-being of our children, than on the individual hard-pressed mother who must find someone to look after her child, or the frightened, possibly fairly ignorant child-minder who doesn't register with the local authority either because she doesn't know that she should or thinks she will be turned down if she does apply. The CHILD-MINDING RESEARCH UNIT estimates that more children are looked after by child-minders than by all the other forms of pre-school care combined, and since most of them are illegal the general standard of care is low. Even those who have registered have often been left to get on with it. The unit has now set up an Action Register to keep local authorities and voluntary bodies concerned with the problem in touch with one another and keep them aware of research and projects going on in different parts of the country. More authorities are putting on special courses for child-minders and are helping them in other ways. The UNIT is also campaigning for a Childminders' Charter.

The women's movement and child care

There have been some interesting child-care projects organized by women in the movement, and they don't believe in leaving it just to the mothers. Men too want to be involved with children, whether or not they are fathers, and a mixed group of adults gives children a better chance of relating to people other than their parents and of avoiding the usual stereotyped impressions of sex-roles with which most children grow up (p. 68ff). Many local groups are campaigning for better child care – it is one of the six demands of the woman's movement (p. 171) – and a few have published helpful accounts of their experience.

THE CHILDREN'S COMMUNITY CENTRE (p. 205) was the first women's liberation child day-care centre to be funded by a local authority (Camden Council). It is run by a full-time paid worker and a rota of parents and other interested people – men and women.

The premises consist of a large terraced house with a kitchen, where the children help to make their own snacks, a room for eating, noisy and quiet rooms and an outside yard with sand, water, things to climb and space. The children also go to the shops, library, swimming pool and parks. They are encouraged to help by clearing their dishes and tidying up and are taught to be considerate to one another. They don't see the adults doing sex-stereotyped jobs, and neither are they shunted into games or creative play according to their sex. A daily journal is kept, and once a week the parents meet to discuss progress and any problems that may have arisen. The centre has produced two pamphlets describing how to set up and run such a centre, and also a film called *One, Two, Three* (p. 216).

Other groups which have written about their experiences are THE CALTHORPE PARK PLAYGROUP (p. 205), which has produced an excellent booklet, *Out of the Pumpkin Shell*, and FERNDALE ROAD ESTATE PLAYGROUP in Brixton, London, which has produced a report on thier successes and failures called *Playing Fair at Ferndale*, available from the London Council of Social Service, 68 Chalton St, NW1. Strictly speaking, the latter scheme isn't within the women's movement, but the report is full of valuable information for anyone planning a scheme on similar lines in an urban community.

GINGERBREAD (p. 206) has printed an information sheet, *Organizing a Summer Play-scheme for Children*, which includes tips about premises, staff, budget and activities.

Mothers

Working mothers

About 22% of working women are mothers with dependent children. Most of these women work because they must, they need the money. Most of them have little choice in the type of work they do; they take what they can, where they can, and earn very little.

Some companies provide crèches, which are all right in theory but they *can* be used as a way of enticing women into badly paid, dead-end jobs. As we have seen in the section on child care, working mothers have many problems finding suitable facilities, and there aren't nearly enough full-time places for under 5s.

Working mothers are often blamed for the ills of society: but research findings have shown that the children of working mothers, far from suffering because of their absent mothers, are often better off than the children of stay-at-home mothers. They are likely to be better adjusted to school life, just as healthy, more independent and there is no difference in delinquency rates between children of working and non-working mothers. One study found that the boys of mothers who *did not* go out to work had a higher incidence of delinquency. They concluded that parental mismanagement or disturbance rather than whether or not the mother was working seemed to be the decisive factor.

MOTHERS IN ACTION was a pressure group founded in 1967 to fight for mothers in all the areas where they suffered discrimination. It exists no longer because it felt that many of the issues it had raised have now been taken up by other groups, but a fitting memorial to its achievements is provided by the following.

WORKING MOTHER'S CHARTER

THE RIGHT TO WORK **Every woman, regardless of family commitments, should have the same right to work as every man.**

SOCIAL SERVICES **Every woman with dependent children should have access to supportive services to allow her to work, and no woman should be deprived of the right to work because of inadequacies in the social services.**

EDUCATION AND TRAINING **No woman should be deprived of the right to work because of lack of education or training. Every woman should be afforded the opportunity to complete or further her education, or to acquire new skills.**

DISCRIMINATION **No employer should be allowed to discriminate against a woman because of her marital status or family commitments.**

VOCATIONAL GUIDANCE **Every woman should be entitled to vocational guidance in order that she may realize her full potential.**

EARNINGS **Every woman should be able to earn sufficient to enable her to be economically independent.**

Unsupported mothers

This includes single mothers, divorced or separated mothers, widowed mothers and mothers whose husbands are incapacitated through illness or imprisonment, are plainly even more vulnerable. The Finer Report, which was published in July 1974 but had still not been debated in the House of Commons by the beginning of

81

1976, revealed an appalling picture of poverty, struggle and loneliness endured by lone parents, of whom 5 out of 6 are women. There are also 100,000 single fathers, many of whom suffer as much hardship as single mothers, but, as Finer points out, the added factors of women's low wages and poor job opportunities make it even harder for women to overcome their problems.

The most important recommendation made by the Finer Committee was that every one-parent family should be offered *as of right* a special cash allowance (guaranteed maintenance allowance) which would be sufficient to give the parent a genuine choice about whether or not to work.

For further information about the report and groups active in helping single parents, see p. 206.

Chronically sick or disabled mothers

This tends to be a forgotten group of women, yet many of them achieve wonders against all the odds in continuing to run their homes and to bring up their children. Groups are organizing to campaign on behalf of these women, who have been denied the disability allowance, and also to do something for women who stay at home to care for disabled relatives but are not recognized as employed nor entitled to an allowance (p. 207).

Adoption and fostering

Adopting

People may want to adopt a child because they can't have any of their own, or they may have completed their own family but would like to take another child, perhaps more than one, if they can afford it, because they love children and enjoy bringing them up. Whatever the publicly expressed reasons a couple may give when presenting themselves to an adoption society, they must be prepared for lengthy and searching interviews. They must expect probing personal questions about their married life, their physical and mental health, and their social and financial circumstances. Their referees will also be questioned closely. For a full list of adoption agencies, both voluntary and statutory, and brief information on how to apply, write to the ASSOCIATION OF BRITISH ADOPTION AGENCIES (p. 207).

Many couples never get as far as being interviewed, not through any fault of their own, but because there are very few white babies now available for adoption (better contraception and more single mothers keeping their babies are the two main reasons). Even if they do get put onto a waiting list, they must be prepared to wait at least 2 or 3 years, possibly even longer. Yet there are thousands of children in care and the numbers increase every year. In 1974 there were 96,000, and many of these children have lost virtually all contact with their natural parents and would be much happier and better-off if they could be taken into a family. In the past, most of these children were considered unsuitable for adoption, either because they were no longer babies, or because they were coloured or handicapped, or their parents had stipulated that they must be brought up in a certain religion or had refused to allow them to be adopted, although they themselves had no intention of looking after their children.

Recent publicity about the plight of these 'forgotten' children has made local authorities much readier to consider requests from people who would like to adopt children falling into one or other of these categories, especially if the applicants already have children of their own and know from first-hand experience the problems as well as the pleasures of bringing up a family. If you are interested in this type of adoption, further advice and information can be got from THE PARENT TO PARENT INFORMATION ON ADOPTION SERVICES (PPIAS) (p. 207), which was started by a group of frustrated would-be adopting parents a few years ago who had discovered how difficult it often was to get any information from local authorities about the children in their care. They have local groups all over the country and, apart from helping people who want to adopt, they also support each other by sharing their knowledge and experience. Another useful agency is THE ADOPTION RESOURCE EXCHANGE (p. 207), which acts as a clearing house for registered adoption agencies all over the country wanting to improve adoption opportunities for coloured children in their care by putting them in touch with people who would like to adopt such children.

If you want to place your child for adoption you can either approach your local authority or go to one of the registered adoption agencies. (Lists available from the ASSOCIATION OF BRITISH ADOPTION AGENCIES, p. 207). In the past, mothers had to wait for 3 months after handing over their child to the adopting parents before signing the legal consent form which formally gave away all their parental rights over the child. Now, under the new Children Act 1975, a mother may give her final legal consent after 6 weeks, provided that she has had an interview with a specially-trained social worker who is satisfied that the mother does mean it and that there is no one in the background, such as the father, for instance, who might suddenly come forward and claim rights. It is hoped that this will take away some of the agony of mind endured both by the natural mother and the adopting parents during the waiting period.

Other important provisions in this Act, often called The Children's Charter because it aims to place the interests of the child first, include:

1. Local authorities may take over parental rights for children who have been left in their care for more than 3 years, thus making them free for adoption.

2. Third party private adoptions, i.e. adoptions arranged through friends or a doctor or some other person who claims to know people willing to adopt, will be banned, unless the child is directly placed with another member of its family, say a grandmother or an aunt.

3. Anyone over the age of 18 who has been adopted will be allowed to see his or her birth certificate. In the past, this was only possible in Scotland, and the whole business of adoption was shrouded in mystery, although for some years parents have been urged to tell their adopted child as soon as it seems right, that s/he has been adopted. Now many social workers make a practice of telling the adopting parents as much as possible about the child's natural parents, which information they can then pass on to the child as and when it's appropriate.

4. Although natural parents may say what religion they would like their child to be brought up in, it's no longer allowed as a condition of adoption.

Many books and articles have been written on adoption, and the ASSOCIATION OF BRITISH ADOPTION AGENCIES (p. 207) will be able to supply you with a recommended booklist. We have mentioned a few of the most important ones in the bibliography (p. 228).

Fostering

Fostering a child is quite different from adopting, and it demands very special qualities of commitment and caring from the foster parents, who are really working in partnership with the Social

Services Department and the natural parents. A foster parent holds a child in trust for its natural parents until they can take over its care once more. It may involve just a few weeks while the mother is in hospital or it may last for months or even years. There are 30,000 foster parents in this country, and the vast majority of them are doing a marvellous and indispensable job which, until recently, was usually given scant recognition. Not only may they be coping with difficult, emotionally disturbed children, but they often help the natural parent(s) to pick up the pieces of a shattered life, caused perhaps by bereavement, nervous breakdown, marriage failure or whatever, so that in due course they are strong enough to make a home once more for their children.

When foster parents accept a child, they sign a form agreeing that they will bring up the child exactly as if it were one of their own and that they will hand it back to the parents as soon as they ask for it, with the consent of the Social Services Department. For this, they get a weekly allowance which varies between local authorities. THE NATIONAL FOSTER CARE ASSOCIATION (p. 207), which has been set up to provide 'a national voice' for foster parents, would like to see this allowance standardized and brought up to a realistic level compatible with today's inflationary cost of living. As it is, too many people who would like to be foster parents and who would do it very well, are prevented from applying because they just can't afford to look after another child on an allowance which would barely keep it in cornflakes and socks. The association has local groups throughout the country which support foster parents in their relationship with the Social Services Department and between themselves.

If you think you'd like to be a foster parent, write or telephone your local Social Services Department. It's very unwise to accept a child privately or vice versa for a mother to place her child in a family without going through the local authority. Many of the unhappy 'tug-of-love' cases which have hit newspaper headlines have been the result of this kind of fostering.

Under the Children Act 1975 long-term foster parents now have certain rights, which include:

1. After 3 years a foster parent can become a custodian, a position half-way between adoption and fostering which means that s/he can make plans for the child's future without consulting the Social Services Department, but not excluding the natural parent.

2. After 5 years, foster parents wishing to apply for adoption can do so without fear of having the child snatched away from them.

After School

Planning your future

1. How to choose

If you were lucky, you were at a school where you were given advice about jobs at an early enough age to allow you to make the right subject choices. Ideally, children should have their first talk about their future with either a teacher or a careers officer in their third year at secondary school, when they are faced with choosing options for CSE or 'O' levels which they'll be taking at the end of the fifth year.

Girls do proportionately better than boys in their CSE, 'O' level and 'A' level exams. In 1972 63.3% of girls got passes at 'O' level compared with 58.3% of boys; 71.4% of girls got passes at 'A' level compared with 68.3% of boys.

In well-run schools, a careers officer, whose job combines giving advice and guidance to pupils and parents as well as helping place school-leavers in their first job, will talk to groups and individuals from the third year onwards. The advantage of consulting him or her is that s/he has good back-up services and should know about local openings for work, training schemes, apprenticeships and other opportunities for gaining qualifications. S/he's there also to help young people either having trouble finding employment or having difficulties in their first jobs.

Although girls do proportionately better than boys in all groups of subjects, especially maths and languages, less girls than boys enter for all these exams and only one-third of the number, compared to boys, qualify in maths and science subjects.

There's a simple explanation for this. In single-sex girls' schools there are fewer science teachers, laboratories and other necessary resources. A recent survey showed that in co-educational schools more than three-quarters of the head teachers (all men) followed a policy of organizing science or engineering-based courses for boys, whereas girls were offered commercial or home-economy type courses. Such science teaching as they might get tends to be unspecialized, and usually they are encouraged to drop science subjects as soon as possible, which means that later on they are unqualified to take up apprenticeships or technical training courses.

Double the number of boys enter university as girls. In 1972 it was 7.6% of all boys and 4.4% of all girls. In the same year there were 3,673 male university professors and only 64 women professors.

Unfortunately, most guidance in schools for careers and jobs is far from ideal, and very patchy. According to a 1973 report by the schools inspectorate, only a few schools see education about future work as part of a preparation for living in the adult world. And if it's bad for boys, this apathy affects girls even more. As from 1 September 1976, schools are no longer allowed to discriminate between boys and girls in any way, but the general view still is that a woman's work 'naturally' takes second place to marrying and bringing up a family. Most parents, most teachers and most future employers think this way, so it's hardly surprising that so many girls reach the end of their schooldays with no clear idea of what they want to do with their lives. And when they do know, they settle mainly for the traditional women's jobs.

More girls than boys go to colleges of technology or polytechnics (12.5% girls, 8.6% boys). Girls do mainly clerical or catering courses, whereas boys mostly follow science-based vocational courses.

One of the problems about choosing a job is that there is such a variety of information, which is often too detailed and confusing for the average person who may not really know what s/he is looking for. Even careers teachers are often bewildered by the huge range of periodicals, guides, books, leaflets, etc., which they are sent.

Three times as many girls as boys go to teacher training colleges, but most head teachers in both primary and secondary schools are men. There are six times as many men teaching full-time in colleges of further education as women.

Here is a guide to help you cut your way through the job jungle. If you have no idea what you want to do:

1. *Look at some books about jobs*
The following is a selected booklist from the hundreds which are available, chosen because they're particularly helpful for girls and women. If you can't afford to buy them, you should be able to find them either in your public library or your local careers office.
Careers Guide, published by HMSO, revised annually. If you want to know more about a particular job mentioned in the guide, check to see whether it is included in the HMSO *Choice of Careers* series. These are informative, accurate and inexpensive. For further details write to the Careers and Occupational Information Centre, 97 Tottenham Court Rd, London W1P 0EP.
Careers for Girls, by Ruth Miller in Penguin paperback. This is a well laid-out, detailed guide to more than 300 jobs.
Careers Encyclopaedia, edited by Audrey Segal published by Cassells.
The Gender Trap, by Carol Adams and Rae Laurikietis published by Virago. This is a series of books about the sex roles imposed on girls and boys in our society. The first volume is on education and work, and tells you about the problems which make it difficult for girls to

"I really wanted to be a mechanic, but there were no apprenticeships for women!"

choose satisfying jobs, and how to overcome them.

Male and Female, CAREERS RESEARCH AND ADVISORY CENTRE (CRAC) (p. 209), Student's book 85p; Teacher's book £1.00, describes just what opportunities women should be making for themselves.

Choosing a Job, CRAC, p. 209, 45p, is a short useful book which will help you to examine your motivations and attitudes. CRAC does not advise individuals, but it organizes conferences, seminars and training courses as well as publishing many useful guides, pamphlets, etc., to help teachers and pupils.

2. *Consult professional job advisory organizations*

A *free* service is provided through the CAREERS SERVICES AGENCY by careers officers throughout the United Kingdom. (Look up the address of your local office in the telephone book or enquire at your local education authority.) A careers officer's main job is to help school leavers decide on a career and find employment, but they can and do advise people of all ages.

THE ADVISORY CENTRE FOR EDUCATION (ACE) (p. 204) runs an advisory correspondence service which includes answering questions about training, job opportunities and choice of 'O' and 'A' levels. Questions *must* be put in a letter, *not* by telephone, and the charge for each question is £9.50 for members and £13.50 for non-members.

ACE also publishes an extremely useful A-Z of the sources on *all* major educational topics *Where to Look Things Up*, £1.00, from the same address (p. 204).

THE NATIONAL ADVISORY CENTRE ON CAREERS FOR WOMEN (p. 209) offers, as its name suggests, advice on jobs and information of special interest to girls and women. Membership is either individual or group (many schools belong and the centre sends lecturers to talk to sixth forms). For further information and a list of publications write to the above address. You don't have to be a member to get information; it just makes it a bit cheaper.

Magazines and newspapers are another useful source of general information, as they often run articles on different jobs. The *Daily Telegraph* probably runs the most comprehensive service, and its CAREERS INTELLIGENCE SERVICE, 1a Camden Walk, London N1 8DY, will answer any written question about careers; it also supplies useful addresses, *all for no charge*. It specializes in advising school-leavers and has also published a helpful guide, *Daily Telegraph Careers A-Z*, published by Collins.

3. *Consider Vocational Guidance*

A *free* and confidential service is offered by the Department of Employment (EMPLOYMENT SERVICES AGENCY) for anyone over 18 who has left school and needs help in finding out what kind of job would suit them in terms of what they're good at, what they like and their circumstances. Guidance officers have had special training and are supported by excellent back-up facilities, like good reference libraries and a constant input of information on local opportunities and information to keep them up to date. There are 43 units in major cities throughout the UK, and you can make an appointment for interview by contacting your nearest unit direct, or by asking at your local job centre or employment office. Women who've used this service speak highly of the care and attention given to their individual case.

ACE (p. 204) gives vocational guidance to anyone over the age of 15. The service consists of a 2-3 hour interview with an occupational psychologist, followed up by an interview with a careers advisor. The first interview can be arranged in London if that's more convenient. Alternatively, an overnight programme in Cambridge can be organized to make it easier for people having to travel some distance.

CAREERS ANALYSTS (p. 209) claims to be the largest and best-known careers guidance organization in the country. The service is brisk, efficient and somewhat impersonal.

THE VOCATIONAL GUIDANCE ASSOCIATION (p. 210) has been going for more than 20 years, and experience in this field is valuable. Follows much the same system as CAREERS ANALYSTS, by giving the person a number of tests to find out interests and special abilities which are then computed, scored and used as the basis of discussion with a consultant. This is followed up by a report.

THE NATIONAL ADVISORY CENTRE ON CAREERS FOR WOMEN (p. 209) does a vocational guidance interview which includes an interest test and a written report.

For a complete list, get the ACE pamphlet called *Organizations Offering Vocational Guidance*, 25p. Fees vary between £20 and £40, depending on the organization and the age and status of the client, but haven't been printed here because of inflation.

More girls than boys leave school at the minimum school-leaving age.

---

2. What next?

1. *Further education*

You may have to get some more 'O' levels or perhaps another 'A' level to qualify for a particular training course or entry to a polytechnic or university. There are something like 600 colleges of further education up and down the country and between them they offer a wide range of courses, both at advanced and basic levels. To find out what's available for school leavers, write to THE DEPARTMENT OF EDUCATION AND SCIENCE FURTHER EDUCATION INFORMATION SERVICE, Room 26, Elizabeth House, 39 York Rd, London SE1 7PH, which will send you useful booklets free of charge. *The CRAC Directory of Further Education* (very expensive so look it up in the library) lists all the opportunities in further education under subject headings.

Far fewer girls than boys take up skilled apprenticeships, and the vast majority of those that do choose hairdressing and manicure.

Maybe it's a specific training you want, rather than an academic course, in which case a good starting point is to look through the CRAC/CBI Yearbook *Education and Training*.

Two out of five girls go into clerical jobs.

---

2. *Vocational training*

This is a specialized training for a wide variety of jobs, anything which comes under the broad heading of 'technical' and can be as diverse as computer programming or catering. It's available in colleges of further education and also in polytechnics and other institutes. Courses can be done part-time, full-time or in the evenings, and they usually lead to qualifications from recognized bodies like the Royal Society of Arts or City and Guilds. Often you can do them with few or no 'O' levels, and they are essentially practical, both in course content and application.

In 1972 only 13.3% of students on sandwich courses were women. In the same year only 28.8% of students on day release courses (also done in employer's time) were women.

---

3. *'On the job' training*

This means that your employer pays for your training, either through an apprenticeship scheme or by releasing you during working hours for a specific course which will increase your skills and qualify you for eventual promotion in the work you are doing. To begin with you'll be earning less money than many of your friends doing unskilled jobs, but the temporary low pay is a good investment for the future.

One-third of girl school leavers go straight into the manufacturing industries, mainly clothing, textiles, food, drink and tobacco.

Since the passing of the Sex Discrimination Act it has become illegal to refuse women and girls access to any apprenticeship or training course they may wish to take up, for instance, in the printing industry, which has hitherto been barred to women. However, although this opens up many new areas of opportunity to women, it will take some time before this right is fully accepted. Providing you have the right qualifications, you're legally entitled to insist on being accepted for the training course of your choice, but if your employer refuses to recognize this right, or your head teacher or careers officer tries to put you off from applying on the grounds that the work isn't suitable for women, you can now take your case as an example of unlawful discrimination to an Industrial Tribunal. (For a full description of how to do this see the Sex Discrimination Act and the Equal Opportunities Commission, p. 123ff.)

Two-thirds of girl school-leavers go into what are broadly called the service industries, which include shops, insurance, banking and finance, and professional and scientific services (nursing, teaching, social work etc).

Your careers officer should have a complete list of apprenticeships and training schemes available in your area, but also look at the *Personnel and Training Year Book* published by Kogan Page, 116a Pentonville Rd, London N1, which covers industrial training courses at every level. It's expensive, so ask for it in your public library.

Another useful source of information about industrial training courses is your local regional training officer. There is a different one for each of the Industrial Training Boards, which were set up under the 1964 Industrial Training Act to represent employers, employees and educational bodies in all branches of industry. The

Education Committees Year Book gives a complete list of the boards and their officers (available in public libraries), and ACE (p. 204) publishes an index of *Industrial Scholarships and Training Schemes*, 60p.

Only 1.7% of girls enter employment leading to a professional qualification, e.g. the law, accountancy, surveying, etc., compared with 3.4% of boys,

---

4. *Training for a profession*

Entrance requirements vary enormously – anything from a minimum of 3 'O' levels to a degree – so it's best to write directly to the relevant professional body for advice and information about any career in which you're interested. (For addresses look at any of the careers guides we have recommended.) Some, like nursing, pay you from the moment you start training. Others, like accountancy, chartered surveying or the law, require certain academic qualifications before you're allowed to enter a firm as an articled clerk, where you'll gain experience and be allowed time off to study for further qualifying exams, while earning a small salary. Here again there's been considerable discrimination against women in certain areas, either by a quota system as in the medical schools, or by quite deliberately refusing to consider applications from women, even when they were suitably qualified. This is now illegal, but there's a lot of ground for women to make up.

5. *Higher education*

You can study for a degree either at a university or a polytechnic. There is a vast number of subjects to choose from and a mass of general information. To help you, we have selected just a few of the most basic and reliable guides. The minimum academic requirements for doing a degree course are usually two 'A' levels, but exceptions are made for mature students and others. (See Starting Again, p. 98.)

Choosing a University, 70p, is intended for those still at school, to help them choose the right 'A' levels for the degree of their choice, but it's also a good basic guide for anyone wanting to know about the actual content of different degree courses and how to apply. When making your choice it's important to remember that some degree courses are essentially academic in content and do not qualify you for a particular job (this is especially true of the older universities). Others combine more than one discipline; for instance, a language may be studied together with history and sociology, rather than from a purely linguistic and literary standpoint, and still others, like law, medicine or psychology, are preliminary qualifications for further training in a specific career. Before you decide on a traditional university degree, it's worth looking closely at the amazing range of courses offered by polytechnics, many of which will fit a course to the individual student's requirements. *Rethink your Plans?* price £1.00 published by CRAC (address p. 209) is a very helpful guide to the wide range of educational opportunity open to people over the age of 18.

For a complete guide to degree courses, consult *Which University?* published by Haymarket Press, which gives details of *all* degree courses, but it's expensive, so look it up in your local library. The UNIVERSITIES CENTRAL COUNCIL ON ADMISSIONS (UCCA) publishes a useful handbook on admissions procedure to universities only; it is available from UCCA, P.O. Box 28, Cheltenham, Glos. GL50 1HY, price 40p post free.

The Compendium of Degree Courses, published by the COUNCIL FOR NATIONAL ACADEMIC AWARDS, 344-354 Gray's Inn Rd, London WC1 8BB, is *free*, is revised every year and is a complete guide to first degree courses in polytechnics. If you want to know more about what goes on inside these universities and polytechnics and to judge whether their facilities, atmosphere, etc., are right for you, it's well worth looking them up in *The Alternative Prospectus of Universities and Polytechnics*, by Vicky Payne and Vivien Lipschitz, published by Wildwood House. Written by two women ex-students, this is a handbook compiled for the student *as a whole person*, not just as a machine for learning, and it takes into account the inbuilt handicaps from which certain students suffer in orthodox circles, like being black, or gay, or a woman. It answers all the questions you'd want to ask but couldn't put on your UCCA form and which your teachers wouldn't know how to answer. Various students' unions are now compiling their own alternative guides, so if there's a particular university or polytechnic which you want to know more about ask the NATIONAL UNION OF STUDENTS (NUS) (address p. 204) if it's got one of these guides.

Approximately 22% of working women and 36% of non-working women who intend to return to work would like some form of re-training.

Mature students are usually people over the age of 25 who may have few or no recognized educational qualifications but want to study: some universities and polytechnics will consider them for a degree course. If they can prove they have followed a systematic course of study, say at a WEA institute (Workers Educational Association) or done one of these induction courses mentioned above, they stand a much better chance of being accepted. They may be asked to write an essay, and relevant experience is also taken into account, especially for jobs in social work or the probation service.

THE OPEN UNIVERSITY is quite literally that: open to anyone, regardless of qualifications, who is over 21 and resident in the United Kingdom. There are 6 faculties – Arts, Social Sciences, Mathematics, Educational Studies, Science and Technology – with over 90 courses at different levels. Study is done mainly at home, with students receiving regular packages of learning materials and doing written work for a tutor who sees the student normally once a week. This is supplemented by television and radio programmes, a few hours a month at a Study Centre and a one-week residential summer school, held at universities, which is compulsory for foundation courses. Three years is the minimum time in which you can work for a BA degree, which you get by earning 6 credits. Most completed courses are worth 1 credit, but it's more realistic to reckon on taking 4 to 6 years.

It's important to apply early – between December and June for courses which start the following January – because places are allocated on a first-come, first-served basis. It costs £10 to register and you have 3 months to decide whether you are doing the right thing before paying the further final registration fee of £15. The fees are kept as low as possible, but Open University students are not eligible for a local education authority grant, although you can sometimes get the cost of the summer school. This is obviously unsatisfactory, as it prevents many people who have little or no income from enrolling – such as pensioners and housewives for instance. The OPEN UNIVERSITY STUDENTS' ASSOCIATION is pressing the Department of Education and Science to make summer school grants compulsory and is also asking for full grants to cover the cost of teaching, books and travel. The association publishes an annual handbook for students and staff and arranges a variety of services, mainly by co-ordinating students on a volunteer basis; anything from organizing special study courses for visually handicapped people to providing a baby sitter. For further information about the Open University write to P.O. Box 48, Milton Keynes MK7 6AB.

It's possible to study part-time for a degree at certain poly-technics and universities. BIRKBECK COLLEGE, part of London University, only accepts students who are in full-time employment, and they attend all their lectures in the evening. London University is the only university which offers the possibility of doing an external degree, a marvellous service for people who are handicapped, or living too far away, or abroad, or for some other reason wouldn't be able to live in at a university. However, unlike the Open University, you must have the minimum university entrance requirements, usually 2 'A' levels. The degree is done by correspondence course (see below). For further information write to the Registrar for External Students, University of London, Senate House, Malet St, London WC1E 7HU.

The National Extension College (p. 209) is the most interesting of the correspondence colleges because it is a non-profit-making body and as such is concerned only to do the best possible for its students. Apart from offering tailor-made courses for GCE at ordinary and advanced level, the University of London external degrees and certain professional qualifications, it has devised some very helpful 'beginners' courses' for people about to study for 'O' levels or for the Open University. Particularly good is the one on 'How to Study Effectively' which can be done on its own (time needed about 2 to 3 months if you work 6 hours a week) or it can be done together with another course. For a complete list of correspondence colleges, write to ACE (address p. 204) for their list, 25p. Don't be fooled by extravagant promises and always read the small print carefully, as people have been known to start on long study courses, only to gain a 'diploma' of doubtful value.

Another way of preparing for university if you don't have 2 'A' levels is to follow a 1 or 2-year course at one of the adult residential colleges dotted up and down the country. RUSKIN COLLEGE, Oxford, is probably the best known and is mainly for people with trade union connections. It gives special preference to anyone who left school at the statutory school-leaving age. HILLCROFT COLLEGE, Surbiton, Surrey, is for women only and has recently broken with the tradition of not preparing students for specific examinations by instituting the (CNAA) Certificate, which has 3 options, Art, Social Science and Social Studies. CNAA (The Council for National Academic Awards) is the only other body, apart from universities, allowed to give degree-level qualifications. The Social Studies certificate is open to women who can show they have had relevant social work experience, either voluntary or as an unqualified paid worker, and its great advantage lies in qualifying you for a professional job in social work or, if you prefer, for going on to do a post-graduate course.

As each of these colleges is very individual, both in its selection procedures and the range of courses offered, it's best to write to them for their prospectuses; you can also visit them by appointment before applying. Others which offer the same type of broadly based non-vocational courses are: NEWBATTLE ABBEY COLLEGE, Dalkeith, Lothian; COLEG HARLECH, Gwynedd; CO-OPERATIVE COLLEGE, Stanford Hall, Loughborough, Leicestershire; and PLATER COLLEGE, Boars Hill, Oxford (mainly for Catholics, but open to others).

If you can't get away on a residential course, it's perfectly possible to attend part-time day or evening courses which may be counted as enough pre-university preparation, providing you can show convincingly that you have followed whatever it is systematically and to some advantage.

Apart from asking at your local college of further education, consider applying to the following bodies: the *extra-mural department* of your nearest university (address in the telephone book); the WORKERS EDUCATIONAL ASSOCIATION (for a full list of district secretaries who can inform you about local classes, write to the WEA headquarters (p. 210) and THE NATIONAL INSTITUTE OF ADULT EDUCATION (p. 210), which publishes a bi-monthly information journal called *Adult Education* and can put you in touch with regional organizers of courses.

If you are very academically inclined and want to pursue a particular research project or to do a higher degree, it's worth contacting the Lucy Cavendish College (Lady Margaret Rd, Cambridge CB3 0BU). This college is for mature women students only, mostly doing post-graduate degrees, but it now also admits up to 50 women doing first degrees. If they are not living in the college, students must live within 3 miles. Fees, etc., cost £300 for UK students and £500 for overseas students, but it's worth trying for an LEA grant.

Starting again

1. Learning

Whether or not she already has a degree or some other specific qualification, any woman wanting to return to work after some years spent at home must think carefully about what she wants to do and whether she can afford to spare time either to train or re-train. The decision is easiest for women who have a job they want to pick up again. It's sensible to keep in touch with your work and with any organizations connected with it (this is easier in the professions), even when you're not working, as many such organizations are now offering special facilities to women members who are temporarily out of action. Apart from refresher courses and information services, it's slowly being realized that *part-time re-training* as well as part-time opportunities for work are essential for women with young children. Where they all fall down badly, even those where the majority of people trained are women, as in the medical ancillary professions like physiotherapy and occupational therapy, is in not offering *part-time training* to late entrants; added to which they also often operate an age bar. There's scope here for investigation by the Equal Opportunities Commission. *Comeback: A Directory To the Professions*, edited by Beatrice Musgrave and Joan Wheeler-Bennett, is a comprehensive and practical guide. It's available from the publishers Peter Owen Ltd, 20 Holland Park Ave, London W11 3QU, £1.10.

Many women either don't have a job they want to return to or decide they would like to start something entirely different. *Returners*, published by the NATIONAL ADVISORY CENTRE ON CAREERS FOR WOMEN (p. 209), 85p, is a useful starting point for anyone who doesn't know where to begin to look or feels doubtful about her chances in a particular area, either because she may not have the right qualifications or because there may not be suitable part-time opportunities, either for training or part-time employment. It's packed with practical advice, information about opportunities for both qualified and unqualified people, and useful addresses.

Before you rush into enrolling for a GCE course at your local college of further education, it's worth consulting the CAREERS

ADVISORY OFFICE (address in your local telephone book) or going to your local job centre, which may either put you in touch with a careers advisor or direct you to an occupational guidance unit (see p. 90 for details). These units are particularly good at helping married women who want to return to work but are doubtful about their skills and have no idea what opportunities might be open to them.

There are also colleges and institutes which offer specially planned courses for women who want to know what is involved in returning to work. Often it's more a question of discovering latent abilities or restoring confidence than having a specific number of 'O' levels. 'Return to Work', organized by Manchester University's extra-mural department, is one such course which has been so successful that it has now been awarded an EEC grant for further research into the whole subject, but there are many other similar ones up and down the country. Find out whether anything similar has been organized in your area, either from your local education authority (address in the telephone book) or by asking at your nearest college of further education.

2. Paying

Money is a big problem for any woman wanting to study. Whether she's single, married, divorced, widowed or separated, she is always assessed as someone's dependant – husband's or parents' – unless she can prove that she's been self-supporting for 3 years (single women only). Married women get the same grants as students living at home with their parents and they are also subject to the 'spouse's contribution' clause, which applies to married men as well, but obviously penalizes women far more often, because their husbands are more likely to be earning above the means test limit. This means that not only are they deprived of the dependants' allowance which a man gets, but they must also rely on their husband's approval and sympathy to do their studies. Many women have already dropped out of courses as a result. Divorced or separated women are assessed as if they were single and they get allowances for dependent children or adults; *but* income from other sources, for instance, a widow's pension or maintenance from an ex-husband, is deducted from the grant. Unmarried mothers get even less, as they're not allowed any personal allowance and they get smaller allowances for their children, in term-time only.

Join the WOMEN'S LIBERATION CAMPAIGN FOR LEGAL AND FINANCIAL INDEPENDENCE (for statement of aims and address, p. 212) if you want to see injustices such as these abolished, which are at the root of women's oppression in our money-dominated society. Meanwhile you need money, so what do you do?

Firstly, *never* be put off applying for a course because you don't have the money. Even before you're given a place, apply to your local education authority. LEAS give *mandatory* (compulsory) grants to anyone who has at least 2 'A' levels and has been offered a place in a university, polytechnic or college of education. This grant pays for the cost of tuition, registration, examination fees and term-time maintenance, but is subject to the deductions and allowances mentioned above. At the time of writing, a grant for a single student living away from home is just over £600, but there's little point in giving a more detailed breakdown of figures as the exact amounts are always changing. Women who have been admitted to a particular course, in other words they have a place in one of the 3 types of institution mentioned above, but who don't have 'A' levels, aren't eligible automatically for a mandatory grant, so they must apply to their LEA for a *discretionary* grant instead.

Discretionary grants are normally given to people who are either doing a course which is below degree level, or who have previously had a mandatory grant, or who, like so many women, have been admitted as mature students on a mature entry scheme without having the usual number of GCE passes. As the name implies, awarding this grant and deciding the amount to be given is left -en tirely to the discretion of the LEA (the one in whose area you live, not where you've got a place). Some are more helpful than others and more sympathetic to the problems of mature students.

However, don't be put off by these difficulties, because LEAS aren't the only source of money. The NATIONAL UNION OF STUDENTS (address p. 204) publishes some useful pamphlets for people who are finding it hard to get an LEA grant: *Mature Women's Grants*, 10p, and *Educational Charities*, 15p. A good comprehensive guide is ACE'S *Grants for Higher Education*, compiled by Judith Booth, which gives detailed information about all the grant-giving organizations, including universities, various industries and the services. A couple worth mentioning, because they offer interest-free loans to women only (repayable when you start earning), are THE SOCIETY FOR PROMOTING THE TRAINING OF WOMEN (p. 210) and THE NATIONAL ADVISORY CENTRE ON CAREERS FOR WOMEN (p. 209).

3. Training

If you've missed out on a training the first time round ('On the job' training and training for a profession, p. 91ff), don't despair. The government-run TRAINING OPPORTUNITIES SCHEME (TOPS) exists for people who are not eligible for a grant or whose employers can't or won't pay for their training. It deserves to be better known than it is. It's open to anyone over the age of 19 and runs more than 500 different courses in a wide variety of subjects in Skillcentres, colleges of further education and employers' establishments. It's immensely flexible in operation because it caters for all the following categories: first-time trainees; people who've decided to switch direction, say from being a clerical worker to a technician or a craft worker; and people who may already have a professional training like teachers and nurses, but want a higher diploma, say in vocational guidance to become a careers officer. Recently it has opened the door to people who want to complete an interrupted course. One thing TOPS doesn't do is to find jobs, but it's attached to local job centres which are run by the EMPLOYMENT SERVICES AGENCY, and this will help you to find something you want to do.

Women ought to take more advantage of TOPS and to extend their range beyond the somewhat narrow secretarial skills which are the most commonly attended courses at the moment. So if you want to be an electrician, a watch repairer, a jewellery maker, a laboratory technician, a carpenter, a plumber, etc., *insist* on being allowed to do the aptitude test, which is fairly basic. If it's necessary for certain courses, you can do a pre-TOPS course to get your language or elementary arithmetic up to standard. Now that we have the Sex Discrimination Act, women can't be refused these jobs and, whatever the economic climate, there'll always be a demand for people with skills to offer. The government has made it clear that this is one area where money will not be cut back, and women have an extra advantage in that the one element of positive discrimination in their favour which has been written into the Act says that women must be given training if they want it, are up to it, and their employer can show that there have been few or no women with a particular necessary skill in his firm over the last 12 months or more.

You get a tax-free allowance, plus allowances for dependants (children or adults), plus other additional benefits if you're eligible (an earnings-related supplement, travel and lodgings expenses, free midday meals and your National Insurance stamp paid). Discrimination against women still exists in two respects: firstly, married women don't get the dependants' allowance, although they probably have to make arrangements for the care of their children, especially if they have to stay away from home for a course; secondly, there are hardly any part-time courses except the occasional secretarial one. This must be brought to the notice of the EQUAL OPPORTUNITIES COMMISSION. For further information about TOPS, see p. 210 or inquire at your local job centre.

4. Lifelong learning

Not as drearily earnest as it sounds. The idea of continuous access to education from childhood to retirement and beyond has been a long British tradition, from the last century when working men's institutes were established to allow men who'd left school at 11 to 'improve' themselves by further education. Nowadays, women are in the majority at evening classes of all kinds, vocational and non-vocational. You can do practically anything – upholstery, car maintenance, karate, child-minding, literary appreciation, women's studies, languages – and if there's something special you want to do which isn't included in your local institute's list, most principals will do their best to set up a course if you can guarantee between 8 and 12 regular participants. This has been the theory, and often the practice, up till now, but the financial future is bleak for non-vocational adult education, and these spontaneous arrangements will be the first to suffer.

Hobbies can be converted into money but watch out for exploitation (p. 107). It's worth inquiring at your local Art College about courses, whether you're artistically inclined or want to develop a talent into a commercial skill. Even if the college doesn't offer the particular course you need, the principal will be able to put you in touch with the appropriate craft association. The Loughborough College of Art, Loughborough, Leics, has been running very successful part-time 2 to 3-year courses in dress design and related subjects, for older married women, which qualify them to work professionally.

Working

Women and their work

Except perhaps for the idle rich, all women work. Some of them get paid for some of it. Most women work for love or because they have to. Until nursery provisions are available for all, and until men share household tasks, women with families will continue to be unpaid servants or 'economically inactive', as the statistics of employment describe them. And those who do a paid job will continue to bear the burden of 2 jobs. Probably only single women without dependants can enjoy any measure of equality with men, and there are fewer and fewer of them; marriage increases in popularity. More women marry and have children at a younger age. They have fewer children. With greater life expectancy, their potential working life is considerably longer than it was a generation ago.

Over 9 million women go out to work in Great Britain today, 35% of the total labour force.

In 1972 there were 5½ million married women at work and their number is increasing.

In 1971 at least 1 in 6 of all households, excluding pensioners, were substantially or completely dependent upon a woman's earnings or benefits.

Most of these households had either children or adult dependants, including husbands. The 1971 census shows that nearly 2 million women under retirement age were the chief economic supporters of their households. This includes 300,000 married women, 520,000 single mothers, and single women including 300,000 with elderly or infirm relatives. These figures leave out the large number of families in which the wife's wage, although lower than her husband's, is crucial to the household budget.

These facts about women's employment hardly support the image of the male breadwinner, yet this myth is still dominant in the minds of the public and is kept going by the State in all kinds of ways,

like social security cohabitation rules, pension regulations and tax benefits. The male 'head of the household', providing for his dependants while his wife/cook/baby-minder/cleaner/washerwoman may do a bit of part-time work on the side for pin money, is the image of the family still kept going by legislators and the media. When did you last see an advertisement, apart from air hostesses serving, showing a woman doing a paid job? Or for that matter, a man in the kitchen? The low pay and poor conditions of most paid work that women do hardly suggests that they are in it for pin money. Most women go out to work because they have to.

Approximately 40% of women work in service industries, about 30% in manufacturing and just over 20% in commerce, mainly the wholesale and retail trades. Of all girl school leavers about 40% go into clerical work.

Of all women in employment, approximately 75% are in jobs which take less than 6 months to learn.

In the professions, women are only well represented in the traditional female jobs: nursing, teaching and social work. For example, only 5% are in the legal profession, under 2% are draughtsmen. Most women do work which is basically similar to housewife's work. They accept jobs requiring little or no training or skill, with low pay and poor conditions. Even highly educated women will do jobs well below the level of which they are capable.

Women's average earnings in industry are approximately half the average earnings of men. The same differential exists in non-manual work.

According to the New Earnings Survey for 1975 published by the Department of Employment just before the Equal Pay Act came into force in January 1976, 10% of women earned less than £23 a week (a man's average pay is now £60.80) and 90% earned less than £56.20.

Women in paid employment meet discrimination at every level and in all kinds of ways. A report published in June 1975 by the Department of Employment, shows that most personnel managers think that a man is more likely than a woman to have the qualities required in an applicant for a job. *Management Attitudes and Practices towards Women at Work*, a survey carried out in over 200 firms by Audrey Hunt of the Office of Population Censuses and Surveys, shows that the predominant attitude towards women workers is that they are likely to be inferior to men.

In an excellent report of one industry, *Patterns of Discrimination against Women in the Film and Television Industries*, prepared by the Association of Cinematograph and Television Technicians, Sarah Benton catalogues in detail the causes of women's inequality.

1. Blatant discrimination against women applying for jobs.

2. Undervaluing of jobs done by women.

3. Educational and social 'conditioning' and the lack of training facilities, which deny women the opportunity, both before and after they enter the industry, to work in a wide range of grades.

4. The job structure of the industry, which makes most women's jobs dead-end jobs and makes movement across and up from the type of work they normally do extremely difficult.

5. Job insecurity and work relationships which make most men see women (and other minority groups) as a threat not only to the existence of their jobs, but also to work relationships.

6. The denial of women's 'right to work' by both State and employers which exclude many women from various rights and conditions of employment because it is assumed their main responsibility lies in the home.

7. The lack of trade union activity against discrimination because women have less time to attend union meetings, and many of their needs and concerns are not regarded as suitable union concerns.

8. The economic and social structure and the inadequacy of legislation which force women into certain economic roles which the law does not alter.

Apart from meeting prejudice at work, women also have to cope with the burden of household chores. Some husbands help a bit, but it will usually be the wife who is ultimately responsible for making sure that the household keeps running. Most men have to be asked and reminded to do these household jobs. Most men don't go to work worrying because they've forgotten to iron a blouse for their daughter's school function that night. They don't *share* the responsibilities of the home, even though they may be prepared to help. And, of course, many men – probably the majority – do practically nothing in the home which they regard as women's work.

A mother with young children who has to go out to work may also suffer the disapproval of neighbours, family and friends, for neglecting her offspring. Dr Mia Kellmer Pringle, influential in ideas about child care, staunchly advocates in her book *The Needs of Children*, that young children need full-time mothers. In fact only 20% of mothers with children under 5 work part-time outside the home, and only 4% full time. It doesn't help these women, probably forced by economic necessity to leave their children with child-minders to be made to feel guilty because their kids may suffer 'maternal deprivation'.

And in the end, many women find that by going out to work they merely replace one form of drudgery with another. The advantages are a small pay packet, some adult companionship and a change from the isolation of the home. Equal pay and anti-discrimination legislation are unlikely to affect this reality for a long time.

Wages for housework

Should housewives be paid? They work. If they weren't there to 'service' their men and rear the next generation of workers, someone else would have to do it.

The Legal and General Insurance Company in October 1975 issued figures claiming that it takes a nanny, housekeeper and cleaning lady to replace a mother, and that their wages would cost £71 a week. Even if there were no family, they reckoned it would cost £31 to have a wife's work done by outsiders.

Some people in the women's movement in this country have advocated that there should be wages for women and men, working or not, married or not. Selma James in her pamphlet, *Women, The Union and Work*, argues that 'when capital pays husbands they get two workers, not one', that most women work hard all the time either for capitalism or servicing workers and should be paid for it. She quotes Mariarosa Della Costa in *Women and the Subversion of the Community*, who says that women must give up the myth of liberation through work, because going out to work is merely another form of exploitation. It means moving from imprisonment in the home to being chained to the desk. THE POWER OF WOMEN COLLECTIVE, a group within the women's movement, describes a woman's 'un-waged' condition as her basic weakness. Wages for housework, they say, would destroy women's dependence on men and therefore destroy their destiny as housewife. They also argue that if women received wages for housework, they would get better pay in employment.

The problem with this argument is that it assumes that every home needs a full-time worker and that the mother should be that worker. With all the conveniences that are available today, house-work does not need to be a full-time occupation. In fact, studies done of housewives show that they spend as much time on housework as they have time for. Women with nothing to do let it become a whole day's work. Women who are busy with other things do it in less. To raise the status of housewifery in this way would, on the one hand, confirm the isolation and boredom which many housebound women feel, and on the other, prevent the possibility of household tasks being shared by all members of the family. For Selma James, a wage implies social recognition. It may make servitude more pleasant but it also establishes it more firmly.

For many women, child-rearing and housework are not the most fulfilling aspects of their lives; in any case, they don't take up all their lives. Many women *have* to go out to work. Many women *want* to go out to work. The advocates of wages for housework are right to say that women can only be liberated when they are economically independent. The best way to achieve that independence is by earning money outside the home.

It is impossible to describe here all the work that is, or should be, available to women. In the chapter 'After School' (p. 86ff), information is provided on career guidance and post-school training facilities. The rest of this chapter will cover some aspects of paid employment as it affects women.

WAGES FOR HOUSEWORK? After eighteen years as a 'perfect mum', Ms Jean Garside of Wetherby was presented with a silver cup, the title of 'Mum of the Realm', and a cheque for £1,000. As the Daily Mirror of 19 November points out, 'Her veterna touch finally paid off...' Well, yes... but at a rate of just over £1 a week...

Homeworking
(sometimes called Outworking)

Some women do work in the home which *is* paid. Nobody knows how many there are; one estimate is about 250,000, but it could be twice that number. Most of them are attached to the garment trade – hosiery, clothing, lace, footwear, etc., but all kinds of other industrial processes – for example, making toys or Christmas crackers – are carried out by women in their own homes. They are usually mothers with young children or elderly or disabled dependants, old-age pensioners, the disabled; a large proportion are immigrants. They are perhaps the most exploited group of workers in this country. 'Sweating', as it was called, was a scandal in the 19th century. The situation has changed little today.

In a study of homeworkers by the Low Pay Unit, *Sweated Labour*, it was found in 1975 that 20% of the sample earned $4\frac{1}{2}$p an hour or less, 80% were getting 30p an hour or less.

They describe a firm selling model football teams for 50p. A woman making them at home got £3.50 per thousand. The company made a profit ratio of 130%. Another woman made lampshades for $1\frac{1}{4}$p, each which retailed at 56p. Arran sweaters, hand-knitted, labelled, pressed and packed for £2 each, retailed for £16.95. Add to this picture the fact that most of the employers concerned have *no* overheads to pay for – no heating, lighting, power, national insurance, sickness or holiday pay, working space, toilets, canteen facilities, accident insurance – because these are borne by the workers themselves, who in some cases also pay for the transportation to their home of the raw materials and the delivery of finished products, and a condition of total and complete exploitation emerges.

Why do women do it? Why don't they protest at their pay and conditions?

– Because it's the only way they can earn any money

– Because they are isolated and frightened of losing the work (frequently different homeworkers are paid different rates for the same work but they don't know about each other)

- Because they're not organized into trade unions. Trade union organization is based on the place of work and the unions are hostile to homework because it undercuts union rates and depresses wages
- Because many homeworkers are immigrants who are doubly isolated by language and cultural barriers from the rest of the community
- Because they may be supplementing inadequate social security benefits or pensions and are frightened that these will be cut once their extra earnings are discovered

And for the employers they provide a buffer against fluctuations in demand: if they want work done, a cheap reserve army of labour is available; if there is no work, they usually have no financial or other obligations to the workers. The homeworkers themselves have no control over the amount and type of work they receive, or if they get any at all. Most of those concerned don't live in spacious houses, so creating work and storage space adds to the inadequacy of their homes. Often the work may be dangerous but they have no insurance.

Attempts to improve the lot of homeworkers have been made for a century with little success. The trade unions believe homeworking should be abolished. Others have suggested that it should be made compulsory for all homeworkers to be registered and their functions timed and valued on the same basis as work done in factories. If you are ever attracted by an advertisement offering work to be done 'in the comfort of your own home', think again. You may need to work from home, but you'll get little reward.

Protective legislation

Various investigations into the condition of factory work at the turn of the 19th century, particularly in the north, where the industrial revolution began, showed the sordid reality of child labour. Children of all ages worked long hours in overcrowded and insanitary conditions and were subject to all kinds of contagious diseases as a result. Reformers and politicians were appalled, and Parliament was eventually persuaded to legislate to prevent the worst aspects of the exploitations of children. At a time when free enterprise meant free enterprise, this was no mean achievement. The first

Factory Acts restricted the hours of work of children in the cotton mills. When children could no longer be exploited so effectively, the factory owners turned to women as a source of cheap labour. Women suffered the same appalling conditions and ill health, particularly during pregnancy. Slowly throughout the 19th century, various Factory Acts were passed to restrict the hours of labour for women, to create safety regulations and to institute a factory inspectorate. All this was achieved against the opposition of an organization of mill owners (which Dickens dubbed the 'Association for the Mauling of Operatives'), and in the 1870s against the opposition of the feminist movement.

The feminist movement in the 19th century was made up mainly of middle-class women whose main problem was that they could not work: they were excluded from the professions. They believed any restriction of women's labour was a restriction on the right of women to work at all. Today, the same debate has emerged again.

Most of the protective legislation passed in the 19th century is still on the statute book in an amended form. Restrictions on women's work are contained in the Employment of Women, Children and Young Persons Act 1920, the Hours of Employment (Conventions) Act 1936 and the Factories Act 1961. Various bodies, including the last Conservative Government, the Confederation of British Industry and sections of the women's movement, have proposed that this legislation should be swept away in return for laws to prevent discrimination against women. They argue that women cannot be equal if special laws exist which treat them un-equally, that it is an infringement of women's liberty to be restricted in their working life, and that, in any case, the social conditions which gave rise to protective legislation have now passed.

Anna Coote in her pamphlet, *Women Factory Workers*, published by the NATIONAL COUNCIL FOR CIVIL LIBERTIES, refutes these arguments. She points out that if women were allowed to work all hours, it would merely add to the double burden they shoulder as workers *and* housewives. The night cleaners, who are not affected by protective legislation, who work through the night for pitiful wages and then go home to look after their families and hope to catch a few hours sleep during the afternoon before they return to work, are a good example of what would probably happen to many women. Because women aren't organized in unions, they have very little strength to fight this kind of exploitation, and protective legislation prevents some of the worst abuses. Shift work and long anti-social hours are only not good for anyone. Protective legislation should not be repealed, but extended to all workers.

The regulations apply only to factories, which means a place where any articles are made, altered, cleaned, washed, repaired, ornamented, finished or adapted for sale by means of manual labour.

It is illegal for women
– **to work for more than 9 hours a day or 48 hours a week**
– **to start work before 7.00 am or go on working after 8.00 pm (1.00 pm on Sundays)**
– **to work more than 6 hours overtime, or 100 hours a year, or work more than 10 hours in any one day including overtime**
– **to work on Sundays, bank holidays, Christmas Day or Good Friday without a day in lieu**
– **to clean machines if this would expose them to risk or injury**
– **to work with certain toxic substances which may be dangerous to their health**

Also, women must have a half-hour rest period after $4\frac{1}{2}$ hours of continuous work, or after 5 hours if they have had a 10-minute break. Women may be exempted from these regulations if their employer applies to the Secretary of State, and he is satisfied that 'it is desirable in the public interest to do so for the purpose of maintaining or increasing the efficiency of industry or transport'. About 2 million women work in factories. Nearly 200,000 are covered by exemption orders.

If you want more information about your job and protective legislation, contact the local Labour Exchange or an office of the Factory Inspectorate, or send for the Department of Employment pamphlet on the Factory Acts to HMSO, 49 High Holborn, London WC1. See p. 126 for the effect of protective legislation on the Sex Discrimination Act.

Health and safety at work

This year 100,000 women will be injured at work or will contract a 'prescribed' industrial disease that will keep them off work for more than 3 days. On average, each will be off work for more than 4 weeks. Most women are not paid when they are sick.

– Of all women who are forced to give up nursing through illness, 40% do so because of back pain. Shortage of money means that lifting aids are seldom available. Shortage of staff means that patients are lifted without assistance. Few hospitals have occupational health services; they get rid of nurses with back trouble.

– Inflammation of the tendons in hands and forearms caused by fast repetitive jobs costs women more lost working days than men, in spite of the fact that there are many more men at work.

– Thousands of women develop varicose veins as a result of standing for long hours at work (and at home).

– Many thousands of women contract dermatitis each year though only about 6,000 are able to prove to the Department of Health and Social Security that it is caused by work and therefore be eligible for injury benefit.

If you are injured at work or contract a disease which could be due to your work, tell your trade union official. If you are not in a union, ring the local office of the Factory Inspectorate, under 'F' in the telephone directory. They have to pursue any enquiry or complaint, even if it is anonymous. They're responsible for the administration and enforcement of the Factories Act of 1961, some premises under the Offices, Shops and Railway Premises Act of 1963, and the Health and Safety at Work Act, 1974. They have the power to prosecute employers who fail to provide safe and healthy conditions for their workers.

For further information look at

The Hazards of Work: How to Fight Them, by Patrick Kinnersly, Pluto Press (p. 229).

The Shop Steward's Guide to Workplace Health and Safety, by Denis Gregory and Joe McCarty, Spokesman Books, (p. 229).

Equal pay

An Act became law on 29 December 1975 which for the first time attempts to make employers pay women the same as men. In the words of the advertisements published by the Department of Employment:

Every woman who does the same or broadly similar work as a man for the same employer at the same place of work has a right to the same rate of pay.

No firms or types of employment are exempted, however small, and the Act applies to part-time and full-time work. It also covers such matters as overtime, bonuses, holidays and sick pay. It does not cover employment conditions relating to retirement, marriage or death.

But although the Act was actually passed by Parliament in 1970, and employers have had five years in which to introduce equal pay, the situation has hardly improved at all. As you can see from the figures quoted on p. 104, just months before the Act came into force women were earning on average about half what men earn in all occupations. The Act itself has serious inadequacies and many employers have found ways to get round it. They have done this

– by grading jobs which only women do differently from jobs that only men do, and paying the latter more

– by reclassifying jobs and giving women's jobs different names so that women can be paid different wages

– by using job evaluation exercises which set higher pay for special aspects of jobs men do (like heavy and shift work) and lower rates to aspects of jobs that women do (like manual dexterity)

– by paying bonuses for something like long service which women cannot claim because their working career is likely to have been broken by childbirth

– by using contract labour for work previously done by female employees

– by transferring women to jobs where there are no male workers to compare themselves with

If you think you're not getting equal pay, you can bring a case before an INDUSTRIAL TRIBUNAL (p. 128). For help with this, contact your union or the ADVISORY, CONCILIATION AND ARBITRATION SERVICE, Cleveland House, Page St, London SW1 (01-222 4383).

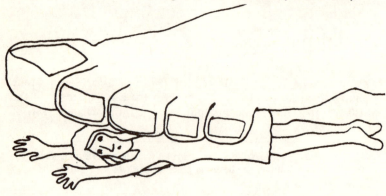

Wages Councils

In Eire, a national minimum wage has been established, as well as an inspectorate to enforce it. In this country minor attempts have been made to make sure that a minimum wage is paid in some trades. Wages Councils meet from time to time to set a statutory minimum wage and holiday pay in certain low-paid occupations, mainly the retail trade, catering and the clothing industry. Under the Employment Protection Act, which comes into force in April 1977, they will also have power to prescribe other terms of employment such as sick pay. The rates are enforced by the WAGES INSPECTORATE, who deal with individual complaints, advise employers, and have to inspect $7\frac{1}{2}\%$ of all establishments concerned every year. There are eight regional offices. Wages in agriculture are dealt with separately by the Ministry of Agriculture.

Contact the nearest offices of the WAGES INSPECTORATE, usually found at the Regional Offices of the Department of Employment, to see if you are receiving the right pay. If you are a member of a trade union, they will advise you. Or write to the Secretary of the Wages Council, 12 St James's Sq, London SW1.

The Wages Councils cover an enormously varied group of trades, which includes many processes surrounding the rag trade, hairdressers, staff of works' canteens, pubs and restaurants, milk distributors, booksellers, and stationers, bakers, newsagents, tobacconists and many others.

Maternity leave

Some women who work in the public sector have been able to claim maternity leave from their employers, which means they have received some or all of their wages for a period before and after childbirth. Most women who work have received no benefits at all. Britain lags far behind the Common Market countries in providing state insurance schemes for pregnancy and in placing legal obligations on employers to keep women's jobs open for them.

The Employment Protection Act which has just been passed by Parliament guarantees a single or married woman 6 weeks' maternity leave if she has worked 2 years with the same employer. It comes into force in April 1977. Provided she tells the employer before leaving, she will be entitled to have her job back up to 29 weeks after the birth of her child. The maternity pay will be nine-tenths of her full pay, less the £11.10 National Insurance maternity allowance.

Apart from the state schemes, you should try to negotiate with your employer for better maternity benefits.

The TUC Women's Advisory Committee has drawn up a list combining the best practices achieved in the public sector. Try to get these agreed in your firm. They are:
- **all women, should be entitled to maternity leave – married and unmarried, full-time and part-time.**
- **women should be eligible for maternity leave after working for a company for 1 year. A period of up to 3 months off work should not count as a break in service.**
- **the best employers in the public sector give 18 weeks leave: 4 weeks on full pay less National Insurance benefit, plus 14 weeks on half pay without National Insurance deduction.**
- **most employers withhold a part of maternity benefit until the woman returns to work. The minimum penalty the TUC found was 4 weeks pay.**

At present if you have paid the full rate of National Insurance contribution, you can claim a maternity allowance and earnings related supplement for 18 weeks.

For further details see *Women's Rights: A Practical Guide*, by Anna Coote and Tess Gill (p. 224), Penguin.

The Working Women's Charter

"—now for the other 40 hours!"

The Working Women's Charter was drawn up by the Women's Sub-Committee of the London Trades Council in March 1974. All over Britain, women and men are setting up groups to promote its aims. In over 27 towns and cities throughout the country, trades councils, tenants' associations, claimants' unions, students' unions and women's groups are organizing around the demands of the Charter. It says:

We pledge ourselves to agitate and organize to achieve the following aims:

1. The rate for the job, regardless of sex, at rates negotiated by the trade unions, with a national minimum wage below which no wages should fall.

2. Equal opportunity of entry into occupations and in promotion, regardless of sex and marital status.

3. Equal Education. Training for all occupations and compulsory day release for 16- to 19-year-olds in employment.

4. Working conditions to be, without deterioration of previous conditions, the same for women as for men.

5. The removal of all legal and bureaucratic impediments to equality, e.g. with regard to tenancies, mortages, pension schemes, taxation, passports, control over children, social payments security and hire purchase agreements.

6. Improved provision of local authority day nurseries, free of charge, with extended hours to suit working mothers. Provision of nursery classes in day nurseries. More nursery schools.

7. Eighteen weeks' maternity leave with full net pay before and after a live child; 7 weeks after the birth if the child is still-born. No dismissal during pregnancy or maternity leave. No loss of security, pension or promotion prospects.

8. Family planning clinics supplying free contraception to be extended to cover every locality. Free abortion to be readily available.

9. Family allowances to be increased to £2.50 per child, including the first.

10. To campaign among women to take an active part in trade unions and in political life, so that they may exercise influence commensurate with their numbers, and to campaign among trade union men, so that they too may work to achieve these aims.

The campaign for the charter

The following organizations have pledged support for the charter as at August 1975:

12 National Unions (NUJ; TASS; NALGO; ATTI; CPSA; ABAS; EQUITY; ACTT; NUS; NSMM; MUSICIANS' UNION; CSA)

58 Branches of other trade unions (ASTMS; AUEW; TGWU; TWU)

33 Trades Councils (e.g. Hackney, Camden, Westminster)

79 'other' (e.g. POLITICAL COMMITTEE OF THE LONDON CO-OPERATIVE
SOCIETY LTD, NALGO ACTION GROUP GLC; BRENT FEDERATION OF
TENANTS' ASSOCIATIONS; BRIXTON WOMEN'S CENTRE; CLPS; CO-OP
PARTIES)

A committee has been elected to co-ordinate the work of the
many Charter activities in the London area. To ensure the broadest
representation by all interested bodies, this co-ordinating committee
will stand for re-election at the next London delegate conference.

There are WWC branches doing similar work now in Bath, Birming-
ham, Bolton, Bradford, Brighton, Bristol, Cambridge, Canterbury,
Colchester, Coventry, East Anglia, Edinburgh, Glasgow, Hanley,
Hemel Hempstead, Lancaster, Leamington, Leeds, London (13
groups), Manchester, Newcastle, Nottingham, Oxford, Reading,
Sheffield, West Lothian and York. WORKING WOMEN'S CHARTER
CAMPAIGN, London Co-ordinating Committee, 49 Lowther Hill,
London SE23 1PZ.

Trade unions

Perhaps the simplest description of a trade union is that it is an
organization of workers established to defend and further its members' interests. They negotiate on behalf of their members and advise
and assist their members on such matters as wages, equal pay,
conditions of work, industrial safety, unfair dismissals and redundancies. Some control terms of apprenticeships; some run educational programmes for their members, and in industrial disputes,
some provide strike pay for their members. Most trade unions
organize workers with particular skills – printers, teachers, garment
workers, and so on – but some of the larger unions have become
general unions; that is, they are beginning to organize all workers
in a particular industry whatever their actual job is – for example,
the TRANSPORT AND GENERAL WORKERS UNION (T&GWU) and the
ASSOCIATED UNION OF ENGINEERING WORKERS (AUEW).

Union structures

Trade unions vary enormously in size, from some with millions of members to some with less than a hundred. Most of the headquarters of the major unions are in London and all national unions have regional offices where the full-time officials are based. It is very difficult to generalize about the structure of different unions, at a national or grass-roots level. The ruling body of all unions is the annual conference. Voting rights are normally in the hands of rank and file delegates from the local organizations. Permanent national officials may be elected or appointed. Regional officers are sometimes appointed by the head office and sometimes elected by the regional membership. The most common pattern of organization at the grass-roots is that individual members make up a branch which may be based on one workshop or office or factory, or more often on a group of workshops or offices in an area, depending on the size of the membership. Each year the members of the branch elect branch officials from amongst themselves – Chairman, Secretary, Treasurer etc. – who officiate at the meetings and carry on the necessary business between meetings. They are not paid by the union.

Shop stewards

Grass-roots union machinery is based on geography and branches usually span a number of places of work. For the purpose of negotiation at *one* place of work, workers elect one or more representatives from among themselves. Where there is more than one union in an establishment, workers of different unions may combine to elect their representatives. Manual workers normally call their representatives shop stewards.

Trade union aims

Although some of the mass media suggest that trade unions are subversive revolutionary organizations, the reality is rather different. Trade unions do not on the whole challenge the basic economic structure of capitalist society (that is, a society based on private ownership of property and the pursuit of profit). They have led struggles against exploitation through the demand for higher wages and reasonable working conditions – without those fights workers would be little different from slaves – and the trade union movement has fought for a century to establish the right to organize and the right to strike. But these struggles have been carried on within the context of capitalist society. Trade unions have accepted that wages are a legitimate measure of people's labour, while improving the worst aspects of that system. They have accepted that some work is worth high pay and some work is worth low pay, which means that differences between grades and between men and women have often been reinforced.

Women and trade unions

The total membership of the TRADES UNION CONGRESS (TUC) is 10 million. 2.4 million of those are women – 24%. There are 23 unions affiliated to the TUC with a mainly female membership, but the leadership of these unions is mainly in the hands of men. There are few female shop stewards and less than 2% of trade union officials are women. But women are joining unions at twice the rate of men.

Some people in the women's movement in this country believe that it is not worthwhile for women to become involved in union activity. Selma James, in *Women, the Unions and Work*, published by the Notting Hill Women's Liberation Workshop in 1972, argues that because trade unions have not been in the forefront of the fight for equal pay and because they have been so backward in organizing and supporting women workers, women should fight their fights outside the trade union movement. Although much of this criticism is justified, the conclusion does not necessarily follow.

"Right, brothers, that's all the business. Now, sister, can we have a cup of tea?"

It would be surprising if the men in the labour movement were very different from other men. They have been subject to the same propaganda which presents the usual kind of discriminatory attitudes towards women and work (that they only work for pin money, that they don't need equal pay because they're not supporting families, that if there are lay-offs women should be the first to go etc.). The response that women make to that situation should not be to opt out, but to fight.

Why join a trade union?

1. Because the more workers who join together to fight for their interests, the stronger they will be. The slogan of the trade unions, 'Unity is Strength', is not an empty one. When wage negotiations are taking place the unions' case is as powerful as the members they represent.

2. If workers don't act in unity, unorganized groups can be used by employers against the union, either by employing scab labour during strikes or people prepared to work for less than the rate demanded by the union at other times. Women have often been a source of cheap labour and have been used to depress wages.

3. Women are in a very weak position in the labour market. They are largely unskilled and have home responsibilities which make it much more difficult for them to bargain actively for higher wages and better conditions. If they are not in a union, their interests will not be represented at all.

4. With the new equal pay and anti-discrimination legislation now in force, major battles will have to be fought to secure women's rights. Trade unions provide the structure within which those struggles can be conducted.

Which union to join

If you work with people who are already in a union, join that one. If you work in a place where nobody who does the same job is in a union (people doing different jobs may be in a union which you cannot join), find out from offices or factories nearby what union other people like you are in and join that. If there is no union at your place of work, it may be possible to start a branch.

If you work in a large organization or factory or in the public sector, you should have little difficulty in finding out which union organizes people with your trade or skill – for example, the NATIONAL UNION OF TEACHERS for teachers, and the CONFEDERATION OF HEALTH SERVICE EMPLOYEES for nurses. A number of unions organize clerical workers – e.g. the T & GWU, the UEW, the ASSOCIATION OF SCIENTIFIC, TECHNICAL AND MANAGERIAL STAFFS (ASTMS), and the ASSOCIATION OF EXECUTIVE, PROFESSIONAL AND COMPUTER STAFF (APEX). If you work in local or central government, there are special unions, such as the NATIONAL ASSOCIATION OF LOCAL GOVERNMENT OFFICERS (NALGO) and the NATIONAL UNION OF PUBLIC EMPLOYEES (NUPE). If you work in a shop, the relevant union is the UNION OF SHOP DISTRIBUTIVE AND ALLIED WORKERS (USDAW).

There is usually a list of local trade unions under 'T' in the yellow pages of the telephone directory. You could ring the local office of one of the major unions, or the TRADES COUNCIL or LABOUR PARTY, and ask their help. Or write to the TUC at Great Russell St, London WC2, for advice on which union to join.

What to fight for

- If you are a member of a trade union, the following are some of the things it is particularly worthwhile for women to fight for within the union.

- that branch meetings be held in work time or at lunch time, and at the place of work, not in a pub in the evenings when most women can't attend

- the election of women as branch officials, delegates to the local trades council, etc.

- the appointment of a women's officer as one of the branch officials with responsibility for the work, pay and conditions of female members

- meetings of female members to plan campaigns on women's issues such as equal pay, the provision of crèches, etc.

- the adoption of the Working Women's Charter (p. 116)

If you meet opposition or cannot get anywhere, contact the national office of your union. Many unions have now appointed women's officers who should help with your problems. Look at *Danger: Women at Work*, National Council for Civil Liberties, 50p.

The Sex Discrimination Act

This chapter deals with the new legislation passed by Parliament during 1975, most of which came into force on 29 December 1975. Many parts of the Act affect matters dealt with in other sections of this book (see chapters on Working, After School).

The legislation is not a solution for all the ills which women suffer. It does not affect pensions, national insurance, social security or taxation. In the field of education, single-sex schools are untouched so the disabilities that girls suffer in such schools – mainly restriction in subjects they can take, due to lack of facilities for science, wood-work, etc. – will still operate. In the field of employment the Act does not apply in many cases: firms employing less than 6 people or in single-sex institutions or where 'privacy' or 'decency' might be threatened. And it will be very difficult for a woman to prove that an employer *intended* to discriminate, and thus be compensated.

In spite of these inadequacies, it is important that women take advantage of the Act and fight for it to be extended and strengthened. There is no doubt that this legislation would not have been introduced and passed so easily if it had not been for the growing pressure of the women's movement over the last 7 or 8 years. But there is a danger on the one hand that those concerned with its enforcement may present it as a total solution to the problem, and, on the other, that some women will adopt a complacent attitude and not feel the need to continue fighting for women's liberation. The Sex Discrimination Act is a minor reform on the way to liberation, and the EQUAL OPPORTUNITIES COMMISSION which it establishes is very unlikely to become the campaign centre for that fight, but the legislation could provide the climate within which entrenched and often unconscious discriminatory attitudes may be changed. Whether or not that happens largely depends on the actions of women, individually and collectively, in the use they make of the facilities it provides. The following guide to the Act is provided in the hope that women will exploit it to the full.

What the Act is about

The Sex Discrimination Act makes it unlawful to discriminate on grounds of sex or marriage in certain situations. It distinguishes between *deliberate discrimination* (for which damages can be sought) and inadvertent, *unintentional discrimination* (which will just be brought to the attention of the perpetrator in the hope that s/he won't do it again). An example of unintentional discrimination would be if a job was only available to employees after a certain period of continuous service. This would have the effect, although it may not have been the original intention, of discriminating against women because many of them will have taken time off for child-bearing. The Act applies to England, Wales and Scotland, but not at the moment to Northern Ireland. It is called the *Sex* Discrimination Act so also applies to men who may bring cases if they feel they have been discriminated against because of their sex.

The Equal Opportunities Commission

The Act established the EQUAL OPPORTUNITIES COMMISSION (EOC), in the words of the Act:

to work towards the elimination of discrimination, and to promote equality of opportunity between men and women generally.

It is now based in Manchester and is expected to have a staff of 400 when fully operational. The 14-strong commission is chaired by Betty Lockwood, who was the Women's Officer of the Labour Party. The government has said that they assume that at least half of the appointments to the Commission and its staff will be female, but this is not written into the Act. *The purpose of the EOC is: to keep the Act under review; to carry out research and conduct formal investigations into problems of sex discrimination, either on its own initiative or on the instruction of the Secretary of State; to make recommendations for changes of policy or procedure.*

The Government has specifically proposed that the EOC, in

consultation with the HEALTH AND SAFETY COMMISSION, should review the provisions of protective legislation (p. 126). Any proposals for change could be achieved by statutory instrument, without the passage of fresh legislation. The EOC has the power to serve notices requiring the production of information and the attendance of witnesses to further their investigations if they believe a person has broken the Sex Discrimination Act or the Equal Pay Act. If in the course of their investigations they discover that a person or company has been discriminating, they may issue a Non-Discrimination Notice requiring that person to stop discriminating and, if necessary, bring proceedings before the courts.

How to use the Act
Employment

This Act does NOT apply to you if you apply for a job or are working

1. In a **private household** (for example, as a cook or cleaner).

2. Where your employer **employs not more than 5 people.** If he employs more than that in different places, for instance 2 shops with 4 employees each, including part-timers, then the Act does apply to you.

3. Where the job is with an **organized religion** if the doctrines of that religion limit employment to men (for example, clergymen in the Church of England).

4. In the police force or prison service, where **height qualifications** disqualify you.

5. If the job is with a **charitable organization** which, under the terms of its charitable status, excludes certain benefits being provided for women.

6. Where **competitive sporting activities** are involved and the physical attributes of women disqualify them from performing.

7. In the **military services.**

8. Where the essential nature of the work requires **authentic male characteristics** and it would be incongruous or ridiculous to employ a woman (for example, a male model or actor).

9. In a situation where **decency or privacy** arises and physical contact with men would be involved, or where the work would involve seeing men undressed (for example, lavatory or changing-room attendants or corset fitters).

10. Where it is necessary to carry out the work to **live on the employer's premises,** like a ship or hostel, and separate sleeping and sanitary facilities for women are not available, and it is not 'reasonable' for the employer to provide such facilities.

11. In a **single-sex establishment** or part of an establishment providing special care, like a male old people's home or a hostel for maladjusted boys, where the job involves close daily contact with the inmates. This would not apply to kitchen or other ancillary staff in such an institution.

12. Where the employee provides individual members of the public with **personal services** to promote their welfare or education (for example, a team, comprising both sexes, of social workers or probation officers may, at any one time, require a man to complete the balance of the team).

13. Where **statutory restrictions on women working** operate. This means in jobs which are affected by the provisions of various Factory Acts. This covers factory jobs which require night work or excessive overtime, working underground in mines, certain jobs involving the cleaning of moving machinery, and jobs that would bring women into contact with certain poisonous substances, like lead manufacturing processes or where doses of radiation may have bad effects on pregnant women. This does not apply, though, if the employer already has enough men in his employment who are capable of doing the work which is affected by this protective legislation.

14. Most of the time or all of the time **outside Great Britain** where because of local customs or laws, the work could not effectively be performed by a woman. This does not apply to ships, planes or hovercraft registered in this country.

15. Where the job is one of two to be held by a **married couple.**

You may have a case if:

1. You have **applied for a job** and feel you were not offered it or not even considered because you are a woman.

2. You have applied for a job and **different criteria** are used to judge you in comparison with a man (for example, there are questions on the application form which are different from those a man has to answer, or, you have to have a medical examination when a man does not).

3. An employer offers you **different terms** than he has offered or would offer a man (for example, the possibility of joining an apprenticeship scheme or attending a day- or block-release course). This does not apply to death or retirement arrangements: that is, pension rights can still be discriminatory.

4. Your employer refuses to offer you opportunities for **promotion, transfer or training** which he has offered or would offer a man.

5. Your employer offers you different **fringe benefits or facilities** than he has offered or would offer a man (for example, cheap mortgages or the use of canteen facilities). This does not apply to death or retirement arrangements.

6. Your employer makes you **redundant, dismisses you** or puts you on **short-time** and does not do the same to men who are in the same position as you. This does not apply to retirement arrangements.

All these situations also apply if you are married and can show that a single woman has been given better treatment than you.

Preparing your case

If you think you have been discriminated against in one of these ways, look up the Department of Employment (under 'E' in the telephone directory) or the Industrial Tribunals (under 'T') and visit or ring the nearest INDUSTRIAL TRIBUNAL listed or your local CITIZEN'S ADVICE BUREAU to get the necessary forms. If you are in a trade union, your shop steward or branch secretary may be able to get you the forms.

The forms must be sent to the INDUSTRIAL TRIBUNAL within 3 months of the action of which you are complaining. This period may be extended in certain situations. They will then send a questionnaire to your employer or potential employer to find out why s/he took the action s/he did so that you have some basic information, to decide whether to bring a case or not. S/he is expected to reply. If s/he does not, then obviously the Tribunal can infer certain things. The employer may provide a perfectly adequate explanation for his/her action which indicated that you haven't been discriminated against because you are a woman. If you're satisfied with this, the matter may rest there. If not, the information s/he provides should be made available to you to help you in the preparation of your case.

At this stage, a Conciliation Officer from the Department of Employment will probably try to reach a settlement between you and your employer privately. Try to have someone with you when you go – a workmate or union representative. If a settlement is reached in your favour at this stage, then that is the end of the matter. But if you're not satisfied, you can insist on a Tribunal hearing.

If you are a member of a trade union, consult your local official, who may advise you and may represent you at the hearing. If you have nobody to help you, you may ask a solicitor for advice under the £25 Legal Aid Scheme. If you ask him/her to represent you at the hearing though, you will have to pay for his/her services. Also, there's provision in the Act for the EQUAL OPPORTUNITIES COMMISSION to help claimants if they feel the case raises an important question of principle or if it's extremely complicated. If you feel your case falls into one of these categories write to the EOC, Overseas House, Quay St, Manchester 3. But even if you have no help from these sources, you can still bring a case to the Tribunal. The Tribunal, unlike a court of law, is very informal and it's not difficult, and in fact is quite normal, for complainants (as you are called) to represent themselves.

The Tribunal hearing

The Tribunal is made up of 3 people: the chairperson who is a lawyer; a representative of the employers' side (a manager or boss); and a representative of the 'workpeople', which usually means an official or active member of a trade union. The government have promised that 1 of these 3 will be a woman. It's important for women to put themselves forward. Also present at the hearing may be a representative from the Department of Employment or the Equal Opportunities Commission, and the Tribunal clerk. The public is allowed to attend but rarely does so. The employers (respondent) and/or their representative will also be present but have no more status than you. It's a good idea to take a friend along to give you moral support if you're not represented.

Procedure varies at different tribunals but usually the chairperson will ask you to describe what has happened and in what way you feel you have been discriminated against. The employers, or their representative, will then reply and either of you may be questioned by any member of the Tribunal.

You must compare your situation with what has happened or might happen to a man in the same position as yourself. It's important that you compare yourself with a man who is similar to you in material ways, that is, ways that are relevant to your case. For example, if you believe that you have not been promoted because you are a woman, you should compare yourself with a man who has been promoted who is more or less the same age as yourself and has the same qualifications and experience. Your situations are materially similar. If you were applying for a job as a youth leader and you are 40 years old, it is no use arguing that the 25-year-old who was appointed is in the same position as yourself. Your situations are *materially* different and no presumption of discrimination should arise.

Take with you any relevant written material to show the Tribunal, like the job advertisement, job description, correspondence with the employer, evidence of your qualifications and experience, references, etc. Any evidence you've given to the Conciliation Officer may be presented if you wish. If you've found evidence of other discriminatory practices by the employer, tell the Tribunal.

The employer may argue that:

* *S/he* was not responsible for discriminating, but that the employment agency only sent men's details, that the personnel manager was responsible, or that other employees refuse to work with women. None of these arguments is justified. The employer is held responsible under the Act for actions by his/her staff, or agents, performed in the course of his/her employment, whether or not s/he knew what they were doing. In other words, s/he can't blame others or claim that nobody told him/her.

* You were not appointed because s/he wanted to maintain a sex balance in the work team or office. This is not a defence, unless the job involves personal services, like social work.The Act does not contain anything which allows employers to impose sex quotas in taking on people.

* You have not been appointed or promoted because men have always done the job before, or it's not a nice or suitable job for a woman. It's precisely this attitude which the Act is intended to remove.

* The work *might* involve night work or excessive overtime for which there are statutory restrictions on women. 'Might' is not enough. Also, s/he can use this excuse only if s/he has no men in her/his employ who could carry out the necessary shift or overtime work.

* S/he has no right to appoint or promote a man because the job falls into one of the Genuine Occupational Qualification categories (see points 8–15 on p. 125ff): for instance that 'leadership' qualities are required, and that this is a genuine male characteristic; that s/he has no toilets for women and cannot afford to provide them, so decency or privacy may be threatened; or that s/he is providing personal services and his/her customers don't like women. None of these arguments is justified under the Act and it's very important to make sure that the Genuine Occupational Qualification clauses are not extended in this way. Also, an employer can claim exemption under the Genuine Occupational Qualification clauses only if s/he does not have sufficient men to carry out the work from which women are excluded.

* Your employer may eventually agree that s/he has discriminated, but claim that s/he did not *intend* to do so. If the Tribunal believes him/her, then they can't penalize him/her. If you believe that this is not the case, and that the employer must have realized that the consequences of his/her actions would be discriminatory, then say so. For example, there may be certain conditions of the job, like regular travelling to other cities or countries, which have prevented women from applying in the past because of their home and family responsibilities. As a result it has become a tradition for men to do the job. It's important to argue that such 'customs', which rapidly become prejudices, must be got rid of, and that the employer is naive to suggest s/he was unaware of their discriminatory nature.

You must tell the Tribunal what you want if they find that the employer has discriminated. This could mean any of the following, depending on your situation:

That you be given the job for which you applied.

That you be able to join the training scheme from which you have been excluded.

That you be promoted.

That you be given the fringe benefits that had not been available to you previously.

If you've been dismissed, that you be reinstated (which means you get the same job back with the same pay and conditions) or re-engaged (which means you get a similar job to the one you were doing before).

If you don't want any of these things or the employer cannot provide them (for example, because s/he has already hired someone in your place), that you be paid money in compensation by the employer. This could be up to £5,200 or 104 weeks' pay.

You cannot be asked to pay any costs to the employer under any circumstances. Also, the Sex Discrimination Act makes it unlawful for someone to be victimized for making a complaint or discrimination or by giving evidence or information to help a workmate who has made a complaint.

Trade unions

The Act makes it unlawful for trade unions, employers' associations and professional associations to discriminate against women in membership, access to benefits, facilities or services, or by 'subjecting her to any other detriment', apart from death or retirement provisions. Two single-sex teachers trade unions are exempted until 1978. Cases can be brought before an Industrial Tribunal (p. 127).

Employment Agencies

It's unlawful for employment agencies to discriminate against women in the provision of or access to their services.

Job training

It's unlawful for any vocational training body to discriminate against women in access to training courses. This provision covers Industrial

Training Boards, the Manpower Services Commission, the Employment Service Agency, the Training Service Agency, employers' associations and any other approved body providing facilities for training. The Act makes provision so that people responsible for training courses can discriminate *in favour* of women to encourage them to take part in training from which they had been excluded before, or where there had been gross imbalance. It's also unlawful for any body which gives authorizations or qualifications to discriminate against women in registration, enrolment, approval or certification.

Education

The Act makes it unlawful for educational establishments to discriminate against women in admissions or terms of admission or in access to benefits, facilities or services in state schools, private and independent schools, special schools, universities, polytechnics and colleges. Single-sex schools or colleges or other educational institutions where only one sex is offered certain courses or boarding facilities are exempted. If such an establishment chooses to become co-educational, they may discriminate in favour of either sex for a period to increase the proportion of that sex within the school or college. Training courses in physical education are excluded from the Act.

This means that if the facilities are there for a male pupil or student, they must be offered to a female pupil or student. Inequalities of provision between different single-sex schools will continue until the resources are made available to assure that everybody being educated has equal access to all facilities. A claim under this section must be made first to the Secretary of State for Education, who may take up to 4 months to investigate the matter or not. Write to him at the Department of Education and Science. If you receive no satisfaction, then make a claim to a county court. (See below under Goods, Facilities and Services.)

Goods, Facilities & Services

The Act makes it unlawful to discriminate in the provision of goods, facilities or services, whether or not they are paid for. This covers:

There are a number of exemptions to this provision as follows:

- access to and provision of public places

- hotel, boarding house and other similar accommodation

- banking, insurance, loans (including mortgages), credit (including HP) or finance facilities

- educational facilities

- entertainment, recreation or refreshment facilities

- transport or travel facilities

- professional or public services

- the selling or renting of living accommodation and premises by private landlords or local authorities.

- the provision for the disposal of premises does not apply to owner-occupiers or small premises where accommodation is shared with the resident landlord or a close relative

- single-sex sections of political parties

- single-sex institutions providing special care, like hospitals or prisons

- single-sex religious institutions or homes

- special services for men where the presence of a woman would be embarrassing, like health clubs or lavatories

- where physical contact between the sexes might be involved

- the provision of goods, facilities or services outside Great Britain (not including ships, hovercraft or planes registered in this country)

- where the services or benefits are provided by a charitable organization which under the terms of its charitable status excludes certain benefits for women

- where competitive sporting activities are involved and the supposed physical attributes of women disqualify them from performing

- in relation to annuities, life assurance policies, accident insurance policies or similar based on actuarial or similar data

- private clubs

Proceedings under this section of the Act should be begun within 3 months through a civil court (a county court in England and Wales, or a sheriff court in Scotland). You may be able to get free legal advice and representation. Ask your local CITIZEN'S ADVICE BUREAU (CAB) for a list of local solicitors and details of the Legal Aid and Advice Schemes. Or go straight to the court (under 'Courts' in the local telephone directory) and ask the clerk to help you in completing the necessary forms.

As with employment cases, you have to prove that the respondent *intended* to discriminate in order to get damages. If discrimination is proved, damages may include compensation for 'injury to feelings'.

Advertisements

The Act makes it unlawful 'to publish an advertisement which indicates or might reasonably be understood as indicating' that jobs, goods, facilities, services or educational provisions are available to only one sex, subject to all the exceptions listed above. This means that, for instance, job discrimination with a sexual connotation (like 'postman' or 'waiter' or phrases like 'a bachelor-type job') are illegal. Cases of discrimination under this section of the Act can only be brought by the Equal Opportunities Commission.

Look at *Rights for Women*, by Patricia Hewitt, National Council for Civil Liberties, 65p, and leaflets published by the EOC, available from EOC or contact an office of the Department of Employment, or your local CAB. The NATIONAL COUNCIL FOR CIVIL LIBERTIES will help women with their cases.

MIS-FIT refuses to conform
MIS-FORTUNE demands equal pay for all women
MIS-JUDGED demands an end to beauty contests
MIS-LAID demands free contraception
MIS-GOVERNED demands liberation
MIS-USED demands 24 hour child care centres
MIS-DIRECTED demands equal opportunity
MIS-QUOTED demands an unbiased press
MIS-TREATED demands shared housework

Money – Our Rights

Women often don't have money which is their own, and even when they're entitled to it they meet with discrimination. We haven't attempted here to explain every aspect of the tax laws or the benefits to which you may be entitled, because this information is available from many sources. Below is a brief guide to the main financial provisions as they affect women and details of where further information can be found. These provisions are fully explained in *Women's Rights: A Practical Guide*, by Anna Coote and Tess Gill (p. 224). There are free leaflets available from government offices, post offices and CITIZEN'S ADVICE BUREAUX (CABS).

Tax

Tax is what is paid from your earnings to the Inland Revenue. You can get certain allowances (for children, mortgages, etc.) which means

part of your earnings are tax-free. These allowances are not given automatically; they have to be claimed. Most people's tax is deducted by the employer under the Pay As You Earn scheme (PAYE). If you are single, your tax position is the same as a single man's. On marriage, you lose the right to fill in your own tax form. An inquiry from the Inland Revenue to a woman states at the top, 'If you are a married woman living with your husband he should complete the form as if it were addressed to him'. You also lose your personal tax allowance, and your husband's allowance is increased. You can get your tax assessed separately from your husband, but it's complicated. If you claim a tax rebate, it will be sent to your husband. *Which? Tax Savings Guide*, and a monthly journal, *Money Which*, are useful reference works on this subject. They're available in all public libraries. For helpful organizations, see p. 212.

National Insurance

National Insurance is the scheme whereby you pay for stamps while you're earning and in return you get benefits while you are not working because of sickness, industrial injury, pregnancy or unemployment. New laws which come into force in April 1978 (the Social Security Benefits Act) will make the benefits more equal for men and women, but a married woman will still not be able to claim extra benefits for her husband or children unless her husband is actually incapable of employment. Patricia Hewitt has written on unfair dismissal and redundancy, as well as maternity leave in *Rights for Women*. Your local CAB will help with National Insurance problems.

Pensions

The size of your state pension is determined by how much money is paid towards it during your working life. Single women have the same rights as single men. Married women are treated as dependants of their husbands whether or not they are the breadwinner or equal contributors to the family budget. Under new laws which come into force in April 1978 (the Social Security Pensions Act), a woman's pension contributions paid while single will be taken into account, and a married woman will not be denied a pension just because she has not paid contributions for half her married life. Widows automatically get a pension because a wife is assumed to be dependent, unless she remarries or cohabits.

Pension schemes controlled by employers or insurance companies also discriminate against women. Very few schemes provide benefits for widowers or for dependent children or relatives of women. The Department of Health and Social Security produces various leaflets on pensions (p. 212); and for organizations that will help, p. 212.

Maternity Benefit

See p. 212 and p. 229.

Supplementary Benefit

This can be claimed as a weekly allowance from the State if you don't have enough to live on. Of those who get it, 68% are women. The amount you get depends on how much you claim and how much other income you have. For married women it's assessed according to the needs of the household, and in most cases your husband must make the claim and will receive the benefit. The 'cohabitation rule' means that if a woman is thought to be cohabiting (that is living as a wife) with a man, she has no right to benefit. As a result many women are harassed and questioned about their sex lives by Social Security officials, checking up on whether or not they're cohabiting.

For help in this area, contact your local CLAIMANTS' UNION, p. 212, the CHILD POVERTY ACTION GROUP (CPAG), p. 212, or the CITIZEN'S RIGHTS OFFICE, p. 212. There are a number of leaflets you can refer to: CPAG leaflets on *The Cohabitation Rule* and *Guide to Supplementary Benefit Appeals Tribunal*; the *Guide to Supplementary Benefits*, by Tony Lynes (Penguin, 40p), p. 229; *Supplementary Benefits Handbook*, HMSO; *Supplementary Benefit Rights*, by Ruth Lister (Arrow, 50p), p. 229; *National Welfare Benefits Handbook*, CPAG, (25p); *Women and Social Security*, CLAIMANTS' UNION (p. 229). For other help, see p. 212.

Widow's Benefit

The amount of Widow's Benefit a woman receives depends on how many National Insurance stamps her husband paid and how old he was when he died. Look at the National Insurance leaflet, *Guide for Widows* and *Widow's Benefits*. For helpful organizations, see p. 203.

Family Allowance

This can be claimed if you have more than one child, whether you are married or single. It's yours by right. A claim form is available from your local Social Security office. For more help, see pp. 206 and 212.

Family Income Supplement (FIS)

This is a weekly allowance for low-income families. How much you get depends on how much you earn. The FIS application form is available from your local Post Office. Check for more information with your local CLAIMANTS' UNION or the CAB (p. 212).

Working women and housewives staged a one-day strike in Iceland on Friday to show that they are indispensable to the country's social and economic life. Shops, newspapers, nursery schools and the telephone service closed down — and many men had to make their own meals

—SUNDAY TIMES

Women: victim and criminal

Victim

The Criminal Statistics for England and Wales show that 54 female children under 16 and 187 women of 16 and over were the victims of homicide in 1974. Homicide means murder, manslaughter and infanticide. The figures for males were 72 and 222 respectively. Of this total, 535, 98 were the son or daughter of the suspect. In 1974, 1,052 cases of rape were known to the police compared to 784 in 1971. 410 men were tried or sentenced in Crown Courts for rape. 90 were acquitted. Of the 317 found guilty, 277 were imprisoned, or sent to borstal or detention centre. Most of the rest received suspended sentences or conditional discharges, went to mental homes, or were put on probation. Also, 3,404 men were proceeded against in Magistrates' Courts for indecent assault on women and 128 for incest.

These figures, which only reveal the cases of assault leading to death or of cases before a criminal court, together with the evidence of wife and child battering which has recently come to light, indicate that for many people home is a very violent place. This chapter will describe two aspects of that violence as it affects women: battering by their husbands and rape.

Battered wives

In October 1975, Judge George Milner, during a trial at Durham Crown Court of a Sunderland man accused of causing bodily harm to a woman, gave him a suspended sentence and said, 'We are doing this because you have been forgiven (by the woman concerned) and because it may be that in the part of Sunderland where you live, this kind of behaviour is not so outrageous as it may be elsewhere.'

A magistrate, Margaret Lampard, speaking at the annual
conference of the National Council of Women in Buxton in October
1975 said, 'I have recently taken a special court case in which I gave
bail to a husband who battered his wife . . . She had deserved it and
he had every reason to batter her.'

The Family Service Unit in their *Quarterly Journal* in 1973 said
that they 'feel that it's important to differentiate between
sporadic "battering" which can be regarded as part of a normal
marriage, particularly in certain cultural groups, and more
persistent beating'.

Erin Pizzey, a fore-runner in setting up battered wives centres and
bringing the issue to the public, in her book, *Scream Quietly or the
Neighbours Will Hear*, quotes a social worker saying: 'It is not the
policy of the social services to interfere with the sanctity of
marriage.'

A committee of MPs looking at violence in marriage were
'disappointed and alarmed by the ignorance and apathy of some
Government Departments and individual Ministers towards the
extent of marital violence.'

How much goes on

In a Report of a Select Committee of the House of Commons,
Violence in Marriage, one estimate given for Wales suggests that
5,000 out of 680,000 married women are battered.

The Report recommends that refuges should be provided at the
rate of 1 family place per 10,000 population. The experience of the
WOMEN'S AID CENTRES is that as places become available they are
filled immediately. It seems that the problem is found in all social
classes.

What kind of violence

The few recorded case histories of battered wives show how very
extreme the violence against them can be. Erin Pizzey's book is a
shattering saga of women suffering vicious and repeated attacks on
their bodies at the hands of their men. Men rape their women, pour
boiling water over them, kick and punch them (sometimes when
they are pregnant), throttle and strangle them, break their bones,
attack them with knives and belts. These men may also batter their
children. They often break up the home and its contents.

Who batters

In what homes does battering occur? Many of the couples involved come from violent homes themselves and, as children, have suffered at the hands of their own parents. There is some evidence that couples who marry very young and have children immediately are particularly at risk. Violence is often triggered by excessive drinking on the men's part. Some of the men are mentally unstable. Some are unemployed. Some battering arises from deep-rooted male chauvinist attitudes by men who see their wives as their property, to be dealt with as they wish. When does the violence occur? It seems to arise in many different ways: the meal isn't on the table immediately the husband comes home; a child cries and cries and irritates the father; a wife rejects the sexual advances of her husband; she goes out without him, and so on. Why has the problem remained hidden for so long? Because of the fear of the women involved, the indifference of the authorities concerned and the reluctance of friends and neighbours to get involved.

Fear of reprisals and humiliation

Battered wives live in genuine and justifiable fear of reprisals from their husbands if they try to take any action. Even if they only run away to parents or friends, the men may follow them and commit further acts of brutality. If the woman considers taking any legal action, not surprisingly she hesitates before revealing in public the awful and degrading treatment she has suffered. She tries to keep up appearances because of her own pride and for the sake of her children. She is ashamed and embarrassed. Also she may feel some love and loyalty for the man who has battered her. It isn't easy for her to make herself responsible for putting behind bars someone with whom she has spent so many years of her life and who is the father of her children.

Action Frustrated

But mainly she does nothing because she can't do anything. She's often isolated from her friends, relatives and neighbours – a situation encouraged or forced by the man – and may believe that her situation is unusual, if not unique. Apart from the major difficulty of getting rented accommodation for women with children, she's unlikely to have sufficient economic independence to pay for another home. Her doctor or the hospital where she goes for help with her injuries tend not to want to give evidence in court. The social services tend not to 'take sides', or they argue that her husband is ill and needs the wife's sympathy and help. (Many of these social workers, however, are happy to recommend their clients to the Women's Aid refuges when their own efforts to support the family fail.) The police usually say that the home is beyond their surveillance (not, it seems, when they suspect that illegal drugs are being used), although they too refer women to Women's Aid Centres. Local Authorities who have a duty (under Section 21 of the National Assistance Act, 1948) to provide temporary accommodation for persons in urgent and unforeseeable need, tell a woman that she is not homeless because she has a marital home. The Social Security offices won't give her any money to find alternative accommodation because her husband is supposed to maintain her. The psychiatrists in the mental hospital where she may end up often believe that she subconsciously needs the violence. Solicitors don't want to be burdened with work that is urgent, takes a lot of time and is not financially rewarding. And even if a woman does take legal action by persuading the police to prosecute, or beginning divorce proceedings, or seeking a separation order, or suing for assault or getting an injunction against her husband, the law will act in its own time, and meanwhile she's vulnerable to further attacks by her husband.

Women's aid centres

For many of these women their only hope is to seek refuge for a period in one of the centres run voluntarily by women in various parts of the country.

In 1975 more than 50 houses provided accommodation for about 550 women and their children, often in short-life properties (p. 213 for further details). Many more are being planned. The centres are havens for women and children where they will meet others who have suffered similar experiences and feel secure amongst people who understand their situation. Many of the women arrive and bring their children and few possessions. Many have made the break after years of battering because of fear that their children are beginning to suffer physical or emotional danger.

The centres are not the most desirable or comfortable residences. The House of Commons Select Committee said: 'We are convinced from our visits to such refuges that they are not places to which women would wish to go unless they were in dire need.' And Erin Pizzey says herself that the overcrowding and primitive conditions of the CHISWICK WOMEN'S AID CENTRE indicates that women must have left unimaginable suffering to bear it. Some of the centres only accept women when they have space. A few maintain an 'open door' policy – anyone will be given shelter at any time of the day or night even when it means 4 children sharing a mattress and the mothers sleeping in the kitchen.

Some of the women come for a few days' temporary relief; others stay for months. They may not take to the cramped communal living, but they have no choice. Many are depressed, feel guilty and are frightened. For some, the shock of their separation enables them to return to their husbands and work out a 'tolerable' relationship. Some return to suffer further violence. Some pursue legal proceedings and gain possession of the marital home. Some find alternative accommodation, occasionally with other women they have met at the centre. Many receive help and advice while in the centre and find strength to fight their own cause with this support.

However adequate these refuges may become, they can never be more than a temporary solution for the women involved. In the long run, most of them must find a legal solution, and all of them must find permanent accommodation for themselves and their children.

The Law

The courts and police are slightly less lenient towards men who assault women who are not their wives. None of these proceedings is easy, cheap or fast. Women will need legal advice and assistance from a solicitor; they will have to make a sworn statement about the way in which they have been assaulted, and this will be read out in court, and they may be questioned about it; they will have to persuade friends and neighbours and perhaps the doctor who treated their injuries and anyone else who witnessed the assault upon them to give evidence in court to back up their story; they may have to fight for custody of their children and for the tenancy of the family home; if the man goes to prison they will have to be prepared to oppose his release at any stage if they don't believe his promises to obey the injunction. It will all take a long time.

THE WOMEN'S AID FEDERATION, p. 214, is the name given to groups working to provide refuge for women driven out of their homes by the violence of the men they live with. They have regular meetings and will also offer help and advice about grants, etc., to women setting up new centres.

A detailed guide to the law on battered women, by Anna Coote and Tess Gill, is available from The Cobden Trust, 186 Kings Cross Rd, London WC1 (1975). It goes through each stage of the legal proceedings involved for married and single women and includes a do-it-yourself guide to single women for getting an injunction in a county court.

Married women, with the help of a solicitor may:

- File a petition for divorce in a divorce court and apply for an injunction. An injunction forbids the husband to assault his wife, to enter the home or to continue whatever behaviour the wife has complained about. If the husband disobeys the injunction he is in 'contempt of court' and may be sent to prison
- Apply for a 'separation order' in a magistrates' court
- Start proceedings for a 'judicial separation' and then apply for an injunction
- Take out a summons for assault against her husband in the magistrates' court

Single women who are assaulted by the men with whom they live may:

- Obtain a summons for criminal assault in the magistrates' court
- Seek an injunction from the county court and claim damages for assault and/or trespass (if the place where they live is in the woman's name)

Rape

Conventional wisdom has it that most women secretly want to be raped and that men must be excused occasional sexual aggressiveness because of their 'uncontrollable' sex drive. In fact, studies in America of convicted rapists show that most crimes are planned. The trial in September 1975 of Peter Cook, the Cambridge rapist, showed the perverse and deliberate nature of his crime.

As with cases of battered wives, one of the reasons for the 'increase' in the rate of rape is probably related to women's growing awareness of themselves as women, the assertion of their rights, and therefore their willingness to report these crimes against them. Not surprisingly, though, many victims are still reluctant to come forward. They will have to suffer the humiliation of a medical examination, probably by a man, within hours of the assault; in court they will be subject to public curiosity about their previous sexual experience and attitudes; and they'll have to convince the jury that even though they didn't struggle (in order to avoid getting injured or killed), they didn't consent.

Rape cases are the only ones where the character of the woman as a prosecution witness comes under scrutiny. The defendant who has been accused of rape cannot – under the rules of evidence – be questioned about his previous sexual life.

The Heilbron Report

A public outcry followed the Morgan judgement in the House of Lords – that if a man *genuinely* believed the woman consented he should not be convicted of rape, no matter how *unreasonable* his belief may have been – and the spectacle of 74-year-old Judge Christmas Humphreys giving a self-confessed rapist a 6-month sentence. As a result the Home Secretary appointed a small committee to 'give urgent consideration to the law on rape . . . and to advise the Home Secretary whether any early changes in the law are desirable'. The committee was chaired by Rose Heilbron, one of Britain's two female High Court Judges, and reported in December 1975. They recommended:

- **anonymity for rape victims from the time of the offence until the trial is concluded**
- **that no evidence about a victim's previous sexual history should be allowed in court**
- **that at least 4 women and 4 men should be on juries trying rape cases**

They upheld in principle the Law Lords' ruling that a man cannot be convicted of rape if he honestly believed the woman consented, no matter how unreasonable that belief. They ruled that a man cannot be found guilty of a serious criminal offence unless he intends to commit the act or is reckless in the sense that he doesn't care whether the woman consents or not. A Private Bill to implement these recommendations is currently going through Parliament.

Rape means being forced to have sexual intercourse against your will. As far as the law is concerned 'sexual intercourse' simply means penetration; the man does not have to ejaculate. Rape involves a fundamental abuse of a woman's body. Enforced intimacy, the physical danger and long-term consequences, like pregnancy, are extremely damaging to a woman's life, emotions and attitudes. The law doesn't recognize rape by a man of his wife unless there's a separation order from a magistrates' court with a non-cohabitation clause or a legal agreement to separate which contains a non-molestation clause.

The problem of rape in America is greater than in Britain. Some American women have taken self-defence courses and others have formed vigilante groups. RAPE COUNSELLING GROUPS have been set up to provide counselling, accurate medical and legal advice and a 24-hour phone service. A similar group has been set up in Britain (p. 214).

An excellent pamphlet published by the National Council for Civil Liberties, *The Rape Controversy*, by Anna Coote and Tess Gill, describes the law with regard to rape, explodes some of the myths about the subject, discusses the Morgan judgement and suggests legal and other reforms to help rape victims. Available from 186 Kings Cross Rd, London WC1, 50p.

Criminal

In 1974, 174,886 females were found guilty of offences in courts in England and Wales, compared to 1,758,763 males. Of those, 11,330 were under 17, and 163,556 were 17 and over. Most of those convicted were fined. The rest received sentences ranging from conditional discharge and probation to suspended sentences and imprisonment.

In a study in 1967, Susanne Dell described the treatment which women receive in the courts. Her book, *Silent in Court*, is a disturbing record of the inadequate advice and assistance which defendants receive. Her researchers interviewed 638 women who went into Holloway Prison, about an eighth of all women received into prison in England and Wales in 1967. She found that

– Only 17% of those women sentenced to imprisonment by magistrates were represented. A third of the girls sentenced to borstal training were unrepresented.

– Of 68 women who were imprisoned because they hadn't paid fines, 57 were unrepresented. Only 16 of these had been allowed time to pay, and of the remaining 52 who were refused time to pay, 20 had either no income or were on national assistance.

– Two-thirds of the sample were *remanded* (kept in prison, awaiting trial or sentence) and not subsequently given custodial sentences; most of those were unrepresented. Of these, 11 were in custody for more than 8 weeks.

– Some were kept in prison for longer than their original remands because they had VD and needed to complete their treatment. One woman who refused to have an operation for cervical cancer, was sentenced in her own interests to 2 months so that she could be persuaded to have the operation.

– Just under half of those sentenced to imprisonment were found to be suffering from some form of mental disorder, but they received no legal assistance because of this.

– 10 of the women couldn't speak English and 6 of those had no legal representation.

– Of those who applied for legal aid in the magistrates' courts, only 43% were successful. The rest made no attempt to get assistance and the courts didn't tell them of their right to do so.

– Even those who got legal aid found the assistance usually consisted of a quick meeting with a solicitor in the court cells just before the hearing.

Why does proper legal advice and representation matter? Most people don't understand how to ask for bail (which means you can apply to stay out of prison before your trial). They plead guilty to charges – often on the advice of the police – in order to get the thing over with, without realizing the consequences of such a plea. Many women are inhibited and bewildered by the court proceedings and don't feel able to speak for themselves (p. 213). All of this is also true for the women who appear in court but don't end up in prison.

How do women react to life in prison?

For a persistent offender imprisonment among her friends and in familiar surroundings may be, at worst, a hazard of her trade and at best a welcome break. For first offenders, particularly a housewife convicted of shoplifting, 'the encounter with her fellow-prisoners may be the most frightening element. She will meet people of whose existence she had never known – drug addicts, prostitutes and lesbians, whose behaviour and attitudes may sicken her; and the uncontrolled behaviour of the more disturbed women, particularly the cell banging at night, will be a source of fear and alarm.'
Susanne Dell

A woman prisoner is cut off from her normal life, deprived of her possessions and locked alone in a cell for hours on end. And what about her children? She will have been taken straight from the court

147

to prison without any means of making arrangements for them or even finding out what's happened to them. 20% of the women in Susanne Dell's sample had dependent children aged 16 or less. 44% of the children were under 5. The social and psychological damage those children suffer is immeasurable.

On 31 December 1974 the number of women and girls in custody in England and Wales was 1,045: 700 adults and 345 young women under 21. This was an increase of over 12% on 1973. There are 2 closed prisons for women (Holloway and Styal in Cheshire) and a secure wing at Durham gaol, 3 open prisons, 3 remand centres, 2 closed borstals and 1 open borstal.

Over half of the women who find themselves in prison each year are on remand.

It's important to recognize that the treatment women receive from the legal and penal institutions of this country is no worse than that given to men. A much larger proportion of men commit crimes (over 10 times more than women), and there's some evidence that women actually receive more lenient sentences from the courts. Many many more men than women have to face the problem of police investigation, inadequate legal advice and representation in court, custodial remands and penal sentences.

'Women aren't usually able to spend Saturday afternoon breaking up the terraces at Trafford Park, or Tuesday evening robbing a bank, or Thursday morning fiddling their tax returns, or Friday evening getting drunk at the local, because they are feeding the children, cleaning the house, cooking meals and so on and so on.'

Prostitution

The incidence of prostitution in this country has gone down considerably since the Street Offences Act of 1959 which 'drove' it off the streets. Only 3,090 cases were proceeded against in magistrates' courts in 1974. The Act has had the effect of involving 'middle-men' in the trade – taxi drivers, hotel porters, café proprietors, etc., extending the call-girl system and increasing the display of small advertisements offering the services of 'masseuses', 'models', 'companions' and 'French teachers'.

Prostitution is a business. Research has shown that a form of apprenticeship operates, that tricks and techniques are shared, that prostitutes have their own 'shop-talk' and that they regard the work as *work*. The problem for those with previous convictions or cautions is that they become by definition 'common prostitutes', and if they're seen on the street talking to a man, the police will arrest them for soliciting, even if the man is a friend.

Prostitution itself is not illegal. It's not against the law for a woman over 16 to have sexual intercourse with a man and be paid for it. It *is* illegal to solicit; that is, to pick up a man in a street or public place for the purpose of prostitution. Of course, if there were no customers there would be no prostitution, but customers are not punished. The client is totally protected by the law: if he is solicited he doesn't even have to give evidence if the woman is charged. Contact the union for prostitutes; PROSTITUTES UNITED FOR SOCIAL AND SEXUAL INTEGRATION (PUSSI).

Shoplifting

It's the aim of modern merchandising techniques to make self-service as easy and attractive as possible. Customers are encouraged to handle and examine goods. Special offers and free gifts to encourage impulse buying mean people often spend more than they can afford, so a bit of impulse shoplifting takes place. The retailers' problem is that if he doesn't tempt the shoplifter, he won't tempt the customer. Supermarkets put great psychological pressures on people and many women, particularly older women or those with young children, find them confusing and complicated.

Shoplifting is thought of as a specifically female crime. In fact, slightly more men were convicted of shoplifting (28,636) than women (28,019) in 1974.

In a Home Office study published in 1973 it was reported that retailers reckon they lose £56 million to £300 million a year by shoplifting and £135 million to £200 million from staff thefts. There is a wide variation in the policies of retailers over finding offenders, reporting them to the police and prosecuting. Most of them concentrate on more efficient detection: plain-clothed store detectives, closed-circuit television, electronic devices which detect the stolen goods on the thief, surveillance mirrors, protected display equipment and fake cameras.

Those who are prosecuted often say that it was an isolated

incident of absent-mindedness or forgetfulness. People put things in their own bags instead of the basket provided by the store by mistake. To avoid prosecution, it is wise to keep your receipt and, if approached by store detectives, to be polite; a hostile response is likely to make them more suspicious. See p. 213 for advice on dealing with the police and information about where to go for legal help.

Child battering

Most people assume that because two people who live together have a child, some instinct teaches them how to care for it sympathetically and automatically to love it. In reality, for many young couples the experience of living together and bringing a child into the world can be very stressful. Young people may suddenly leave the familiar environment in which they have been brought up, and are expected to become a self-sufficient *family*, just like that. The woman, for the first time in her life, may find herself house bound and isolated. Her child, which she may not have wanted, demands her total attention. She may be lonely and frustrated and may become depressed and anxious. The child may become the butt of her frustration.

We're all horrified to read stories of children being badly treated and neglected. Yet no one who has brought up children of their own can truthfully swear that never once have they ever felt like hitting their children really hard. Fortunately, for most parents, the expression of their exasperation stops short of real violence. In some societies violence against children is unknown, yet the Department of Health and Social Security estimated that there were 5,700 cases of child abuse in the last 9 months of 1974. About 400 a year suffer permanent brain damage, many as a result of severe shaking. Probably as many as 700 children die annually. A study conducted in Birmingham showed that 15% of the children studied developed spasticity, paraplegia and other neurological damage that required long-term rehabilitation. There is the possibility, therefore, that battering is responsible for a large proportion of mentally-handicapped children. The killing of children who are battered seems often to happen accidentally: few baby batterers deliberately intend to kill the child, but sometime their ill-treatment leads to it.

More women than men batter their children. They are often young people who are exposed to excessive stress. They may have been neglected in their own childhood. As a result, they often make great demands on their own children by expecting uncritical love, obedience and good behaviour. Battered children are rarely neglected in the sense of being under-fed or badly clothed. On the contrary, excessive concern by the parents with neatness or cleanliness is common. The children must be a credit to their parents. Jean Renvoize in her book, *Children in Danger*, said that

'Most baby batterers are emotionally immature people who expect too much from their children, who punish them too severely for faults that in reality do not exist, but who often nevertheless fuss over them, sometimes with over-protective fanaticism.'

It's because in so many respects parents who batter their children are normal, and seem so concerned with the welfare of their children, that most child abuse is unrecognized. Busy family doctors, social workers and hospital staff are inclined to believe the explanations the parents provide for the injuries which their children suffer, however unlikely they may sound. Even parents who seek help by continually taking the child to the doctor for non-existent ailments, but who can't actually say that they've hurt it, often just irritate the doctor. And those who may have the courage to confess their behaviour to a social worker or doctor are likely to be put off by stories of prison sentences which other baby batterers receive. In September 1975, Judge Michael Argyle sent a woman to prison for 18 months for causing injury to her son when he was a few weeks old. Apart from the fact that that woman needed help, not punishment, such a sentence can only have the effect of putting off other parents who injure their children from getting help.

The Maria Colwell and Stephen Meurs cases showed that even when an incident of child abuse is known to social workers, teachers and neighbours, terrible consequences may not be avoided. The problem goes far deeper than the supposed faults of individual social workers; there is a contradiction between the desire to protect privacy and expecting the social services to prevent such tragedies.

It's not a simple task for the relevant agencies to deal with in any case, and many problems arise because of lack of liaison between them. Health visitors and social workers complain that the police barge in and accuse the distraught mother at a time of tragedy in the family, and that police interference prevents more humane solutions being found. The police complain that social workers are middle-class do-gooders who become emotionally attached to the parents and are more concerned with keeping the family together than with preventing possible deaths. The police also argue that unless there are sanctions against the parents, they'll go on battering. Obviously, for the parents to be sent to prison and the children taken into care is a failure on the part of the social worker. But many social workers are expected to assume full responsibility for such cases before they are properly trained, and they're all over-worked.

Apart from the statutory social services, some agencies who are concerned with this problem include

The NATIONAL SOCIETY FOR THE PROTECTION OF CRUELTY TO CHILDREN (NSPCC) (p. 213), and THE FAMILY FIRST TRUST, The Croft, Alexandra Park, Nottingham.

Legal Advice

This section has dealt with some aspects of the law as it affects women in particular. If you need legal help, either as the victim of crime, or if you are charged with an offence, the following may be able to help:

NATIONAL COUNCIL FOR CIVIL LIBERTIES, RELEASE, your local CITIZENS' ADVICE BUREAUX, MARY WARD CENTRE, your local neighbourhood law centre or THE LEGAL ACTION GROUP and BIT (p. 196). Look also at *Alternative London* and *Civil Liberty: The NCCL Guide*, by Anna Coote and Lawrence Grant (p. 230).

Dealing with the police

1 The police cannot detain you to ask questions without first arresting you. You do not have to answer questions or 'assist the police with their inquiries'. But if you are driving a motor vehicle, you must give your name, address and age if requested.

2 You do not have to make a statement. If you do make one, make sure it is accurate before signing it. It is often better to write it yourself.

3 If you are arrested, the police should tell you what you are charged with, allow you to telephone your family, a friend or a solicitor, and allow you to talk to a solicitor in private.

4 Your person may be searched by the police only for the purpose of obtaining evidence of the crime with which you have been

charged, or to safeguard damage or injury to persons or property. Women can only be searched by female police officers.

5 If you are arrested, ask for bail. The police should grant this unless the offence is very serious.

6 Do not make any deals with the police – for example, agree to plead guilty in return for bail, or admit to a minor offence in return for not being charged with a more serious one. Such deals are probably illegal and are unlikely to help you.

7 If you are appearing in court, get legal advice and assistance from a solicitor. If you appear in court without a solicitor, ask for a remand (an adjournment until you can get advice), ask for bail, and ask for legal aid.

8 Keep your cool at all times.

Celebrations

Film

Women have always been in the forefront of development and experimentation in film. With the growth of women's consciousness the traditional picture of women as decorative stars only in the cinema has been rapidly changing. Bolstered by a whole network of women's film events, women have been rewriting their own history and making what was concealed dramatically visible. Alice Guy Blache's films were among the first fictional works in the history of the medium. In France at the turn of the century, she turned out hundreds of 'one-reelers', from fantasies to comedies. In New York she founded her own company and became the most powerful executive-director in the business. She made a version of Poe's *The Pit and the Pendulum*, and a science-fiction work in which women rule the world, *In the Year 2000*. Lotte Reiniger made the first successful silhouette animation films in Germany in 1919; *Prince Ahmed* is a classic of this genre. Germaine Dulac was in the forefront of the surrealist movement in France. *The Smiling Madame Beudet* (1923) looks into the consciousness of an outwardly meek and model wife, while in *The Seashell and the Clergyman* (which caused Artaud to call her a cow in public) she used Freudian symbolism to attack masculine sexual fantasies. In Russia, Olga Preobrazenskaya, an actress turned director, directed short children's films and made, in 1928, a feature length film *Peasant Women of Ryazan*, with a wholly non-professional cast – very relevant to understanding the Russian women's movement before and after the Revolution. Also in Russia, Esther Shub, rescuing bits of discarded film from the cutting room table, discovered the principles behind the compilation film; *The Fall of the Romanovs* (1927) is a key work.

In America during the teens and 20s, before the importance of the still very new and flexible film industry had been fully realized, women were actively encouraged to direct or write and direct. Often stars directed their own films, e.g., Mabel Normand and some of the films in which she performed with Chaplin. Ida May Park was a

writer-director (*The Fires of Rebellion* and *Bondage*), as was Lois Weber, an early feminist. She was head of Universal's Bosworth studios and wrote and directed *Raffles*, among her more conventional films, as well as a series of outspoken films on women's issues like abortion, birth control and the white slave traffic (*The Sensation Seekers*, *The Marriage Clause*, etc.).

During the late 20s, Dorothy Arzner made films in which female behaviour and reactions are accepted as the norm, while masculine behaviour is examined from the point of view of female consciousness. *The Wild Party* (1929) stars Clara Bow. About a group of college girls, it is notable for its sense of solidarity. In *Merrily We Go To Hell* (1932), Arzner shows the break-up of a marriage. In *Dance Girl Dance* (1940), showbusiness and the conflicts produced by the stereotyped roles open to women and their own desires are examined. Katherine Hepburn is the heroine of a tale of marital infidelity and female professionalism in *Christopher Strong* (1933). *Craig's Wife* (1936) is about the sterility of a woman's total devotion to her home. Arzner was a marvellous director of actresses and perfected the technique of exploding the 'happy ending' by leaving unresolved conflicts, a sense of being trapped, in the air.

Leontine Sagan made her only German film, *Maedchen in Uniform*, with an all female cast (1931). It's set in a Prussian girl's school, and looks at female solidarity, lesbianism and authoritarianism. Ida Lupino made 8 successful, often witty films within Hollywood; they include *Not Wanted* (1949), about illegitimacy, *Never Fear* (1950), about a dancing team, *Outrage* (1951), about rape, and *The Bigamist* (1953) about a man who defies convention by marrying two women instead of keeping one as a mistress.

It's hardly surprising, given the industry's notorious resistance to new ideas, as well as its particular resistance to employing women behind the camera in positions of authority, that women should have been attracted to the freedom of self-financed experiments. Maya Deren, during the '40s in America, made non-narrative *avant garde* films. In *Meshes of the Afternoon* (1943), she plays a woman shaken by a series of incidents escalating to the terrifying. She made several films on dance, including *Meditation on Violence* (1948), around the Chinese martial arts.

Fresh possibilities coming with the New Wave and the events of '68 led to more public acknowledgement of some women directors. Mai Zetterling began a series of films about female sexuality. *Loving Couples* (1964) hinged on the idea that marriage is like 'falling asleep for the rest of your life'; there were also *Night Games* (1966) and *The Girls* (1968). The czech Vera Chytilova made *Something Different* (1963) about a woman gymnast and a housewife; *Daisies* looks at the lives of 2 anarchic heroines. Liliana Cavani's films try to contrast fascism with a belief in the truth of physical and emotional experience; thus *Galileo* (1968) and *Cannibals* (1970). In France, Marguerite Duras scripted *Hiroshima Mon Amour* (1959) and directed films such as *Detruite Dit Elle* (1970) and *India Song* (1974). Nelly Kaplan's vengeful heroine in *La Fiancée du Pirate* (1968/9) sweeps all before her; Kaplan is not afraid to break the bounds of good taste. In *Papa Les Petites Bateaux* (1972) she jokes against the male way of showing gangsters as 'things of beauty'. In Hungary, Marta Meszaros directed 3 films full of joy in and love for her own sex.

Although there is an increasing number of women working in Hollywood at the moment as screenwriters (Joan Tewkesbury on Robert Altman's films, Eleanor Perry at first on her husband Frank Perry's, now she works independently) or as co-screen writers or as assistant directors (once a male-only preserve), there are still very few directors (as in the European industry too). Exceptions are Elaine May (*A New Leaf* and *The Heartbreak Kid*), where female characters battle comically against stereotyped roles, and Stephanie Rothman, whose films are entertaining and staunchly feminist. *The Velvet Vampire* turns the tables on the vampire myth; *Student Nurses* has a realistic abortion and a marvellously liberating ending, while *Knuckle-Men* is a women's prison film and *Working Girls* is about prostitutes.

Though the emphasis here has been on directors, we shouldn't ignore the considerable achievement of all the women working in other fields within the cinema, most notably perhaps those actresses (like Bette Davis, Joan Crawford and Jane Russell) who, by uncompromising performances, have forced the audience to question the more conventional elements in their films.

Problems remain. Both Perry and May have stressed the difficulties over script-writing; May records the tendency of producers to take out the most crucial portions of the script. Perry recalls being told by another producer 'It takes balls to direct – why not be a script girl, kiddo'. Though *La Fiancée du Pirate* was a commercial success, Kaplan hasn't got the finance for her long-cherished project *The Necklace of Ptyx*. Despite the commercial success of Lupino's films, she hasn't been invited back to direct more. Blache's power waned when she passed the studio over to her husband; she died forgotten in a home. All this casts the achievements of women in the cinema in an even more remarkable light. All that can be done here is to point to the existence of a whole world of grass-roots film-making by women; to a wealth of investigative feminist-political film making; and large numbers of women working inside the experimental tradition. Also note the women film-makers working in films about the Third World (Sarah Maldoror's *Sambizanga* about the Angolan resistance, for example), about Vietnam, China, Eastern Europe, Japan, Hong Kong, etc. Such work should be sought out, seen and discussed. For more films, etc., see p. 215ff.

Theatre

Women actresses have been around since the 17th century. The tastes of the court at the time of the Restoration were French tastes, and the French liked women actresses. Many Restoration comedies were written by women.

Celebrated women in the theatre today are invariably actresses, and because of the public nature of their profession, they, if not their work, are usually widely known. There are the great dames, the likely dames of the future, the many actresses of slightly less front-page fame, but with solid well-deserved reputations. There is the newer generation of actresses establishing themselves within and by the 'establishment' theatre (i.e. major subsidized companies and the commercial West End), and those who have mixed their careers in all the media, yet keeping one foot firmly on the stage.

While these actresses are arguably celebrated enough not to need cataloguing here, they deserve mention for 'making it' (or trying to, for regardless of sex, the acting profession is notoriously oversupplied and under-employed) in a ruthlessly exploitative system. Also, unlike other professions, skill is only one of several necessary qualifications, the others being the ubiquitous (iniquitous) attributes of beauty, charm, charisma and sometimes sex appeal. The person of the actress, or actor for that matter, is a commodity in a buyer's market, self-exploiting and exploited. Fame is the spur.

At the same time acting is one of the few 'professions' (like wife-hood and housewifery) which is indiscriminately open to women and will be as long as there are roles for women in plays. In other areas of the theatre women have played a relatively small role, with writers, directors, designers, critics and particularly technicians few and far between in the past and, with a few important exceptions, still today.

There have been no 'major' women playwrights (with the possible exception of Lillian Hellman). In the wake of the 1956 New Wave drama, Shelagh Delaney and Ann Jellicoe emerged with Osborne, Wesker, Arden, *et al.*, but neither has proceeded to produce a body of work on a par with their male contemporaries. Since then only Caryl Churchill has achieved remotely similar stature. It's not easy to say why.

There have been no 'major' women directors, at least not in establishment theatre, though Buzz Goodbody became a Royal Shakespeare Company director in her 20s and began to establish a reputation, until she took her life last year. There have been few major designers: Motley (3 women) have designed primarily for the commercial theatre since the '30s; Tania Moisiewitsch and Tazeena Firth work regularly for the Royal Shakespeare Company and the National Theatre respectively; and Jocelyn Herbert and Deirdre Clancy have worked primarily at the Royal Court. But theatre design is still underpopulated with women. There have been no female Tynan's or Bentley's of drama criticism, though Penelope Gilliat, Helen Dawson and Hilary Spurling made respectable reviewing reputations for major newspapers.

In management, curiously, a number of women have made their mark. The grand lady of them all was Lillian Bayliss, conceiver and creator of the Old Vic and its tradition of Shakespeare. Italia Conti founded the child acting school which bears her name; A. E. F. Horniman founded the 'Manchester School', promoting new writers in the early part of the century; the late Caryl Jenner founded the Unicorn children's theatre company. Successful female managers exist in USA too, with Zelda Fichandler of Washington's Arena

Stage and Ellen Stewart of New York's La Mama being two current examples.

There are many women agents, the most notable being Margaret Ramsey, whose talen for spotting playwrights in the '60s has made her one of Britain's most influential agents. Gloria Taylor, Genista Streeten and Sue Rolfe have made careers as press reps.

A very special kind of theatrical 'management' has produced the only 'major' female figure and influence in British theatre this century: Joan Littlewood. She was the inspiration, as well as the creative and organizing force behind Theatre Workshop, especially in its halcyon days in the '50s at Stratford East, producing Brendan Behan and Shelagh Delaney and *Fings Ain't Wot They Used T'Be* and *Oh, What a Lovely War*. In addition to promoting new writers, Joan Littlewood was before her time in her political, social and community commitment and in her pioneering and experimenting with collaborative and 'co-operative' methods of rehearsing and production.

In fact, a variety of developments of politically- and socially-orientated theatre and co-operative production now characterize much of the most interesting work – and in many cases women's work – in theatre. The two most well-known companies happen to be non-British, but, significantly, woman-inspired: Ariane Mnouchkine's Theatre du Soleil in France and the San Francisco Mime Troupe in the USA, which has been recently reorganized on a collective basis by Joan Holden. In England, the WOMEN'S THEATRE GROUP has produced two excellent collectively-created shows, one on sex education, which toured schools, and the other on women's work roles. The people involved in these companies have deliberately chosen to work outside establishment theatre, and they are among the most radical in structure, working methods, and material. Even when the alternatives in alternative theatre (and there are over 100 companies in Britain now) are less radical, the most interesting current work is of a social, political, feminist or aesthetically experimental nature. And women are playing an increasingly important role in it and in previously male-dominated roles.

There are many directors: Jane Howell who created a socially conscious repertory at the Northcott Theatre, Exeter; Penny Cherns, who is concerned to pursue this policy; Pam Brighton, who directed brilliantly on the 'fringe' in the '50s and is doing community-committed theatre at the East End's Half Moon Theatre; Frances Rifkin, who began directing on the 'fringe' and then turned Recreation Ground into a company committed to the group creation of anti-fascist plays; Denise Coffey, who has written, acted in and directed many plays for young people at the Young Vic; Nancy Meckler, who founded the Freehold Theatre; Chattie Salaman who runs the community-orientated Commonstock Company; Sue Todd who is committed to feminist theatre.

There are designers who work in fringe and alternative theatre: Di Seymour particularly, Sue Plummer, Rita Furzey. Actresses who commendably seem to prefer alternatives to mainstream include Carole Hayman, Jennie Stoller, Mary Sheen, Caroline Hutchinson, Dinah Stabb. Critics like Naseem Kahn, on *Time Out* and the *Evening Standard*, and myself, in *Tribune* and *Theatre Quarterly*, have chosen to cover alternative theatre often in preference to establishment theatre. There is an increasing number of women writers in alternative theatre: Margaretta D'Arcy, Olwen Wymark, Pam Gems, Mary O'Malley, Jennifer Phillips, Dinah Brooke, Michelene Wandor – women who often want to write about women. And there are many women in partnership with men, who have established and run the best of the fringe and alternative venues: Joan Crawford at the King's Head, Verity Bargate at the Soho Poly, Thelma Holt at the Open Space, Shirley Barrie with the Wakefield Tricycle Company.

One thing is certain. In the '60s women may have begun to find in fringe theatre opportunities to work in previously male dominated areas closed to them in establishment theatre. Now it would appear that the alternatives might be a matter of positive choice. Perhaps women realize that outside of establishment constraints they are freer to create not only their own roles, but also models of working which are progressive and, perhaps most important, sexually undiscriminating.

Novels and poetry

It is arguable that writers are more different from other people than men are from women. And, as that early psychologist Galton put it in 1869, 'Poets are clearly not the founders of families'. Nor does anyone ask if Fielding could boil an egg or if Richardson was fond of his poultry. Because men are thus, men who want to write slam the door, take opium, ring for the servants in the middle of the night, go off on walking tours, get their valets to dress them and sit them down at 4.30 am – and all in the name of literature. Willy did it for his wife, Colette, with mediocre results. Otherwise, hounding their wives to write is not usually the kind of thing husbands expect to do. So women have to deal with the fierce impulse to write within a rigid time-table of housekeeping and child care. 'Marriage,' said Hardy, in spite of being a man, 'is your mind clear and your pen sharp and a great black bonnet coming round the door saying it wants to go for a walk.' And for women the black bonnet is being tied to your children's needs as well. The drain on the mind and the resources is well shown by the terrible experiment conducted on board US *Nautilus*. A doe rabbit, on shore, gave birth to a litter; the babies were immediately taken on board the submarine and killed at random intervals in the depths of the sea thousands of miles from the mother. She reacted every time. Women with children are like that sad, furry animal. Medea may have killed her children to punish Jason, but women who are also writers want to try and satisfy both urges. Sometimes they have solved it by making the creativity wait. Dangerous. Others have solved it by not marrying at all.

There *were* women writers before the 18th century. They were aristocrats polishing a dilettante talent in friendly competition with brothers or husbands in an era when literature itself was a mere accomplishment. The only known writer who produced criticism of society was, interestingly, Christine de Pisan (in the 14th century) who had been left a widow at 25. She was writing to earn a living.

Even in the 18th century, patronage was not easy to come by and not always satisfactory when you got it, *viz.* Dr Johnson. But he helped Charlotte Lennox and Anna Selward, championing them in his difficult trade. Fanny Burney was the one with a job at court and her *Evelina* and diary found the most favour. She showed the way to the many women who wrote novels as the century closed; Ann Radcliffe, who wrote *The Mysteries of Udolpho* and many other powerful Gothic fantasies, was perhaps the most distinguished. Mrs Radcliffe's novels usher in Jane Austen herself and her 6 matchless novels. In joyful competition with one another, the Brontë sisters produced *Wuthering Heights, Jane Eyre, Agnes Grey* and *Villette*. It's now well known that they had to give men's names when presenting their work to publishers; it's perhaps less well known that, although they all obviously fell in love, it was only when Charlotte married that she sickened and died! Jane Austen too nearly married, as a second best, but flew out in the morning to take back her promise.

Writers do need to be heard, though. Maria Edgeworth managed with a brother and Susan Ferrier with a father until their novels were widely known. Dorothy Osbourne wrote enchanting letters to a lover absent in the Civil War; Madame de Sévigné to a beloved daughter; Lady Mary Wortley Montagu wanted us to know exactly what it was like in a Turkish harem. That quiet genius, Dorothy Wordsworth, stored every experience, every vision of mountain and lake for her beloved brother to make into poetry. Anais Nin told everything to her diary. As writers, women in the past have shaped their talents towards an immediate outlet. But Dorothy Wordsworth lost her mind; can't even brothers tolerate an equal genius on the hearth?

Mrs Gaskell was married, it is true, and had several children for whom she cared, as well as writing prolifically. She was buoyed up by her sense of performing a public duty in bringing social evils to society's notice. *Mary Barton* was a successful and realistic novel. The conflict for Mrs Gaskell between writing and domesticity was probably less severe than for a woman who is 'merely' satisfying an urge to write for 'art's sake'.

Then comes George Eliot, that noble writer. She found a lifelong companion in a man who believed in her genius and was willing to support her through periods of depression. Virginia Woolf too found such a companion in her husband, someone willing to set aside his gifts in favour of nurturing hers. Emily Dickinson is another example of a writer who never married (although she clearly fell in love), but wrote her poems sheltered by father and sister. In this century, Marianne Moore was asked by her southern fiancé to give up 'that writing nonsense' when she married. She died old, successful and unmarried.

The 20th century shows it at last possible for a woman to write for a living. Dorothy Parker managed, so did Vera Brittain. But Katherine Mansfield, involved in her tormenting love relationship, became ill, and died feeling that she had never written as much as she had wanted to. Simone de Beauvoir eschewed marriage and writes books, many a source of inspiration to women. Colette wrote about the choice between love and art in *La Vagabonde*, showing that in the very act of writing she had already made the choice. Zelda Fitzgerald was superbly able to value her husband Scott as well as to love him, but he was not able to tolerate her production and insisted on near suppression of her work. Doris Lessing writes sensitively about the dilemmas of being a woman. Sylvia Plath compelled with her poems.

Now at last we are moving into a time when a woman writer

can legitimately satisfy the fierce and joyful desire to write, as well as to love and care for others. Now that each can be fulfilled less rigidly, it is far from remarkable that so many novelists are women. Moreover, it is becoming more and more of an intrusion to ask of women writers how they are balancing the two sides of their natures. It is certainly no longer cause for comment that so many women do write. The impertinence of questions about age or domestic arrangements recedes correspondingly. For example, among many others, none of the following writers are answerable on their age or their companions: Doris Lessing, Patricia Beer, Nell Dunn, Ruth Prawer Jhabvala, Alison Lurie, Olivia Manning, Iris Murdoch, Muriel Spark, Edna O'Brien. They stand or fall as writers.

Music

Music can be put to an individual purpose or to the purpose of the group. In either case it is rooted in magic and religion. A love song has an individual purpose. Once it would have taken the form of a charm, bewitching the soul of the loved person. A requiem has a social purpose. Once it would have been a request from the group to the dead man to go to his appointed place and not haunt the living.

Group music has naturally always been associated with official religion, which has in turn reflected and upheld the laws of the group. Since Christ's day Europe has had a Christian, male administration, and church musicians have been male. Today small churches use female organists, and some church choirs have women in them, but no woman holds a high musical post in the Roman Catholic or the Anglican Church, and few choir schools are open to girls. This is of little importance since most of our musical activity now takes place outside the Church. But in Bach's day almost all the work available to musicians was of the *Kapellmeister* type: the musician would write and put on music for his church, play the organ, and teach the choirboys to compose and perform. Private, secular music coexisted with sacred music, but since the Church was responsible for most serious musical training, and for composition in particular, important practitioners of secular music were likely to be church musicians too. Even musicians employed by courts had usually to cater for the court chapel and had therefore to be men.

In the 18th and 19th centuries, musical patronage gradually moved into the hands of the public, and there was a demand for secular music that could be played on serious occasions to a large audience. The music that resulted (the large-scale works of Mozart, Haydn, Beethoven, Brahms, Berlioz, Wagner, Tchaikovsky, Mahler and others) still had, in effect, a sacred purpose. The composer combed together many strands of individual and group experience into a model of his society's consciousness; he was a prophet. He was also, still, a man.

Composers still attempt to reflect society in their music, but there has been no generally agreed musical language since the turn of the century, when conventional harmony was abandoned by many. This, combined with our increasing confusion over national and traditional loyalties, has made it difficult to know what modern 'great' music would be. Women have missed the chance to compete with Beethoven, but they start as equals with men in the present period of breakdown and discovery in composition. Prejudice against women composers has been strong, but is less so now. Most composers outside the pop field make their living by a combination of academic work, music-copying, commissions and state subsidies. In these areas women nowadays theoretically have the same chances as men, and indeed composition is the most convenient musical career for a woman, since it can be done at home. The 1975 *British Music Yearbook* listed about 50 female composers in this country, although male composers still exceeded them by more than 10 to 1. Thea Musgrave, Elisabeth Lutyens, Elisabeth Maconchy and Priaulx Rainier are admired figures included – they all started their careers when prejudice against them was strong. A specifically female use of musical language could conceivably arise this century, although so far as it has not. One American composer, Pauline Oliveros, is known as a radical feminist as well as a creator of musical events in the Dada tradition popularized by John Cage.

While public music has been foundering, along with our group identity, private music (the individual, erotic lyrical tradition that gave rise to the lute songs of 17th-century England and the *lieder* of 19th-century Germany) has had another great success under the name of pop. One might suppose that if there were lingering problems for women in official 'serious' music, they might nevertheless shine here, and they do. The stars of pop music are singers, and secular singing has in any case always been open to women. But, more interestingly, some of the most successful pop composers have been women, and some, like Joni Mitchell and the remarkable Laura Nyro, are major artists by any standards. Some women pop composers, like Dory Previn, have introduced unusually personal subject matter into their music.

Careers in performance, with their commitments to travel, practice and evening work, conflict with child-rearing and will therefore not attract as many women as men while this is the responsibility so largely of women. Positive discrimination against women is, however, almost dead. Perhaps the most conservative bodies in this respect have been the big symphony orchestras, but most of them now admit women, though sometimes in small numbers. For the Chicago Symphony Orchestra, for example, one of the world's best, players now audition from behind screens to ensure fairness.

The female virtuoso is a less recent phenomenon than the female rank and file player. Singers led the way. Even the *castrati* in their heyday could not entirely substitute for the range, timbre and sexual allure of female opera singers. In Mozart's day there were already famous female violinists and keyboard players. However, only in the present century have the conventions which prevented women from travelling and earning alone broken down sufficiently to make the itinerant female virtuoso more of a commonplace. We have had artists like Wanda Landowska, Fanny Waterman, Annie Fischer; in the newer generation, Kyung Wha Chung and Marta Argerich; and among many opera singers, Sena Jurinac, Elizabeth Schwarzkopf and Joan Sutherland. Conducting, with its peculiar demands and savage commercial pressures, has attracted few women – Nadia Boulanger, the great teacher and world-famous conductor, is one. Performing careers, though now more generally open to women, still suffer from the conflicts which are part of all women's lives: the choice between work and domestic commitments.

Painting and the visual arts

There is very little to be found in any art history books that defines women as artists. This does not mean that women have never been artists. In fact they have always been. There are many cultures in which all the art is or was made by women; Navajo blankets are woven by women and almost all American Indian basketry and pottery was done by women. The women of the Mathila in India have been painting for 3,000 years (recent exhibition in the Musée des Artes Decoratifs, the Louvre). In the Mapuchi tribes of Chile, it was the women who traditionally did the weaving, pottery and basket-making. In most simple societies women are potters and have produced work ranging from the beautiful ceramic art of ancient Crete to the erotic pottery of Peru. Women have also produced the huts of the Australian, the black camel-hair tents of the Bedouin, the earth lodges of the Omaha, and the *yurta* of the nomads of Central Asia.

It is only in relatively recent Western culture that 'art' has been abstracted from the process of day-to-day experience, so that delineations like embroidery, dress-making, quilting, knitting, patchwork, weaving, and pottery became 'women's work' and fine art became man's territory. However, in spite of the difficulties for women in pursuing fine arts, there have been women at various times who have successfully become defined as painters or sculptors, although they have often faded into obscurity after their deaths. Examples are Artemesia Gentileschi, a 17th-century Italian who painted many biblical themes such as 'Judith Beheading Holofernes;' the strength and character of her women was unusual for that period; Elisabeth Vigée Lebrun was a court painter in 18th-century France, and her patron was Marie Antoinette; Rosa Bonheur, a 19th-century French painter, had to go to slaughterhouses and horse fairs in order to study anatomy, because women were excluded from anatomy classes in the academies. Her painting, 'The Horse Fair', was the first work by a living artist to go into the National Gallery in London.

In the 20th century, many more women have risen to prominence as artists and sculptors: Barbara Hepworth, Bridget Riley and Laura Knight in England, and in America Georgia O'Keefe, Louise Nevelson, Grace Hartigan, Elaine de Kooning and many others.

The situation for women artists in terms of the art establishment in Britain is still very poor. In recent Arts Council exhibitions of contemporary British art at the Hayward Gallery, there have been only 20 women artists as compared with 156 men. In general there are far more men than women on all the grant-giving panels of the Arts Council and teaching in art colleges.

Most interesting at present is that groups such as WOMEN'S FREE ARTS ALLIANCE, p. 220, and the WOMEN'S ART HISTORY COLLECTIVE, p. 220, are finding out more about women artists of the past and exploring our connections with them. The WOMEN'S ART HISTORY

COLLECTIVE has been working on a feminist critique of cultural history, researching, for example, into the Old Mistresses which are mostly hidden in the basement of the National Gallery. The WOMEN'S FREE ARTS ALLIANCE runs seminars, open to all women, which include discussion of the work of women artists, past and present, of themes such as female archetypes and stereotypes, and of 'living architecture', the integration of art into daily life.

Since the start of the women's movement five years ago, women artists have begun to create their own networks of support and to work towards establishing their own art forms. In the USA, progress has been immense, with centres established in most of the major cities. Progress has been slower in Britain, but recent events have been encouraging. In the last few years there have been several all-women exhibitions, in 1973 at Swiss Cottage Library, in 1974 the Women's Workshop of the Artists Union exhibition at the Arts Meeting Place; and in 1975 the first multi-media exhibition of women's art in Great Britain, *Sweet Sixteen and Never Been Shown*, was produced by the WOMEN'S FREE ARTS ALLIANCE.

One of the most exciting recent developments in the visual and performance arts is the extended use of the 'conceptual' form (the focus being on the *idea* as primary, with permanence and formality not being of great concern). This is a way of working in art which includes as many women working and exhibiting as men – a first in the annals of art history. In general, the emergence of a more balanced and accurate appraisal of women in the arts is beginning.

why would a married woman
want a mortgage in her own
name? We'll have husbands
doing the housework next!

The Women's Movement

This section describes groups and campaigns of the women's movement. The present movement grew from a few small groups of women who met in the late 60s to talk about what it meant to them to be women in their daily lives and how they could organize together to improve women's lives and to struggle for women's rights. Some were inspired by what they knew of women's groups and activities in the USA; some were disillusioned by their experiences in student and other groups, which too often concentrated on men's interests and left women doing the chores. Some were women who felt isolated and dissatisfied with their lives and who wanted to work together with others to change the assumptions about women's roles which they felt were shaping their lives.

The WOMEN'S LIBERATION WORKSHOP emerged in 1969 in London as a co-ordinating centre for women's groups (p. 184) which were then starting up all over the country. London groups became involved in actions like mounting a sticker campaign against advertisements insulting to women, participating in the Equal Pay Rally and demonstrating against the Miss World contest in 1970. At the same time women were meeting in small groups to read, talk, share their experiences as women and understand better the position of women. A monthly women's liberation magazine, *Shrew* (p. 192), was started with a different group producing each issue. In February 1970 the first women's liberation conference was held at Oxford, attended by 600 women from all over the country. Groups with special interests in women's history, sexuality, education and art began to meet. In March 1971 on International Women's Day there was a women's liberation rally and demonstration in London. The campaign for the first 4 basic demands of the movement (for equal pay, equal education and job opportunity, free abortion and contraception on demand, and 24-hour nurseries) was launched. From that time the movement grew rapidly, and later, in 1974, the fifth and sixth demands for financial and legal independence and the right to a self-defined sexuality were added.

Today women's groups are working in almost all the areas discussed in this book: for equal rights, job opportunities, education and vocational training, and legal and financial independence; and for the right to choose when and whether to have children and for access to free and safe contraception and abortion facilities. They are also active in education, the media and trade unions. They are concerned to live sexually and socially according to what they feel is right for them and to fight prejudice on these issues.

At the core of the women's movement there are even deeper issues. In trying to gain more control of their lives and the decisions which affect them, many women in the movement have come to see the need for a more fundamental challenge to the way things are. Women don't simply want to do everything men can do now; the roles men are expected to play are not a great deal better than women's; the society men largely run is often destructive and does violence to humans and to other life. It's more a question of working for a society in which people are freer to express themselves and less dominated and exploited by what is expected of them. 'Politics' is no longer just part of government and political parties, or even just factories and trade unions. It's part of how we live our daily lives, in the home, in housework, in bed, in bringing up children and in the way we express love and anger. It isn't just 'society out there' which is being challenged. This awareness has strengthened the women's movement as women have come to feel that their concerns are important and relevant to 'real' politics and to 'real' social issues.

The women's movement is about celebrating women's good qualities and strengths as well as fighting issues and situations which are oppressive to them. It means women getting together to enjoy themselves as well as struggling for change. There are groups of women writing, reading, painting, making music, dancing, talking and having fun together because they enjoy being together as women. All this is an important part of the women's movement.

The structure of the movement

The movement is a loose collection of groups, and it isn't easy to say where it begins and ends, because it isn't an organized network. Groups come together when they need to work on a campaign and when they want to share experiences and learn from one another. There is no central organizing body, nor are there leaders, officers or even official spokeswomen, although individual women and groups will sometimes talk publicly about what women's movement means to *them*.

A strong, flexible, countrywide (and international) movement has been created, relying on a growing sense of the sisterhood of all women rather than on conventional political structures. At the same time, some women feel a need for better communication and co-ordination so that women can keep in touch more easily and work together more effectively. There are a number of general information centres that co-ordinate information about campaigns and groups, helping them to keep in touch with one another as well as helping individual women to find groups (p. 172).

Small groups

The basic form of òrganization within the movement is the small group, in which a few women (perhaps as many as 20) meet together regularly. The wide variety of such groups is indicated in the lists in this section of the book. Some groups meet weekly as 'consciousness-raising' groups. These provide a space in which women can explore in various ways their feelings about being women, usually drawing on the personal emotional experience of their lives, both past and present, and exploring what sexism means to them. Others meet as study groups, reading and studying literature, history, politics, feminist and other writings. Other groups are organized around particular campaigns: abortion, day nurseries, sex discrimination etc. There are groups concerned with health, free pregnancy testing, art, rock, writing, education, sexuality; others are producing newsletters and magazines, running information centres, child-care centres and battered women's refuges. Each has some consciousness of being part of a broader movement of social change and will support in varying degrees what other groups are doing. Individual women are often active in more than one group. Groups are formed as women feel a need to work together in a particular way, and they may be open or closed to new members. Groups adapt to members' needs: a group usually stops meeting when it has achieved its aims or is no longer found satisfying; alternatively, it may change its activities or join with another group.

Conferences

Various women's conferences, taking place in different parts of the country, are another source of unity and communication. There have been 8 national women's conferences since the first one (p. 184). These are meeting places for women from all over the country, where they can discuss progress on campaigns, share experiences in special interest groups and buy books, pamphlets and newsletters. They also provide an opportunity to see the women's movement as some kind of a whole, and to discuss how the movement should develop. Special conferences have been called on almost every campaign in which the movement is involved (p. 186). There are occasional regional conferences where women from one area of the country meet together between national conferences.

The six demands

- Free 24-hour nurseries
- Equal pay
- Equal education and job opportunity
- Free contraception and abortion on demand
- Financial and legal independence
- End to discrimination against lesbians and the right to a self-defined sexuality

These demands are a major unifying force in the women's movement. Groups have concentrated on different issues, and since the demands were first formulated much has been achieved in changing policies and attitudes. Much remains to be done. We have discussed the fuller implications of these demands throughout the book.

Newsletters

The publication and circulation of newsletters and pamphlets creates another communication network which keeps women in touch with what groups elsewhere are doing, and they are often sources of new ideas. Most towns have their local women's liberation newsletter, as do most campaigns and special interest groups. As well as news, they include articles, reviews, poems and letters. There are also a number of news magazines which cover the movement nationally. They are an integral part of the women's movement (p. 191).

Women's centres

Finally, there are women's centres, meeting places whose main purpose is to provide a way for groups and individual women to communicate. They also offer services, such as pregnancy testing, abortion referral, etc. The WOMEN'S LIBERATION WORKSHOP is a co-ordinator for London groups and keeps addresses of groups. At the Manchester national women's conference it was agreed to set up a similar information centre for the whole country and WIRES (p. 173) in Leeds is the beginning of that service. Local women's centres do some of the same things, on a smaller scale.

How to find the group you want

- Look in the *Local Group* section (p. 173ff). Your local group will be able to tell you whether they are open to new members, or whether there is one even nearer to you.
- If there isn't a local group near you contact one of the GENERAL INFORMATION CENTRES (below) or a WOMEN'S CENTRE (p. 173ff). They will be able to give you local contacts, tell you about special activities and local newsletters.
- Write to *Spare Rib* (p. 193) asking for contacts in your area. Their information will be roughly the same as the women's centres, but they may publish your letter and so put you in contact with other readers who may be looking for a group in your area. They have a section in the classified ads listing new groups
- If you're interested in a particular campaign, problem or activity, look up the Resources section (p. 196). This is grouped under sections and includes resources from inside and outside the women's movement.

General information centres

These co-ordinate and keep lists of local contacts all over the country.

AWARE, *c/o South London Women's Centre, 14 Radnor Ter., London SW8* (01-622 8495). Feminist information service; files on abortion, contraception, campaigns and organizations relevant to the women's movement; battered women's refuges; contact addresses for groups; several research groups including information collective, women's research index, women and psychiatry, women's art history collective and an advertising group; operates from SOUTH LONDON WOMEN'S CENTRE; open evenings for women to telephone or call in.

LONDON WOMEN'S LIBERATION WORKSHOP, *38 Earlham St, London WC2* (01-836 6081). Information and co-ordination centre for groups in London, usually the best place to find a women's group in London; one of oldest women's groups in country; began 1969 as federation of few small women's groups which had begun to meet in different parts of London; helps with setting up of new groups; arranges speakers for groups; deals with press inquiries and co-ordinating production of women's liberation journal, formerly *Harpies' Bazaar*, now *Shrew* (p. 192); workshop has grown with growth of women's movement; has reading room, bookshop, and rooms for meetings. Weekly Workshop newsletter.

SCOTTISH WOMEN'S LIBERATION WORKSHOP, *4 Fleming Pl., St Andrews, Fife, Scotland*. Co-ordinating centre for the women's movement in Scotland; monthly Scottish national newsletter.

WIRES, *c/o 30 Blenheim Ter., Leeds 2*. The women's movement national information centre set up in April 1975; not a policy-making organization or an official central organization of the movement; answers women's inquiries about groups, campaigns and issues; central contact point for the women's movement building up a comprehensive address list; produces fortnightly newsletter; both information service and newsletter financed by subscriptions from groups and individuals.

WOMEN IN RURAL WALES, *Geulan Felen, Pentre Cwrt, Llandyssul, Dyfed*. Contact centre for women living in rural Wales interested in women's movement who want to make contact with other women living near them.

Local groups and women's centres

This section lists women's groups according to region. The women's centres in large towns in each region are likely to know of groups throughout the area, and the kind of groups you will find in any

particular district can vary widely. Where the group is called a women's group or women's liberation group, the name has been left
out, and only the address given.

Regions

1. Scotland
2. North
3. North East
4. North West
5. Northern Ireland
6. North Midlands
7. Wales
8. South Midlands
9. East Anglia
10. South West
11. South
12. Central
13. London

Scotland

The women's movement in Scotland is closely linked with groups in
England, Wales and Northern Ireland, and involved in the general
campaigns, newsletters and magazines shared by the movement as a
whole. The SCOTTISH WOMEN'S LIBERATION WORKSHOP (p. 175) co-
ordinates information and activities for Scottish groups; and there
are Scottish NAC and WOMEN'S AID conferences. Contact the WORK-
SHOP for more information.

One particular problem of the movement in Scotland is the very scattered population: apart from a few main centres, women are often living in isolated situations. If you contact one of the groups listed here, they may know of individual women living near to you who are interested in women's groups. Also contact COUNTRYWOMEN, (p. 192) which was started as a contact point for women living in isolated rural situations; it publishes an address list with every issue of its newsletter.

SCOTTISH LESBIAN FEMINISTS, contact EDINBURGH WORKSHOP, *31 Royal Ter., Edinburgh*. Produce newsletter called *Red Herring*; regular meetings.

SCOTTISH WOMEN'S AID FEDERATION, contact WORKSHOP (below) for details. WOMEN'S AID GROUPS (p. 214) in Dundee, Dunfermline, Drumchapel, Edinburgh, Falkirk, Glasgow, Perth.

SCOTTISH WOMEN'S LIBERATION WORKSHOP, *4 Fleming Pl., St Andrews, Fife* (St Andrews 5705). Central contact point for Scottish women's groups: up-to-date list of *Liberation Newsletter*; occasional workshop meetings attended by women from all over Scotland; bi-weekly meetings.

ABERDEEN, *30 King St, Aberdeen*. Involves women from town and university; consciousness raising; women's studies; media; women's aid; monthly general meetings.

DUNDEE, *1 Lynnewood Pl., Dundee*. Battered women's refuge; regular meetings

EDINBURGH, *31 Royal Ter., Edinburgh* (031-556 5655). One of main centres of activity in Scotland. Discussion meetings; working women's charter group; health and sexuality groups; literature group; new members group; Marxist study group; women's studies; women and media, consciousness raising; NAC, sex discrimination, SCOTTISH LESBIAN FEMINISTS

GALLOWAY, c/o *Laurieston Hall, Castle Douglas, Dumfries and Galloway*. 2 women's groups meet regularly; women living in Laurieston Hall have had women's week there for past 4 years (p. 187)

GLASGOW, WOMEN IN ACTION, *89 Gibson St, Glasgow G12 8LD*. Working women's charter; women in media; legal and financial independence campaign; abortion campaign; health; women in education; street theatre; women's aid; library; newsletter, *Glasgow Women's Liberation Newsletter*; regular meetings

SKYE, *12 Balmoral Rd, Portee, Skye*

ST ANDREWS, *4 Fleming Pl., St Andrews, Fife* (St Andrews 5705). Discussion and consciousness raising; campaigning for day nursery at university; NAC; running market stall, running SCOTTISH WOMEN'S LIBERATION WORKSHOP; student women's action group; regular bi-weekly meetings

STIRLING, *C.S.A., Stirling University, Stirling*

THURSO, THURSO WOMEN IN ACTION, *5 St Olaf Rd, Thurso, Caithness*. Very small group. Acts as women's centre for whole Caithness area

WEST LOTHIAN, *39 Philingstone Rd, Bo'ness, Lothian*

North of England

BATLEY, see Dewsbury

BINGLEY, *4 Norfolk St, Bingley, West Yorks.* Discussion; consciousness raising, poetry, film-making, body-awareness and relaxation; have started playgroups; written introduction to group; regular meetings

BRADFORD, *c/o 4th Idea Bookshop, 14 Southgate, Bradford 1, West Yorks.* Socialist women's action group, women's aid group; women's centre, 149 Little Horton La. (Bradford 21413)

CALDER VALLEY, *8 and 10 Castle Gate, Mytholmroyd, West Yorks.* (Calder Valley 3943)

DEWSBURY/BATLEY, *65 Halifax Rd, Staincliffe, Dewsbury, West Yorks.* Regular women's page in community paper, *Shoddy News,* different topic from women's movement each issue; no regular meetings, but new contacts welcome.

DONCASTER, *51 Park Dr., Doncaster, South Yorks*

HARROGATE, *25 Poplar Grove, Harrogate, North Yorks.* NAC; women's aid

HUDDERSFIELD, *84 Upper Clough, Huddersfield, West Yorks*

HULL, THE WOMEN'S CENTRE, *17 Park Av., Hull, Humberside*

HULL WOMEN'S LIBERATION, c/o *University House, The University, Hull.* Also women's aid group

KEIGHLEY, *9 Sun La., Lumbfort, Stanbury, Yorkshire*

LEEDS, TOWN WOMEN'S GROUP, *19 Broomfield Cres., Leeds 6;* WOODHOUSE WOMEN'S GROUP, *45 Hartley Cres., Leeds 6.* Lesbian group, radical lesbian group, health (*25 Lucas Rd, Leeds 6*), working women's charter, rambling group, non-sexist children's books collective; women's aid; consciousness raising; babysitting rota, NAC, student groups; newsletter produced by each group in turn. *Bread and Roses* ; *WIRES; Feminist Books* ; monthly all-Leeds meetings

SHEFFIELD, *194 Brunswick Rd, Sheffield 3.* NAC; Working Women's Charter; health group; WACC; women in news (*c/o Radio Sheffield*), women's aid, women in the NHS; pamphlet produced on rape; several women's studies courses in Sheffield; group setting up women's centre; monthly newsletter

YORK, *3 Fairfax St, York.* Health group; NAC; women in trade unions; gay women; women's aid; women's studies course in York; monthly newsletter

North East of England

CLEVELAND, CLEVELAND WOMEN'S ACTION, *Newport Community Centre, Newport Rd, Middlesbrough, Teesside*

DARLINGTON, *85 Stanhope Rd, Darlington, Durham*

DURHAM, *Dunelm House, New Elvet, Durham.* NAC; umbrella group for Durham activities; weekly bookstall; newsletter

GRANTHAM, *25 Commercial Rd, Grantham, Lincs.* Discussion, consciousness-raising, street theatre

GRIMSBY, *10 Abbey Dr. West, Grimsby, South Humberside.* Contraception group; better conditions for homeless women and their children; NAC women's aid; regular meetings

MIDDLESBROUGH, MIDDLESBROUGH WOMEN'S ACTION GROUP, *15 Taunton Vale, Cleveland*

NEWCASTLE, *223 Jesmond Rd, Newcastle-upon-Tyne 2.* Advice and information, free pregnancy testing, rape crisis centre, self-defence, abortion campaign, lesbian feminist group, consciousness raising, discussion, socialist women; *Women's Struggle*, containing articles on women and the crisis, equal pay, abortion etc, available from 11 Callerton Pl., Newcastle-upon-Tyne 4

SCARBOROUGH, *Flat 2, 6 Seamer Rd, Scarborough, Yorkshire*

SCUNTHORPE, *24 Chaucer Av., Scunthorpe, South Humberside.* Campaign for battered women's refuge

SUNDERLAND, *30 Grosvenor St, Southwick, South Shields, Tyne and Wear*

TYNESIDE COAST, *33 Grosvenor Av., Whitley Bay, Tyne and Wear*

North West of England

BLACKBURN, *c/o Amamus Bookshop, 1–3 Market Street La., Blackburn, Lancs.* Free pregnancy testing and advice; weekly meetings

BLACKPOOL, *27 Carnforth Av., Bispham, Blackpool, Lancs.* Includes women's aid group

BOLTON, *3 Lightburne Av., Bolton, Lancs.* Working women's charter, group preparing local guide for women; regular meetings

BURNLEY, *8 Mill Lane, Hapton, Burnley, Lancs.*

GLOSSOP, *4 Manor Park Rd, Glossop, Derby*

HEBDEN BRIDGE, *68 Bridge La., Hebden Bridge, West Yorks.*

LANCASTER, LANCASTER WOMEN'S CENTRE, *The Plough, Moor La., Lancaster* (0524-63967). Information centre; battered women's refuge; consciousness raising; theatre; Working Women's Charter; writing group; older women's group; lesbians; NAC; health; education; self-defence classes at university; women's studies course at university; WEA course in town; monthly newsletter

LIVERPOOL, MERSEYSIDE WOMEN'S CENTRE, *49 Seel St, Liverpool 1,* (051-709 4141). Advice and information on contraception and abortion; women's rights advice; free pregnancy testing; gay women; open discussion meetings; monthly general meetings; meetings on running the Centre; local groups in Hoylake, Sefton, Bootle (at university, at polytechnic); women's studies group; monthly newsletter

MANCHESTER, MANCHESTER WOMEN'S CENTRE, *218 Upper Brook St, Manchester 13* (061-273 2887). Co-ordination centre for Manchester women's groups. Monthly business meetings, discussions, education groups (national women and education newsletter produced in Manchester, p. 193); women's rights; NAC; Women's Aid; women and socialism; self-defence; women and literature; women's rights stall in Salford market weekly; small groups at Didsbury, Chorlton, Oldham, Moss Side, North, Central, South Manchester, Manchester Polytechnic; groups share in producing newsletter, running information service, talking in schools, organizing publicity and meetings for new members

OLDHAM, *133b Chew Valley Rd, Greenfield, Oldham, Lancs.*

PRESTON, *5 Lefton Rd, Waltham-le-Dale, Lancs.*

ROCHDALE, *67 Harewood Rd, Norden, Rochdale, Lancs.*

SALE, *51 Barnfield Cres., Sale, Cheshire*

STOCKPORT, *8 Earl Rd, Heaton Moor, Stockport, Cheshire* (061-442 9204). Women's aid; NAC; several women's groups

TODMORDEN, TODMORDEN WORKING WOMEN'S CHARTER GROUP, *24 Lime Av., Todmorden, Rochdale, Lancs.*

Northern Ireland

NORTHERN IRELAND WOMEN'S COMMITTEE, *c/o Students' Union, Queen's University, Belfast 7*

NORTHERN IRELAND WOMEN'S RIGHTS MOVEMENT, *c/o Eileen Eveson, Dept. of Social Administration, the new University of Ulster, Coleraine, Co. Londonderry.* Formed in May 1975. Drafted a Women's Charter for Northern Ireland, along lines of Working Women's Charter, adapted to situation in Northern Ireland. (See p. 117 where the Charter is reprinted.)

BELFAST, *c/o Students' Union, Queen's University, Belfast 7*

COLERAINE, *c/o Eileen Eveson, Dept of Social Administration, the new University of Ulster, Coleraine, Co. Londonderry.* Involved in campaign to have Northern Ireland included in Sex Discrimination Bill; weekly meetings

See also information on women's groups in Eire (p. 190). There are a number of women's groups in Britain concerned with Northern Ireland (p. 188)

North Midlands of England

DERBY, *15 Chevin Rd, Milford, Derby.* Some women setting up a rape crisis centre.

HANLEY, *494 High La., nr Tunstall, Stoke-on-Trent, Staffs*

LEICESTER, *c/o Link, 122 Humberstone Rd, Leicester.* Town group: university group; WWC; NAC; pregnancy testing and contraceptive advice; feminist teachers' group (p. 204); women's aid

LOUGHBOROUGH, LOUGHBOROUGH WOMEN'S RIGHTS GROUP, *23 Kirkstone Dr., Loughborough LE11 3RN.* Not a regular group; women give talks on women's rights to other local groups; produced an exhibition called 'What are little girls made of?' and a game, Womanopoly

NEWCASTLE/NORTH STAFFS, NORTH STAFFS WOMEN'S ACTION GROUP, *15 Heath St, Newcastle-under-Lyme, Staffs.* Working Women's Charter campaigning for women's centre; NAC; consciousness raising; weekly meetings for business and discussion

NOTTINGHAM, NOTTINGHAM WOMEN'S CENTRE, *26 Newcastle Chambers, Angel Row, Nottingham.* Anti-discrimination; NAC; Working Women's Charter; nurseries campaign; women and writing; women's art centre; monthly newsletter (from *41 Cromwell St, Canning Circus, Nottingham*) *Women Now* (Nottingham women's monthly journal); regular discussion meetings

STAFFORD, *12 Tixall Rd, Stafford.*

Wales

There is no one centre for the women's movement in Wales; the larger centres such as Cardiff and Swansea have information about most other groups. South Wales regional conferences are held quite regularly. For details contact one of the groups listed below. Because many women in Wales live in quite isolated rural situations, a contact network for women in rural Wales has been set up.

CONTACT, WOMEN IN RURAL WALES, *Geulan Felen, Pentre Cwrt, Llandysul, Dyfed (Llandysul 3407).* See also *Country Women's Newsletter* (p. 192)

OAKLANDS WOMEN'S CENTRE, *Glasbury, nr Brecon.* A house in the country given to the women's movement for use as retreat for study weekends and workshops. For details, booking arrangements, contact the London Women's Liberation Workshop, *38 Earlham St, London WC2*

ABERGAVENNY,
The Old Gardens Cottage, Panty-y-goytre, Llanfair Kilgeddin, nr Abergavenny, Monmouthshire (Gobion 240)

ABERYSTWYTH, WOMEN'S ACTION GROUP, *13 Chalybeale St, Aberystwyth, Dyfed*
ABERYSTWYTH, *Murmur y Coed, 10 Penglais Ter., Aberystwyth, Dyfed*
ABERYSTWYTH, TOWNSWOMEN'S GROUP, *c/o M. Vincentelli, Visual Arts Dept, University of Wales, Aberystwyth, Dyfed*

BANGOR, *2 Frowhellog, Glanrafow, Bangor, Gwynedd*

BARMOUTH, *7 Maes-y-Geddi, Bala Gwynedd, Barmouth, Gwynedd.*

CARDIFF, CARDIFF WOMEN'S ACTION GROUP, *c/o 108 Community Bookshop, 108 Salisbury Rd, Cathays, Cardiff* (0222-28908). Housing group; self-help group (has put together a health handbook); consciousness-raising; Women's Aid; women's studies; study group; NAC; bookshop has large stock of feminist literature; organizing a playgroup; newsletter; several women's studies courses available; regular meetings

LLANAFON, *Eillinbach, Brynafon, Llanafon*

LLANDYSSUL, *Geulan Flelen, Pentre Cwrt, Llandyssul, Dyfed* (Llandyssul 3407). Consciousness-raising and contact centre; regular meetings

LAMPETER, *c/o Mary Alderson, St David's University College, Lampeter, Dyfed*

NEWPORT, *48 Brynglas Rd, Newport, Gwent*

POWYS, *The Flat, Ashgard, Talybont on Usk, Brecon, Powys*

South West Midlands of England

BIRMINGHAM, *76 Brighton Rd, Birmingham 12.* Good regional contact centre. Meeting place; community and information centre; new members group; women's liberation playgroup in Calthorpe Park; produced booklet on running playgroups (p. 205); NAC; women artists; women and health; socialist women; gay women's group; reading group; anti-discrimination group; women and psychiatry. Groups at Aston and Birmingham universities, North Birmingham polytechnic; regular general meetings

COVENTRY, *41 Kirby Rd, Earlsdon,*

Coventry, Warwks. Lesbian group; Women's Aid; regular meetings

KIDDERMINSTER, *30 Hathfield Rd, Bewdley, Worcs.* Discussion and consciousness-raising; NAC; theatre; weekly meetings

LEAMINGTON, *c/o The Other Branch, 7 Regent Pl., Leamington, Worcs.*

MALVERN/WORCESTER, *Birchwood Hall, Storridge, Gt Malvern, Worcs.*

WOLVERHAMPTON. *313 Dudley Rd, Blakenhall, Wolverhampton, Staffs.*

WORCESTER, *Students' Union Office, College of Education, Worcs.*

East Anglia

BASILDON, *450 Whitmore Way, Basildon, Essex.* Also Women's Aid

BOXFORD, *6 Holbrook Barn Rd, Boxford, Colchester, Essex* (Colchester 210707)

CAMBRIDGE, *48 Eden St, Cambridge.* Education group (organizes visits to schools); feminist reading group (discussing the work of contemporary women writers); marxist reading group: gay women's group; wages for housework; newcomers' group; Working Women's Charter; Women In Media; consciousness-raising; discussing setting up battered women's refuge and rape crisis service; contraception and pregnancy advisory group; free pregnancy testing; contraceptive advice and information about local doctors and contraceptive facilities; regular discussion and planning meetings; monthly newsletter; NAC; nursery action group

CHELMSFORD, *1 Coppins Cl., Chelmsford, Essex*

COLCHESTER, *39 Charles St, Colchester, Essex*
COLCHESTER, WORKING WOMEN'S CHARTER GROUP, *31 Heath Rd, Wivenhoe, Colchester, Essex*

ELY, *42 Sun St, Isleham, nr Newmarket, Cambs.*

GRAYS, *10 Arthurtoft House, New Rd, Grays, Essex*

HORNCHURCH/ROMFORD, *46 Shaftesbury Av., Romford, Essex.* NAC; local claimants' union; women against torture (p. 188); men's group started in this area (contact at *223 Collier Row Lane, Romford, Essex*); women's studies course; weekly discussion meetings

ILFORD, *74 Westwood Rd, Goodmayes, Ilford, Essex* (01-597 2964)

KINGS LYNN, *c/o Jennifer Dunton, Marshland Smeeth, Kings Lynn, Norfolk* (0945-73276)

NORWICH, *'Seagulls', Braymeadows La., Little Melton, Norwich NR9 3NQ* (Norwich 810458). Drop In Centre

(*Charing Cross Centre,*
St John Maddermarket, Norwich),
open Tuesdays, Wednesdays 10 am–
1 pm for mothers and young children;
NAC; Working Women's Charter
group (working on demand for more
nurseries); street theatre; Women's
Aid; hoping to start regional network

South West of England

ANDOVER, WOMEN'S CRISIS AND
SUPPORT CENTRE, *17 New St,*
Andover, Hants.

BATH, *The Basement, 13 Johnstone St,*
Bath. Open Fridays 10am–2pm.
Informal place for women to meet,
talk, have lunch, for children to play;
free pregnancy tests; information;
Women's Aid; NAC; Working
Women's Charter; health groups;
women's studies course (WEA);
weekly meetings

BOURNEMOUTH, see Poole

BRISTOL, *Second Floor,*
59 Lower Union St, Bristol 1, Avon
(0272-22760). Good regional contact
point, centre open 10–4 weekdays.
Free pregnancy testing; books and
pamphlets to buy or borrow;
several local groups; newcomers
meetings; gay women's group;
Working Women's Charter; wages
for housework; NAC; WACC;
Women's Aid; sistershow theatre;
women and socialism; socialist
discussion group; women's film
group; child care outside school
hours (CCOSH); several women's
studies courses; occasional journal,
Enough; monthly newsletter

CHELTENHAM,
c/o The Horse and Groom,
30 St George's Pl., Cheltenham, Glos.
Group meets Wednesdays 7.30 pm
Horse and Groom

CHIPPENHAM, *78 Lowden, Chippenham,*
Wilts. SN15 2BS. Special interest
groups include political; women's

and conference for East Anglia;
regular newsletter; weekly meetings

PETERBOROUGH, *37 Winwick Pl.,*
Westwood, Peterborough. Small
groups; NAC; monthly meetings

SOUTHEND, *67 Burnham Rd,*
Lee on Sea, Essex

aid; consciousness-raising; health
group (the last runs a free pregnancy
testing service); women have visited
schools, other local groups to talk
about women's liberation; involved in
scheme to teach illiterate adults to
read; other local projects; meets
fortnightly

CORNWALL, *28 Woodlands View,*
West Looe, Cornwall PL13 2AW.
Not an active group; contact point
for women in Cornwall

DARTINGTON,
Dartington College of Arts, Totnes,
Devon

DEVIZES, *89 Southbroom Rd,*
Devizes, Wilts.

DEVON, *161 Barton Ter., Dawlish,*
Devon

EASTLEIGH, WOMEN'S ADVICE CENTRE,
21 Desborough Rd, Eastleigh, Hants.

EXETER, EXETER WOMEN'S ACTION
GROUP, *9 Alexandra Ter., Exeter,*
Devon, EX4 6SY. Women's Aid;
weekly meetings

PLYMOUTH, *36 Julian St, Cattledown,*
Plymouth, Devon

POOLE AND BOURNEMOUTH, *9 North Rd,*
Parkeston, Poole, Dorset

SOUTHAMPTON, *82 Cranbury Av.,*
Bevois Valley, Southampton, Hants.
Street theatre group;
consciousness-raising; NAC;
Women's Aid; silkscreen workshop;
university group; newsletter; weekly
meetings

SWINDON, *46 Dixon St, Swindon, Wilts.*

TOTNES, *4 Puddavon Ter., Totnes, Devon*

WESTON-SUPER-MARE, *1a Ashcombe Rd, Weston-super-Mare, Avon*

South of England

ABINGDON, *44 Baker Rd, Abingdon, Oxon* (Abingdon 3537)

BANBURY, BANBURY WOMEN'S ACTION GROUP, *113 Bloxham Rd, Banbury, Oxon.*

BASINGSTOKE, BASINGSTOKE WOMEN'S RIGHTS GROUP, *20 Old Worting Rd, Basingstoke, Hants.* Working Women's Charter; campaigning locally against cutbacks in nursery provision; NAC Basingstoke, *20 Cotswold Cl., Basingstoke*

BECKENHAM AND BROMLEY, *1 Florence Rd, Beckenham, Kent* (01-460 6818 or 01-778 3246). NAC; Women's Aid; arrange outings with their children; new members and help welcome; consciousness-raising; monthly discussion and planning meetings

BEDFORD, *Flat 7, 14 St Andrew Rd, Bedford, Beds.*

BRACKNELL, *30 Ambassador, Great Hollands, Bracknell, Berks.*

BRIGHTON, *79 Buckingham Rd, Brighton, West Sussex* (0273-27612)

BROMLEY, see Beckenham

BYFLEET, Daniele Hart, *6 Winern Glebe, Byfleet, Surrey KT14 7LT.* No group but contact for women interested in forming one

CANTERBURY, RADICAL WOMEN'S GROUP, *c/o Students' Union, University of Kent, Canterbury, Kent*

CHESHAM, *9 Broadlands Av., Chesham, Bucks*

CRAWLEY, CRAWLEY WOMEN'S ACTION GROUP, *5 Camber Cl., Pound Hill, Crawley, Sussex*

FARNHAM, *c/o Gill Allen, West Surrey College of Art and Design, The Hart, Farnham, Surrey*

GUILDFORD, *c/o Student's Union, University of Surrey, Guildford, Surrey*

HASTINGS, see St Leonards

HARROW, *57 Warham Rd, Harrow Weald, Middx.* (01-427 2885)

HATFIELD, *Queenswood, Harfield, Herts*

HEMEL HEMPSTEAD, *c/o South Hill Annex, Heath La., Hemel Hempstead, Herts*

HIGH WYCOMBE, *21 Castle St, High Wycombe, Bucks*

KETTERING, *41 Pollard St, Kettering, Northants*

LEWES, *20 St Edwards Rd, Lewes, Sussex*

LUTON, *34 Dallas Rd, Luton, Beds*

MAIDENHEAD, *c/o Liz Smith, Bramleys, Altwood Cl., Maidenhead, Berks*

MEDWAY, *13 Mansel Dr., Borstal, Rochester, Kent.* Consciousness-raising and pressure group; NAC; petitioned against recent rape ruling (p. 144); in touch with Women's Aid Group at Bridgewood, Rochester

MIDDLESEX, *57 Warham Rd, Harrow-Weald, Middx.* Group acts as co-ordination centre for other women's groups in Middlesex

MILTON KEYNES, *Simpson Lodge Farm, Milton Keynes, Bucks.* (or via Open University). Women's Aid; nurseries; health; consciousness-raising. Also Open University Women's Group, (c/o Lee Taylor, The Open University) with regular discussion and study meetings

MONKS RISBOROUGH, *Old Rectory Cottage, Mill La., Monks Risborough, Bucks*

NORTHAMPTON, *c/o Ann Stirland, General Studies Dept, Northampton College of FE, Booth Lane South, Northampton, Northants*

NORTHWOOD, *14 Frithwood Av., Northwood, Middx*

ORPINGTON, *42 Broomhill Rd, Orpington, Kent*

OXFORD, *34 Cowley Rd, Oxford.* A number of groups active in Oxford, including gay women's; health; women and socialism groups

PORTSMOUTH, PORTSMOUTH WOMEN'S ACTION GROUP, *c/o Community Advice Centre, 157 Lake Rd, Portsmouth, Hants.* Also a group at polytechnic

READING, *57 Watlington St, Reading, Berks.* (Reading 64594)

ST LEONARD'S/HASTINGS, *34 Upper Park Rd, St Leonards, Sussex*

SHOREHAM, *154 Harbour Way, Shoreham Beach, Sussex* (Shoreham 61680)

SOUTHSEA, *41 St Andrews Rd, Southsea, Hants*

STEVENAGE, *Lansdale Court, Stevenage, Herts*

TWICKENHAM, *21 Cambridge Rd, Twickenham, Surrey*

WATFORD, *93 Oxney Ave, Bushey, Watford, Herts.* (Watford 44042)

WEYBRIDGE, *48 Waverley Rd, Weybridge, Surrey*

WINCHESTER, *176 Stockbridge Rd, Winchester, Hants.* Action NAC group

WORTHING, *c/o Ashdown Community Centre, Worthing, Sussex.* Centre open alternate Friday evenings; regular study group Worthing, *31 Clive Av., Goring-by-Sea*

London

This section is compiled differently from other areas. There are over 100 women's groups in London alone. Many specific interest groups have originated in London and are still co-ordinated from there. Many of the major women's liberation publications (p. 191ff) and some of the best bookshops and libraries (p. 221ff) are in London. The LONDON WOMEN'S LIBERATION WORKSHOP keeps an up-to-date list of women's groups in London, and you can find out the address of your nearest group by phoning them, so individual groups are not listed here. AWARE (p. 172) and WIRES (p. 173) also keep lists of London groups. A number of women's centres in different parts of London are listed below.

LONDON WOMEN'S LIBERATION WORKSHOP, *38 Earlham St, London WC2* (01-836 6081). Information and co-ordination centre for groups in London, usually the best place to find a women's group in London; one of oldest women's groups in the country; began in 1969 as federation of few small women's groups which had begun to meet in different parts of London; helps with setting up of new groups; arranges speakers for groups; deals with press inquiries; co-ordinates production of women's liberation journal, formerly *Harpies' Bazaar*, now *Shrew* (p. 192); workshop has grown with growth of women's movement; reading room; bookshop; rooms for meetings; *Weekly Workshop* newsletter

ACTON WOMEN'S CENTRE, *c/o Priory Youth Centre, Petersfield Rd, London W4* (01-994 4244 or 01-994 3275)

BRENT WOMEN'S CENTRE, *134 Minet Av, London NW10* (01-965 3324)

BRIXTON WOMEN'S CENTRE, *207 Railton Rd, London SE24* (01-733 8663)

ESSEX ROAD WOMEN'S CENTRE, *108 Essex Road, London N1* (01-226 9936)

GRAFTON ROAD WOMEN'S CENTRE, *158 Grafton Rd, London NW5*

LEWISHAM WOMEN'S CENTRE, *c/o Lewisham Town Hall, Rushey Green, London SE6*

NORTH KENSINGTON WOMEN'S CENTRE, *13 Auckland Ter., London W8*

SOUTH LONDON WOMEN'S CENTRE, *14 Radnor Ter., London SW8* (01-262 8485)

WALTHAM FOREST WOMEN'S ACTION GROUP, *161 Markhouse Rd, Walthamstow, London E17.* Community centre

Gatherings

In addition to regular women's groups, there are all sorts of occasional women's gathering which bring women in the movement together to talk, plan, act, relax and have fun. There are women's socials and discos; women's football games; women's weekends where small groups of women get together to talk, write and relax; women's art exhibitions and festivals; women's marches and demonstrations; and women's conferences of all kind. The larger events are listed here. They are part of a growing culture around the women's movement living, working and playing together. You can find out about many of them through local women's centres and publications.

National Conferences

Going to a national women's conference is one way of introducing yourself to the women's movement, since women representing a wide range of interests go to them. It can also be frightening to see so many women together, appearing to know everybody else! Since the women's movement began to grow again in the late 60s, there have been 8 national conferences of the Women's Liberation Movement.

February 1970 Women's Conference, Ruskin College, Oxford
NCC **set up**
September 1971 Skegness; NCC **dissolved**
March 1972 Manchester
November 1972 London
July 1973 Bristol
June 1974 Edinburgh
April 1975 Manchester
April 1976 Newcastle

A National Co-ordinating Committee was set up at the first conference at Oxford, in February 1970, to co-ordinate activities of the women's movement; but was disbanded at the next conference in September 1971 because it was seen by many women no longer to represent the movement as a whole. Since then there has been no central national organization of the women's movement, and national conferences are the only time when the movement 'as a whole' gets together. The organization is informal: there are no conference delegates; any woman is free to come. Each conference has a different atmosphere about it, is held in a different place and has a different timetable and topics for discussion, but there is a roughly similar programme. There is usually a series of 'workshops' (small groups discussing a particular topic and planning future action) organized by women from different small groups who want to meet women from other parts of the country with similar interests and involved in similar projects. Workshops cover most of the topics listed on pp. 5–6. There are also a number of 'plenary' sessions in which everyone at the conference meets together in a big hall, and there is discussion of important issues which have arisen at the conference, or which women have brought to the conference.

The Six Demands (p. 171) were adopted by the movement at conference plenary sessions. At each conference the group responsible for planning and organizing the next is decided upon. This group then makes the arrangements, with a number of planning meetings which women from groups all over the country attend. A crèche is organized for children. There are social events; women's folk and rock music; women's theatre; exhibitions and dance; stalls selling books, pamphlets, posters and badges. Accommodation is provided in church halls, schools and the homes of the local women involved. A collection of papers and workshop reports is usually made after each conference, so that a record is available. Most women feel that there is a lot to gain from meeting together as a national group, for the sense of unity and size this gives, for the chance to make personal contact with women from all over the country, and to celebrate the growth and strength of the women's movement. For information about future national conferences, contact local groups or see newsletters, *Spare Rib*, *Women's Report* or *Women's Liberation News*, where they are widely advertised beforehand.

Some past conferences

Women's Abortion and Contraception Campaign	**January 1973 Liverpool and March 1975 Nottingham**
National Lesbian Conferences	**April 1974 Canterbury and Autumn 1974 Nottingham**
Structure and Organization in the Women's Movement	**April 1974 Coventry**
Women and the Media	**July 1974 Bristol**
Sexuality	**August 1974 Bristol**
Women and Health	**October 1974 Sheffield**
Women and Psychiatry	**February 1975 Malvern**
Sexism and Education	**March 1975 Nottingham**
Children at Conferences	**Spring 1975 Newcastle**
Childcare	**May 1975 Nottingham**
Women's Arts	**July 1975 London**
National Abortion Campaign	**September 1975 London**
Girls and Science Education	**Autumn 1975 London**
Women against Torture	**November 1975 London**

Regional conferences

Held irregularly, they are worth going to when they do occur. They give a good idea of what the women's movement is like in a particular region, and because they're usually small it's fairly easy to get to know people. For details contact local women's centres.

Special subject conferences

There have been national conferences in almost every area of interest to women in the movement (see p. 186 for a list of some conferences which have taken place). These are opportunities for interested women from all over the country to work on particular issues together, to discuss in detail some of their shared experiences in organizing particular campaigns and to arrange to co-ordinate future activities. For details contact either local women's centres (p. 173ff) or groups involved in particular issues (p. 173ff). The booklets of conference papers and reports of discussion give useful summaries of activity in the movement in particular areas.

International Women's Day March

Each year since 1972 there has been a women's march, in early March, through London on International Women's Day, in solidarity with the struggles of women everywhere for liberation. It's a tremendous feeling to be walking in such a large group of women. Details from women's centres and in newsletters.

Laurieston Women's Week

Laurieston Hall, Castle Douglas, Dumfries and Galloway, Scotland. There has been a women's week at Laurieston Hall (a community of men, women and children) each year since 1972, organized by the women who live there. It is a time when women from all the country meet to talk, work, live and have fun together. Send SAE for details.

Women and socialism

The women's movement in Britain has always had links with socialism. Many of the women involved in the first women's groups in the late 60s had previously been, or were still, involved in socialist groups. There are a number of socialist women's groups active within the movement, and many women who see themselves as socialist are working in other groups and campaigns. For local groups see p. 173ff. These groups may be primarily study groups or may be involved in any of the many activities of the women's movement, attempting to organize and to understand their activities and aims within the framework of a socialist theory. There have been a series of 'Women and Socialism' conferences, bringing together women from all over the country, considering topics of importance in the women's movement and discussing the relationship between feminism and socialism. Papers from these conferences are available. There has also been a series of 'Women and Socialism' one-day workshops. A lot of discussion on the aims, organization and theory of the women's movement has come out of these meetings. For socialist women's publications see p. 191ff.

Support for struggles in other countries

The groups listed here are campaigning in various ways in support of women in other countries who are fighting against oppression of one kind or another.

CAMPAIGN FOR THE RELEASE OF INDIAN POLITICAL PRISONERS, *Sonia Khan, 22 Boundary Rd, London NW8* (01-382 2332)

WOMEN AGAINST TORTURE, *c/o Amnesty International (British section), 55 Theobalds Rd, London WC1.* Aims to draw attention to plight of women prisoners of conscience and to help combat the alarming increase in the use of torture

WOMEN'S CAMPAIGN AGAINST FACIST SPAIN, *c/o Women's Liberation Workshop, 38 Earlham St, London WC2.* Collective of Spanish and British women initially informing people about conditions of life under fascism, and showing links between sexism and fascism

WOMEN'S CAMPAIGN FOR CHILE, *91 Alderney St, London SW1.* Campaign of protest for the hundreds of women still in prison in Chile

following military coup in 1973. Mainly letter-writing campaign, to the authorities and prisoners; also 'adopting' prisoners, to find suitable jobs for them in Britain, obtain their release from prison, get visas etc. Participated in the Chile Committee for Human Rights

WOMEN'S COLLECTIVE ON IRELAND, *20b Batoum Gdns, London W6.* Involved in publicizing facts about situation in Northern Ireland. Will visit women's groups to talk about political issues; slide show, photographic exhibition and music

WOMEN IN INDOCHINA, *49 Florence Rd, London N4* (01-272 7043)

Women and racism

There are several groups of women fighting racism in Britain.

RACE TODAY: monthly journal published from within the black community in Britain. Has published articles on Caribbean women and the black community in Britain, and on Asian women

RACE TODAY WOMEN'S GROUP, RACE TODAY, 74 Shakespeare Rd, London SE24.

BLACK WOMEN'S GROUP, 65 Barnwell Rd, London SW2

INDIAN WOMEN'S LIBERATION GROUP, c/o Amrit Wilson, 10 St Mary le Park Court, Albert Bridge Rd, London SW11

The women's movement abroad

There is not enough space in this book to give contact addresses or information about the women's movement in other countries. Women are organizing together all over the world, and you are likely to find women's groups in almost any country you visit. *Women's Liberation News* and *Women's Report* give a good coverage of news from other countries. They also have initial contact addresses for many countries (see p. 192). Also try the LONDON WOMEN'S LIBERATION WORKSHOP and WIRES (p. 173) for foreign contact addresses.

WOMEN'S LIBERATION HOUSE, 25 Alberta St, Sydney NSW 2000, Australia

MOUVEMENT DE LIBERATION DES FEMMES, 1 rue Guy de la Brosse, Paris 5, France

LA LIBRERIA DELLE DONNE, Via Doghana 2, 20123 Milan, Italy

FRAUENZENTRUM, 1000 Berlin, Hornstrasse 2, W Germany

NATIONAL ORGANIZATION FOR WOMEN, National Office, 5 South Wabash, Suite 1615, Chicago, Illinois 60603, USA

CANADIAN WOMEN'S EDUCATIONAL PRESS, 218 Bloor St, West Toronto, Ontario, Canada

ISIS, *Isis Suisse, Case Postale 301, 1227 Carouge, Switzerland.* International communications centre for women's groups and activities. Has lists of women's groups all over the world.

AIM Group Women's Centre, *44 Lower Mount St, Dublin 2.* AIM (action, information, motivation) formed in Dublin in 1971 to campaign for Family Law Reform. Centre has coffee bar and space for meetings and discussions; advice on legal and social aspects of marital breakdown; research and reading library with women's books and newsletters from women's groups abroad; information and discussion groups on women's health and employment; and 'events' board. Open to all women.

WOMEN'S LIBERATION GROUP, *14 Screen Rd, Dublin 7*

FEMINIST ALLIANCE, *c/o Students' Representative Council, University College, Cork.* Women's rights group, publishes a magazine *Aware*

IRISH WOMEN'S AID, *Box 791, 54 Harcourt St, Dublin 2.* Provides refuge for battered women; house was given by developer on indefinite lease; interest in setting up other refuges around the country; accepts children with mothers; provides nursery facilities and help with rehousing

IRISHWOMEN UNITED, *c/o 12 Lower Pembroke St, Dublin 2.* Formed in April 1975. Umbrella for women's liberation groups from the universities, self-help group, health group, social welfare group, theatre, consciousness-raising groups; marches on abortion and contraception, workshops on women's history and women and trade unions

When ladies were ladies they would never have dreamed of standing at a bar by themselves and drinking —

MR CHRISTOPHER MITCHELL, OWNER OF EL VINO —

The women's movement and men

Women's groups are usually closed to men, because women have felt the need for a space away from the daily pressure of men (and children) to begin to find the insight and energy to struggle to change their lives and themselves. But women's liberation obviously affects men. As women begin to make new demands and to see themselves differently, the people around them are forced to become involved in these changes. For many men, contact with the women's movement through the women they know and live with has been disturbing and even frightening. Men's groups have been formed in some places, partly as a response to the women's movement and as a way of coming to terms with the changes it is throwing up for men. They are also a way for men to begin to challenge their own roles as men, and to understand how they themselves are stereotyped and confined by the social roles they are expected to play. For some men they are an opportunity to be more open with other men and to experience the openness, gentleness and vulnerability which boys are usually taught to control or to hide. There have been several issues of a men's magazine, *Brothers/Men Against Sexism*, and several men's conferences. For details of men's groups all over the country contact *7 Muswell Av., London N10* (01-444 0711), or *55 Grove Av., Birmingham 13* (021-449 5939). Local women's centres may know of men's groups in their area. RISING FREE (p. 222) has a book-list on men against sexism.

Magazines and newsletters

Reading the magazines and newsletters of groups is an excellent way of becoming familiar with the issues, concerns and activities of the women's movement. Most of these are produced collectively by small groups of women who work for little or no pay, aiming to spread information as widely as possible and to cover costs rather than to make a profit. Some groups publish their own newsletter. Here we list only the wider-ranging publications, available either singly or by subscription. Some, like *Spare Rib* and *Women's Report*, are available nationally in women's centres, alternative/left-wing bookshops (p. 222) and some newsagents. They are all available by post from the addresses given below. Price details for 1976.

BREAD AND ROSES,
Bread and Roses Collective,
29 Glossop St, Leeds 6. Quarterly,
free (surviving on donations),
produced by group of women in
Leeds as outlet for women to publish
their work. Articles, poems,
information about activities

COUNTRY WOMEN'S NEWSLETTER,
Dumb Toms, Ingleton, Carnforth,
Lancashire. Each issue produced by
women in different part of country.
Means of making contact for rural
women in the movement. Contact
address list of subscribers in each
issue. Discussions of particular
contributions country women can
make to movement, how movement
can be part of country life

IGNITION, *53 Lime Walk, Headington,*
Oxford. Proposed new lesbian
feminist magazine; news, articles,
poems, reviews

IMAGES OF WOMEN NEWSLETTER,
Angela Martin, c/o 62 Dean St,
London W1, 12p including postage.
Information and addresses on all
areas connected with images of
women (film, art, video, books etc)

LIBERTARIAN WOMEN'S NETWORK,
1 Lynnewood Pl., Dundee, Scotland

LINK

LINK, *16 King St, London WC2.*
10p or subscription 70p from Central
Books, *37 Gray's Inn Rd, London*
WC1X 8PS. The Communist Party
Women's Journal

MOTHRA, *158 Grafton Rd,*
London NW5. Poetry, prose and
pictures

NATIONAL LESBIAN NEWSLETTER
COLLECTIVE, *41 Cromwell St,*
Nottingham. Group producing
national newsletter for lesbians in the
movement.

WOMEN'S LIBERATION NEWS
20b Batoum Gdns, London W6.
Monthly, 60p for 6 months. Good
succinct regular news from women's
movement in Britain and abroad

NEW WOMEN'S MONTHLY PAPER,
57 Lucas Av., London E13. Non-
sectarian forum for open discussion
of ideas and exchange of experience
by and for women in the movement.
Non-profit making

RED RAG

RED RAG, *22 Murray Mews,*
London NW1. Quarterly, 20p;
subscriptions £1 for 4 issues.
Interesting forum for deeper
discussion of campaigns, activities
and organization of women's
movement. Socialist feminist
orientation. Also produce pamphlets

SAPPHO, *39 Wardour St,*
London W1V 3HA. Monthly, 35p.
Lesbian feminist magazine, until
recently the only one in Europe.
Aims to break down isolation of gay
ghettoes, to support all minority
groups; acts as clearing house for
lesbian groups and publishes
information about existing groups,
articles, short stories and poems

shrew

SHREW, *c/o The Women's Liberation*
Workshop, 38 Earlham St,
London WC2. Price varies. Original
paper of the London Women's
Liberation Workshop. Each issue

produced by different group, with different topic. Workshop sells back copies, interesting record of the movement's growth and development in London. Past issues have included topics such as sexuality, children, socialism and feminism, radical feminism, night-cleaner's campaign, work, women in East London, women in the Third World etc

Socialist Woman

A JOURNAL OF THE INTERNATIONAL MARXIST GROUP AUTUMN 1975

SOCIALIST WOMAN, *21 Highview Court, College Rd, Harrow Weald, Middlesex*. 10p or 70p subscription from above address. The women's paper of the International Marxist Group

spare Rib

SPARE RIB, *9 Newburgh St, London W1A 4XS*. Monthly, 30p; subscriptions £4.44 from *Spare Rib* Subscriptions, c/o *Linda Phillips, 114 George St, Berkhamsted, Herts PH4 2EJ*, or order it from your newsagent. Started 1972, now collectively produced by group of women, some full and some part-time workers. Honest, serious discussion of events and issues of great interest to women. Book and film reviews, women's activities etc

WOMEN AND EDUCATION NEWSLETTER, *4 Cliffdale Dr., Crumpsall, Manchester 8*. Comprehensive, covering all aspects of education from pre-school playgroups to universities. Has lists of women and education groups throughout country. Extremely informative on developments, issues and happenings in education, and publishes reports,

articles, book reviews etc.
Non-Sexist Teaching Resources Report available from newsletter (an account of discussions at 1974 conference)

WOMEN'S REPORT

WOMEN'S REPORT, *14 Aberdeen Rd., Wealdstone, Harrow, Middx*. Bi-monthly, 20p (from the Women's Liberation Workshop), or subscription £1.50 (direct). A comprehensive feminist analysis of current issues and events. Includes excellent up-to-date information about women's activities, women's organizations in Britain and abroad, legal, educational, medical matters concerning women, book reviews, diary of forthcoming events, and more

WOMEN SPEAKING, *The Wick, Roundwood Av., Hutton, Brentwood, Essex*. Quarterly, 20p. Articles, news and reviews. 'A unifying periodical for women's activities and problems', concerned broadly with women's rights

WOMEN'S STRUGGLE NOTES, *from Big Flame Women's Group, 21 Wayland Av., London E8*. News of women's campaigns, strikes etc

WOMENS VOICE

WOMEN'S VOICE, *61 Tylney Croft, Essex*. 5p. Paper of International Socialist women.

Other Women's Organizations

This is a list of women's organizations which don't fit into the section on the women's movement, although some of them are directly concerned with the struggle for women's rights and for improving the position of women in society. There is a vast number of organizations concerned with the interests of women in many areas. A fuller list is published periodically by *Women's Forum*, an associated group of the NATIONAL COUNCIL FOR SOCIAL SERVICE (26 Bedford Square, London WC1). Their list includes professional, religious and international organizations and women's sections of political parties.

COUNCIL FOR THE STATUS OF WOMEN, *Hillcrest, Stillorgan, Co. Dudlin.* Composed of women from 23 organizations; aims to implement recommendations of Commission for the Status of Women, published by government in 1972

THE FAWCETT SOCIETY, *27 Wilfred St, London SW1E 6PR* (01-828 4966). Stands for equal rights and responsibilities for women and men, working to remove all inequalities and discrimination based on sex; the Fawcett Library has a wide range of literature on interests, activities and achievements of women currently and throughout world history; newsletter and other publications

FEDERATION OF WOMEN'S INSTITUTES OF NORTHERN IRELAND, *Northern Ireland War Memorial Building, South Waring St, Belfast 1* (Belfast 26335). To enable women to take more effective part in rural life and development, and to encourage fuller education and cultural development; local groups throughout Northern Ireland; monthly publication

THE HOUSEWIVES TRUST, *3 Sloane Terrace Mansions, London SW1X 9DG.* Aims to represent and protect the interests of housewives to official bodies, wholesale and retail organizations, manufacturers and government; and to make information available to members; newsletter (*Insight*)

MARRIED WOMEN'S ASSOCIATION, *87 Redington Rd, London NW3 7RR.* Aims to promote recognition of a wife as equal legal and financial partner during marriage

NATIONAL COUNCIL OF WOMEN OF GREAT BRITAIN, *36 Lower Sloane St, London SW1.* Working for women's rights and co-operation among women to promote human rights and the welfare of women and all people

NATIONAL FEDERATION OF WOMEN'S INSTITUTES, *39 Eccleston St, London SW1 9NT* (01-730 7212). Aims to give all countrywomen chance to work together to improve the conditions of rural life, and opportunity for members to develop their talents and widen horizons educationally and socially; branches all over England; monthly publications

NATIONAL JOINT COMMITTEE OF WORKING WOMEN'S ORGANIZATIONS, *Transport House, Smith Sq., London SW1.* Composed of representatives of 26 national organizations. Aims to promote interests of working women and to encourage their representation on any committees or similar bodies established by government or other authorities to deal with matters where women have a special interest; also conducts campaigns on subjects of national importance which may benefit from combined action by women

SCOTTISH TRADES UNION CONGRESS (WOMEN'S ADVISORY COMMITTEE), *12 Woodlands Ter., Glasgow G3 6DE.* Works to extend trade union organization among women workers and to encourage their full participation in trade union movement

SCOTTISH WOMEN'S RURAL INSTITUTES, *42 Heriot Row, Edinburgh EH3 6EU* (031-225 6490). Provides educational and recreational opportunities for women who live and work in the country or who are interested in country life; local groups throughout Scotland; monthly magazine

THE SIX POINT GROUP, *61 Barton Court, London W14.* Non-political party organizations; objective is betterment of society by emancipation of women; the 6 points are: equal pay, equal partnership in marriage, equal opportunity, equal education, equal retirement, equal basis for pensions

THE SUFFRAGETTE FELLOWSHIP, *14 St Augustine's Mansions, Bloomburg St, Vincent Sq., London SW1.* Perpetuates memory of pioneers and outstanding events connected with women's emancipation, especially militant suffragette campaign; and to secure women's political, civil, economic, educational and social status on the basis of equality of the sexes

TRADES UNION CONGRESS (WOMEN'S ADVISORY COMMITTEE), *Gaywood House, 29 Gt Peter St, London SW1* (01-222 3776). Concerned with interests of women workers and with unionization of women

UNION OF TOWNSWOMEN'S GUILDS, *2 Cromwell Pl., London SW7* (01-589 8817). 3,000 local guilds; provide meeting places and encourage social, cultural, and educational activities among women; monthly magazine

WOMEN IN MANAGEMENT, *4 Mapledale Av., Croydon CR0 5TA, Surrey.* Voluntary group working for the improved use of the nation's womanpower

WOMEN'S INTERNATIONAL LEAGUE FOR PEACE AND FREEDOM, *29 Gt James St, London WC1N 3ES* (01-242 4817). Aims to bring together women of different political and philosophical tendencies to abolish the political, social, economic and psychological causes of war, and to work for a constructive peace; occasional seminars; campaign on a wide range of issues. Branches throughout Britain; newsletter

WOMEN'S NATIONAL COMMISSION, *Queen Anne's Chambers, 41 Tothill St, London SW1H 9JX.* Aims to ensure informed opinion of women is given its due weight in deliberations of government on both national and international affairs

195

Resources

General information

BIT, *146 Great Western Rd,
London W11* (01-229 8219). Free
information service. Also produces
useful information guides: (*Overland
to India and Australia, Overland
through Africa, Overland through
Central and South America*). Guides
to cheap travel with information about
accommodation, food, transport,
visas, health precautions etc.
European and British address network
Squatters' handbook

CITIZENS' ADVICE BUREAUX,
*National Council of Social Service,
26 Bedford Sq., London WC1.* Advice
and information on anything and
everything. Look in the phone
directory for local addresses

CONSUMER ASSOCIATION (CA),
14 Buckingham St, London WC2N 6DS
(01-839 1222). Publishers of *Which*
and many useful handbooks for
women

NATIONAL COUNCIL FOR CIVIL
LIBERTIES (NCCL), *186 Kings Cross Rd,
London WC1* (01-278 4575). An
organization fighting to defend and
extend civil liberties. Provides legal
advice and representation. Women's
Rights Dept publishes rights
information, provides individual
advice on legal employment and
other women's problems (particularly
Sex Discrimination and Equal Pay);
lobbies government on women's
rights issues

PEOPLE'S NEWS SERVICE, *PO Box 1949,
197 King's Cross Rd, London WC1.*
Regular publication of news: local,
national and international. Good
insight into news that other
newspapers often gloss over or
ignore: about people's struggles of
many kinds in this country and
abroad, and about government and
corporation activities. Good
alternative to conventional news
media

RELEASE, *1 Elgin Av., London W9 3PR*
(01-289 1123, 01-603 8654 emergency
outside office hours). Help and advice
on legal and welfare rights, and access
to reliable solicitors if necessary.
Also offer pregnancy counselling.
Book-list on women

Our bodies, our minds

Many women's groups and women's studies courses spend time
exploring ideas and feelings about sexuality. Contact local groups
(p. 173ff) for details. See also p. 215ff for films.

Health

There is a strong network of women's health groups across the country in which women are learning basic self-help skills (p. 20ff).

AWARE HEALTH COLLECTIVE,
c/o South London Women's Centre,
14 Radnor Ter., London SW8

BIRMINGHAM, *50 Blenheim Rd,*
Moseley, Birmingham, Warwicks.

BRISTOL, *contact the Women's Centre,*
59 Lower Union St, Bristol BS1 2DU,
Avon

CAMBRIDGE PREGNANCY ADVISORY
SERVICE, *48 Eden St, Cambridge,*
Cambs.

HACKNEY, *51 Buckingham Rd,*
London N1

LEAMINGTON SPA GROUP,
c/o 10a Beauchamp Av.,
Leamington Spa, Warks.

LEEDS, *25 Lucas St, Leeds 6, Yorks.*

LIVERPOOL, *c/o The Women's Centre,*
49 Seel St, Liverpool 1

MANCHESTER, *contact the Women's*
Centre, 21 Upper Brook St,
Manchester 13

YORK, *3 Fairfax St, York*

HEALTH EDUCATION COUNCIL,
78 New Oxford St, WC1

Sex, contraception, abortion and pregnancy

The abortion and contraception campaigns are working for freely available abortion and contraception facilities, for improvements in methods and techniques and to publicize any harmful side-effects of commonly used contraceptives such as the Pill and IUD (p. 35ff).

Abortion
Branches of NAC in most towns. Local contact addresses available. Information on how to campaign locally. Fighting for improved abortion facilities to be available to *all* women. 'The aim of NAC is to build a mass national campaign to defeat all restrictive legislation on the basis of a woman's right to choose whether to continue or terminate a pregnancy.' (*Spare Rib*, No. 42, p. 20)

NATIONAL ABORTION CAMPAIGN (NAC),
30 Camden Rd, London NW1

SCOTTISH NATIONAL ABORTION
CAMPAIGN, *c/o G. Smith, 54 Grant St,*
Glasgow G3 6HN (041-333 0318)

WOMEN'S ABORTION AND
CONTRACEPTION CAMPAIGN (WACC),

c/o Merseyside Women's Centre,
49 Seel St, Liverpool 1. WACC started in order to co-ordinate the activities of local groups. Newsletter available from Merseyside Women's Centre, containing medical news about abortion and contraception methods as well as reports of local and

national campaigning. (Back copies available from BRISTOL WOMEN'S CENTRE, *59 Lower Union St, Bristol BS1 2DU,* 7p + postage)

A WOMAN'S RIGHT TO CHOOSE, *88a Islington High St, London N1*

(01-359 5200 or 01-359 5209). Works closely with the NAC and with MPs involved in abortion legislation. Host for the new international information bulletin on abortion law reform. Has list of publications on abortion.

Contraception, Pregnancy, Pregnancy Testing groups

THE FAMILY PLANNING ASSOCIATION, *Margaret Pyke House, 27/35 Mortimer St, London W1A 4QW* (01-636 9135). Voluntary organization, registered charity. Largest medical agency outside the NHS. Has built up nationwide professional service for people with wide range of needs. Provides advice, help with birth control for everyone over 16 years, including examination and regular medical supervision, and a cervical smear test service. Campaigns to spread information on family planning and runs clinics for people with sexual problems. Pregnancy testing. Free leaflets available on methods of contraception: booklist on subjects related to family planning and sexual relationships. FPA clinics in most towns. Addresses in the phone book.

FERTILITY RIGHTS, *c/o Spare Rib, 9 Newburgh St, London W1A 4XS.* Criticizes population-control policy from feminist point of view. Supports women's right to choose to have children (and to have the material conditions to make this a possible choice) as well as to choose not to

NATIONAL ASSOCIATION FOR THE CHILDLESS, *318 Summer Lane, Birmingham*

BRITISH PREGNANCY ADVISORY SERVICE. Non profit-making charitable trust. Clinics in a number of cities,

offering free pregnancy tests, advice on abortion, contraception, vasectomy and sterilization. Main centres: Birmingham 021-643 1461; Brighton 0273-509 726; Leeds 0532-443 861; Liverpool 051-227 3721; Manchester 061-236 7777

BROOK ADVISORY CENTRE, *233 Tottenham Court Rd, London W1* (01-580 2991). Gives advice and counsels on contraception, abortion referral. Particularly good for young unmarrieds. Centres all over the country

PREGNANCY ADVISORY SERVICE, *40 Margaret St, London W1* (01-409 0281). Registered charity

WOMEN'S ABORTION AND CONTRACEPTION CAMPAIGN, *Women's Centre, 2nd Floor, 59 Union St, Bristol 1.*

CAMBRIDGE: Telephone Cambridge 59798 or 52871 to find out where to go

ROCHDALE HEALTH GROUP, *c/o 67 Harewood Rd, Norden, Rochdale, Lancs*

STEPNEY HEALTH GROUP, *c/o 196 Jubilee St, Stepney, London E1*

WOMEN'S RELEASE, *1 Elgin Av., London W9 3PR* (01-289 1123). Offers pregnancy counselling and help with obtaining abortions, contraception and sterilization

Childbirth

ASSOCIATION TO IMPROVE MATERNITY SERVICES (AIMS), Secretary:
Mrs A. Taylor, *West Hill Cottage, Exmouth Pl., Hastings, Sussex*

THE NATIONAL CHILDBIRTH TRUST, *9 Queensborough Ter., London W2 3TB*. Prepares expectant parents for childbirth; co-ordinates research, information and experience relevant to preparation for childbirth.

Publishes books and pamphlets for teachers and parents.

KATE RUSSELL, *75 Leigham Court Rd, London SW16* (midwife who delivers babies by the Leboyer method)

SOCIETY TO SUPPORT HOME CONFINEMENTS, *274 Merton Rd, London SW18* (01-874 7940)

WOMEN'S CHILDBIRTH PROJECT, *140 Adelaide Av., Brockley, London SE4*

The Menopause

ABERDEEN: Gynaecological Endocrine Clinic
BELFAST: Samaritan Hospital (Dr J. F. O'Sullivan)
BIRMINGHAM: Queen Elizabeth Medical Centre
BRIGHTON & HOVE: The Lady Chichester Hospital
BRISTOL: South Jead Hospital
DURHAM: Dryburn Hospital
EDINBURGH: Royal Infirmary
GLASGOW: Glasgow Royal Infirmary
LEEDS: General Infirmary; Women's Hospital
LIVERPOOL: Women's Hospital
LONDON: Chelsea Hospital for Women; St Thomas's Hospital; Dulwich Hospital; King's College Hospital
MERTHYR TYDFIL: St Tydfil's Hospital
NOTTINGHAM: City Hospital
NUNEATON: George Eliot Hospital
OXFORD: John Radcliffe Hospital
SHEFFIELD: Jessop Hospital

Look up the hospital in the phone book and ask for details.

WOMEN'S HEALTH CARE (WHC), *7 Coniston Court, Carlton Dr., London SW15 2BZ* (01-788 2733).

Information and pressure group for better health care for menopausal women

Cystitis

U & I CLUB, *22 Gerrard Rd, Islington, London N1* (01-359 0403). Advises on all aspects of urinary infection; leaflets on cystitis and thrush (Angela Kilmartin)

Cancer

MASTECTOMY ASSOCIATION,
1 Colworth Rd, Croydon, Surrey
(01-654 8463). Advice and support to
women who've had breast cancer
(Betty Westgate)

WOMEN'S NATIONAL CANCER CONTROL
CAMPAIGN, *9 King St,*

London WC2E 8HN (01-836 9901)

BRITISH UNITED PROVIDENT
ASSOCIATION (BUPA),
Medical Centre Ltd, Webb House,
210 Pentonville Rd, London N1
(01-278 4651, 01-278 4565,
appointments)

Lesbian groups

There are many local lesbian groups. These may be contacted through
local groups (p. 173ff). See also p. 191ff for newsletters and magazines.

ACTION FOR LESBIAN PARENTS,
address as above. Group formed
from GAY WIVES AND MOTHERS
COLLECTIVE, SAPPHO, the NCCL and
representatives from women's
movement and ONE PARENT FAMILY
GROUPS. Aims to mount a national
campaign to publicize the plight of
lesbian parents in custody cases and
to lobby for changes in the
administration of the law

GAY WIVES AND MOTHERS COLLECTIVE,
c/o 39 Wardour St, London W1
(01-434 1801). Formed in 1973. Aims
to campaign against injustice in

lesbian custody cases; to attempt to
break the isolation felt by lesbian
parents/wives; to educate the gay
world and the general public about
the problems of lesbian wives and
mothers; and to provide counselling
and advice. *Sisterhood*, the newsletter
of the Gay Wives and Mothers
Collective, is available from
182 Uxbridge Rd, Harrow,
Middlesex

KENRIC, *B/M Kenric,*
London WC1V 6XX. Arranges
meetings, visits and talks for lesbians,
mostly in members' homes

Gay groups

The following is a list of gay switchboards, telephone numbers you
can ring for information, advice or simply someone to talk to. It is
not a complete list of gay groups in Britain. They will be able to tell
you about local gay groups and gay publications. So will women's
centres, p. 173ff.

BIRMINGHAM (021-449 8312), evenings
7–10pm

BRIGHTON (0273-278 78), Wed/Fri/Sat
8–10pm

BRISTOL (0272-712 621), evenings
8–10pm

DUBLIN (0001-764 240) Thurs/Fri/
evenings 7.30–9.30pm Sat 3–6pm

GLASGOW (041-204 1292), evenings 7–9pm except Tues

LEEDS, LEEDS GAY INFORMATION CENTRE, *153a Woodhouse Lane, Leeds 2.* No phone, but will answer letters

LONDON (01-827 7324), 24 hours

MANCHESTER (061-273 3725), evenings 7–10pm

BEAUMONT SOCIETY, *BM Box 3084, London WC1V 6XX.* Self-help group for transvestites

CAMPAIGN FOR HOMOSEXUAL EQUALITY (CHE), *PO Box 427, 28 Kennedy St, Manchester* (061-228 1985)

FRIEND (01-603 6293). Counselling service for homosexual women and men

GAY RIGHTS COMMITTEE, *c/o NUS, 3 Endsleigh St, London WC1.* Organizes gay societies in universities and colleges

GAY WORKING PEOPLE'S COLLECTIVE, *134a Woodhouse La., Leeds 2.*

Produces a newsletter which also lists gay groups

ICEBREAKERS (01-603 6293). Telephone counselling service for homosexual men and women. 7.30–10.30pm

INTERGROUP, *Unitarian Hall, Hoop La., London NW11.* Arranges meetings between heterosexuals and homosexuals (men and women) centred round Unitarian church

IRISH WOMEN UNITED, *4C Millmount Av., Dublin 9.* For gay and straight women. Meets every Sunday

NORTHERN IRELAND GAY RIGHTS ASSOCIATION, *4 University St, Belfast 7*

SCOTTISH MINORITY GROUP, *60 Broughton St, Edinburgh EH1 3SA,* or *214 Clyde St, Glasgow G1 4JS*

TRANS-SEXUAL ACTION ORGANIZATION, *c/o The Peace Centre, 18 Moor St, Queensway, Birmingham B4 7UH* (021-449 8305). For trans-sexuals, friends, relatives, social workers

Sexual problems

MARRIAGE GUIDANCE COUNCIL, *National Marriage Guidance Council, Little Church St, Rugby, Warks.* (0788-72341). Runs clinic for couples (married or not) with sexual problems, using Masters and Johnson techniques

THE ASSOCIATION OF SEXUAL AND MARITAL THERAPISTS, *79 Hurley St, London W1T 2U*

Pre-orgasmic therapy groups are being organized by Eleanor Stephens, *c/o Spare Rib, 9 Newburgh St, London W1*

Mind

LONDON WOMEN AND PSYCHIATRY GROUP, *c/o The Women's Liberation Workshop, 38 Earlham St, London WC2*

PSYCHIATRY AND EVERYWOMAN,

194 West Malvern Rd, West Malvern, Worcester

LONDON WOMEN'S CO-COUNSELLING GROUP, *c/o The Women's Liberation Workshop, 38 Earlham St, London WC2*

WOMEN AGAINST AGE LIMITS,
40 Cork Rd, Lancaster. One aspect of
the creation of a stereotyped 'ideal
woman' by the media, advertising
and the fashion industry is the idea
that women, once they begin to get
old, are somehow obsolete as
attractive human beings. Along with
this go other problems which older
women particularly have to face:
the problems of the menopause, and
the way in which this is approached by
doctors; the adjustment which takes
place as children grow up and leave
home; the experience of going back
to work after a break of several
years; and often a sense of having
lost years of life, of futurelessness
(p. 53 for a discussion of these
problems). There are a few women's
groups in different areas which are
concerned specifically with women's
experience of growing older, although
as yet this perspective has not been
given much direct emphasis within
the movement. The above is an
address for women who would like to
make contact with other women to
share experiences on this subject.
See *Countrywomen's* issue on
'Older Women's Liberation' (no. 11,
June 1974)

WOMEN AND PSYCHOLOGY,
*Janet Seed, Dept of Psychology,
University of Manchester,
Manchester M13 9PL*

AL-ANON FAMILY GROUPS,
61 Great Dover St, London SE1
(01-403 0888). For wives/husbands
and children of alcoholics

ANOREXICS AID, *c/o 1 Pool End Cl.,
Macclesfield, Cheshire*. Organizes
local groups for parents and children
affected by anorexia nervosa

ANXIETIES ANONYMOUS,
*The Christian Telephone Ministry,
228 Oving Rd, Chichester, Sussex*
(0234-82572)

ASSOCIATION FOR RELATIVES OF THE
MENTALLY, EMOTIONALLY AND
NERVOUSLY DISTURBED (AMEND),
*Glebe End, Warnham, Nr Horsham,
Sussex*

COPE, *11 Acklam Rd, London W10*.
Meetings, therapy sessions, mutual
support. Alternative to psychiatric
in-patient treatment

DEPRESSIVES ANONYMOUS,
50a Masson Av., Ruislip, Middlesex.
Originally formed to help women
suffering from post-natal depression,
but has now broadened its scope;
local groups

HORIZON SOCIAL CLUB, *8 Sussex Rd,
New Malden, Surrey*. Self-help club
for psychiatric patients

MENTAL PATIENTS UNION HACKNEY,
*c/o 177 Glenarm Rd, Clapton,
London E5*. Sends out pamphlets on
the mental health services, and
*A Directory of the Side Effects of
Psychiatric Drugs* (25p or less or free)

MENTAL PATIENTS UNION HULL,
*c/o 16 Clifton Gdns, St Georges Road.
Hull HU3 3QB*. Has lists of local
MPU groups

MIND (NATIONAL ASSOCIATION FOR
MENTAL HEALTH), *22 Harley St,
London W1N ZED* (01-637 0741).
Publishes *Mind Bulletin*; also papers
on Women and Depression
Conference

NARCOTICS ANONYMOUS,
*17 Lordship La., East Dulwich,
London SE22* (01-693 4780, day,
01-692 4880, night)

PEOPLE NOT PSYCHIATRY,
*18 Russell Garden Mews,
London W14* (01-603 4042). Free
therapy centre

PHOBIC TRUST, *51 Northwood Av.,
Purley, Surrey CR2 2ER* (01-660 0332).
Forms local groups; finances research;
aims to establish mobile clinic

PHOBICS SOCIETY, *4 Cheltenham Rd,*
Chorlton-cum-Hardy,
Manchester M21 1QN (061-881 1937).
Helps all phobics, especially
house-bound agoraphobics who
remain untreated through lack of
domiciliary service

PSYCHIATRIC REHABILITATION
ASSOCIATION, *21A Kingsland High St,*
Dalston, London E8 (01-254 9753).
Group homes and hostels; research;
after care; day centre

SAMARITANS Phone number in your
local telephone directory (or call the
operator). Telephone service for
people who feel desperate for any
reason

Living together, living alone

Most of the resources for this section will be found under OUR BODIES
OUR MINDS; OUR CHILDREN; MONEY – OUR RIGHTS. For films, see
p. 215ff; for books, p. 227.

NATIONAL COUNCIL FOR THE SINGLE
WOMAN AND HER DEPENDANTS,
166 Victoria St, London SW1 5BR
(01-828 5511). Aims to promote the
welfare of single women in need, and
of dependants. Bi-monthly newsletter

COMMUNES NETWORK, *31 Wood View,*
Manningham, Bradford, West Yorks

CRUSE, *Cruse House, 126 Sheen Rd,*
Richmond, Surrey. An organization
for widows

NATIONAL ASSOCIATION OF WIDOWS,
65 Eastgate St, Stafford
(0785-57150)

Children

This chapter includes resources on children and their parents.
For books, see p. 228; for films, p. 215ff.

CHILDREN'S RIGHTS WORKSHOP,
73 Balfour St, London SE17
(01-703 7217). Concerned with rights
of children over a wide area: legal,
educational and family. Produces
booklists on children's rights and on
racist, sexist and class stereotyping
in children's books.

CAMPAIGN TO IMPEDE SEXUAL
STEREOTYPING IN THE YOUNG (CISSY),
24 Cresside Rd, London N19. Formed
in 1971. Has made surveys of sexism
in reading primers, picture books for
under-5s, elementary science
textbooks, education books and career
novels; surveys published in *Shrew,*
October 1973 (see p. 00). Also
published pamphlet *Cissy talks to
Publishers,* available *35a Eaton Rise,
London W2,* 15p plus postage.
Contribute regularly to reviews of
children's books in *Spare Rib*
(see p. 193) and has written a number
of other articles

Children's books

A number of groups aiming to improve the quality of childrens' books.

THE CHILDREN'S RIGHTS WORKSHOP (Book Project), *73 Balfour St, London SE17* (01-703 7217). Publishes lists of children's books with comments on content. Concerned with wider roles, including class and racial bias as well as sex-role stereotyping. Produces literature and a list of groups looking at sex roles in children's books in Britain

THE WRITERS AND READERS PUBLISHING COOPERATIVE, *14 Talacre Rd, NW5 3PE*

(01-485 1949). Have published non-sexist children's books.

NON-SEXIST CHILDREN'S BOOKS COLLECTIVE, *22 Stanmore Rd, Leeds 4* (0532-755984). Produces regular newsletter reviewing children's books. Contribute reviews to *Spare Rib*

NATIONAL BOOK LEAGUE, *7 Albermarle St, London W1X 4BB* (01-493 9001/4). Houses a reference library of children's books published in the last year. Provides booklists

Schooling

There are women and education groups in many towns. Activities range from organizing women's studies courses to visiting schools to talks on the position of women. For details of activities in your area contact the local women's groups (p. 173ff). See also the sections on children (p. 66ff) and women's studies (p. 208ff).

NATIONAL UNION OF SCHOOL STUDENTS, *c/o National Union of Students, 3 Endsleigh St, London WCLH ODU* (01-387 1277)

SCHOOLS ACTION UNION, *c/o 75a Acre La., Brixton, London SW2*

WOMEN AND EDUCATION NEWSLETTER (see p. 193). Includes a pre-school page and news about sexism in children's books

FEMINIST TEACHERS, *61 Kirkby Rd, Leicester*. Group of teachers in the women's movement

ADVISORY CENTRE FOR EDUCATION

(ACE), *Dr White House, 32 Trumpington St, Cambridge CB2 1QY* (0223-51456). Research and information centre for parents and students

CONFEDERATION FOR THE ADVANCEMENT OF STATE EDUCATION (CASE), *81 Rustlings Rd, Sheffield S11 7AB* (0742-662467)

HOME AND SCHOOL COUNCIL, *c/o 81 Rustlings Rd, Sheffield S11 7AB*. Set up by ACE, CASE and NCPTA, produces a variety of publications for parents

NATIONAL CONFEDERATION OF PARENT-TEACHER ASSOCIATIONS (NCPTA), *1 White Av., Northfleet, Gravesend, Kent* (0474-60618)

The child care campaign

The provision of free nurseries available 24 hours a day is one of the Six Demands (see p. 171).

CALTHORPE PARK PLAYGROUP,
c/o 65 Prospect Rd, Birmingham 13.
Started by women from the women's movement in Birmingham. Have produced a 50-page booklet, *Out of the Pumpkin Shell* (see p. 228), an account of their experiences

CHILD CARE OUTSIDE SCHOOL HOURS,
c/o Bristol Women's Centre,
59 Union St, Bristol BS1 2DU.
Campaigning for better provision for the care of school-age children with working mothers, outside school hours and in school holidays

THE CHILDREN'S COMMUNITY CENTRE,
123 Dartmouth Park Hill,
London NW5. Started by women from a women's group. Run by paid workers and a rota of parents and other interested people, men and women.

PRE-SCHOOL EDUCATION GROUP,
33 Demesne Rd, Whalley Range,
Manchester M13 8HJ. Campaigning for improved facilities and supports the challenging of sex-roles

BRITISH ASSOCIATION FOR EARLY
CHILDHOOD EDUCATION,
Montgomery Hall, Kennington Oval,
London SE11 5SW (01-582 8744).
Works to increase quality and quantity of nursery provision. Free information and advice to visitors. Free quarterly newsletter to members

CHILDMINDING RESEARCH UNIT,
32 Trumpington St,
Cambridge CB5 1QY (0223-51456).
Publishes an Action Register, which lists local authorities social service departments and voluntary

organizations instigating action or projects with childminders

CHILDREN AND YOUTH ACTION GROUP,
16–20 Strutton Ground,
off Victoria St, London SW1. National resource centre providing information and advisory service to anyone involved or interested in out-of-school educational and recreational activities for children. Annual directory of children's play activities. For same service in Scotland contact CYAG, *18–19 Claremont Cres.,*
Edinburgh HE6 4QD (031-556 8886)

COUNCIL FOR CHILDREN'S WELFARE,
183/189 Finchley Rd,
London NW3 (01-624 8766).
Interested in day-care schemes for pre-school children and runs occasional conferences on childminding

NATIONAL CAMPAIGN FOR NURSERY
EDUCATION, *33 Hugh St,*
London SW1 (01-828 2844).
Vigorous pressure group now campaigning against the cuts

NATIONAL PLAYING FIELDS ASSOCIATION,
57B Catherine Pl., London SW1E 6EY
(01-834 9274/5). Issues a register of holiday playschemes county by county, their names and addresses, the authority or organization responsible for them, times of opening and the person to contact for further details. Research and resource centre. Does not include London or Scotland

NURSERY STAFF ACTION GROUP,
St Peter's Toddlers Club,
St Peter's Church, Eaton Sq.,
London SW1

PRE-SCHOOL PLAYGROUPS ASSOCIATION, *Alford House, Aveline St, London SE11 5DJ* (01-582 8871) and *7 Royal Ter., Glasgow G3 7NT* (041-331 1340). Formed to encourage mothers to establish playgroups for themselves. Advises, helps and encourages all affiliated playgroups either directly through a local branch or through an area organizer. Write for list of publications or name of local branch

Mothers

ASSOCIATION FOR DESERTED AND ALONE PARENTS (ADAPT), *PO Box 673, Dublin 4, Eire.* Information service. Social gatherings and outings. Monthly meetings

CHERISH, *2 Lower Pembroke St, Dublin 2, Eire.* Association for unmarried mother and her child. Lobby for social and legal reform; has house where an unmarried mother can take her child after birth, to give her time to decide whether or not to keep the child and to make necessary arrangements

CUSTODY GROUP, *c/o Women's Liberation Workshop, 38 Earlham St, London WC2.* Offers support to women who are fighting to gain custody of their children

GINGERBREAD, *9 Poland St, London W1V 3OG* (01-734 9014). Social and welfare help to single people with children; referrals, legal advice, welfare rights, tax problems; 200 local groups throughout Britain

MATERNITY LEAVE CAMPAIGN, *5 Amherst Rd, London W13.* Group campaigning for improved maternity leave provisions for women doing paid work, e.g. a guaranteed period of maternity leave, and protection for pregnant women against losing their jobs

THE MOTHER'S AND CHILDREN'S GROUP, *West Green Community Centre, Stanley Rd, London N15.* Meets twice a week to share child care and talk together

NATIONAL COUNCIL FOR ONE PARENT FAMILIES, *255 Kentish Town Rd, London NW5 2LX* (01-267 1361). Working to improve conditions for one-parent families. Finer Joint Action Committee based with this group; pressing for urgent help for one-parent families in light of recommendations of Finer Report

PRISONERS' WIVES AND FAMILIES SOCIETY, *14 Richmond Av., London N1* (01-278 3981, 01-883 2001). Provides overnight accommodation for wives and families visiting prisoners; short-term accommodation (up to 3 months); nursery open 8.30–5.30; 2 caravans in Clacton for free holidays for prisoners' wives; advice service 10–5; local branches in Northampton, Surrey and Wales

SCOTTISH COUNCIL FOR SINGLE PARENTS, *44 Albany St, Edinburgh EH1 3QR* (031-556 3899). Working for the well-being of single-parent families in Scotland

WORKING ASSOCIATION FOR MOTHERS (WAM), *16 River View Gdns, Twickenham, Middx.* Self-help co-operative in south-west London; aims to help women isolated by changing patterns of housing, work and growing families by giving them social contacts and new outside interests

WORKING MOTHERS' ACTION GROUP, *25 Milton Rd, London N6.* Campaigning for economic, medical and legal needs of working mothers. Campaigning for better day-care facilities, leave to look after sick children etc.

Disabled mothers

ACTION FOR THE DISABLED ASSOCIATION, *26 Barker Walk, Mount Ephraim Rd, Streatham, London SW16.* Militant pressure group campaigning on behalf of both disabled housewives and women who have had to give up employment to look after disabled relatives

DISABLEMENT INCOME GROUP (DIG), *Queen's House, 180–182A Tottenham Court Rd, London W1P 0BD* (01-636 1946/7)

THE DISABILITY ALLIANCE, *96 Portland Pl., London W1*

NATIONAL SOCIETY FOR MENTALLY HANICAPPED CHILDREN, *Pembridge Hall, Pembridge Sq., London W2 4EP* (01-229 8941). Help and information centre. Co-ordinates regional groups who give help and support to parents of mentally handicapped children

Adoption, fostering

ADOPTION RESOURCE EXCHANGE, *Cranmer House, 39 Brixton Rd, London SW9* (01-582 9802)

ASSOCIATION OF BRITISH ADOPTION AGENCIES, *4 Southampton Row, London WC1B 4AA* (01-242 8951)

NATIONAL FOSTER CARE ASSOCIATION, *5 Talacre Rd, Kentish Town, London NW5 3PH* (01-485 8201)

PARENT TO PARENT INFORMATION ON ADOPTION SERVICES (PPIAS), *26 Belsize Gr., London NW3* (01-722 9996)

Students

There are student women's groups at almost all universities in Britain, and at many polytechnics and some colleges of education. They can be found through the student union of each particular college, and usually publicize their activities at the beginning of each academic year and when big campaigns occur. More and more colleges and universities are starting women's studies courses. In some towns there are no separate student women's groups, and women from town and college or university meet together in a single group.

NUS WOMEN'S CAMPAIGN, *c/o National Union of Students, 3 Endsleigh St, London WC1H 0DU* (01-387 1277). Campaign in various ways on wide range of women's issues, including married women's grants, provision of nurseries, contraceptive advice and abortion, job opportunities, women's courses and the position of lesbian students. Contact the above address for details WOMEN AND EDUCATION NEWSLETTER (see p. 193), *63 Clyde Rd, Manchester 20*

Women's studies

'Women's studies' is a general term for groups and courses which concentrate on studying the world from the point of view of women or which give special emphasis to the roles women play. It includes the study of women and culture, women and art, women's roles in different societies, women's biology and physiology, women and history, and women and literature. Women's studies offers important new perspectives in all of these areas.

There are women's studies courses at universities, polytechnics, colleges of education and further education, and adult education centres. They usually start on the initiative of women who want to share feminist perspectives with their students, or are founded by groups of women who want to learn more about women's activities and experiences in some subject area. Some have a more distinctly feminist approach than others. Some are a part of the official system, with exams and coursework assessment; others are more flexible and experimental, run collectively by women's groups. There is discussion in the women's movement about the value of women's studies courses taught within the traditional structure, and some courses attempt to bring this discussion about the value of the present education system into the course itself, directly questioning the role of teachers, exams and 'objective facts' in learning about ourselves and the world we live in. To find out about courses in your area:

– Contact local colleges and adult education centres and ask what courses they offer on women. If there isn't a women's studies course you may be able to get one put on for you, if enough people are interested, either through the WORKERS' EDUCATION ASSOCIATION (WEA) or through the local education authority.

– Contact your local women's group or centre and ask if they know of any courses. They may be willing to start a women's course or study group.

– Get a copy of *Women's Studies in the UK*, by Oonagh Hartnett and Margherita Rendel, ed. Zoe Fairbairns, available from THE LONDON SEMINARS, *c/o Dr M. Rendel, 71 Clifton Hill, London NW8 0JN*. This is a guide to women's studies courses in the UK, listing over 60 courses. For information about teaching materials, see p. 215ff.

LIBRARIANS FOR SOCIAL CHANGE FEMINIST GROUP, *35 Hardy Rd, London SW19 1JA*. Women working in libraries interested in improving conditions of work for women librarians, and in combating sex-roles in library work, including sexism in children's books. Produces

Librarians for Social Change journal
(67 Vere Rd, Brighton, Sussex,
15p + postage)

THE LONDON SEMINARS,
c/o Dr M. Rendel, 71 Clifton Hill,
London NW8 0JN. 'The seminars are
open to all women from this country
and abroad, and exist to provide a
forum for discussion of issues
concerned with women's studies
courses, sex-role stereotyping and
opportunities for women in the
educational professions and
occupations' (*Women Studies in the*
UK)

LONDON WOMEN'S ANTHROPOLOGY
GROUP, *c/o Pat Caplan,*
23 Court House Rd, London W12

NATIONAL REGISTER OF TEACHING AND
RESEARCH INTERESTS, *c/o Miki David,*
24 Stanley Rd, Bristol 6. A register
of teaching and research interests of
women social scientists

WOMEN AND HISTORY,
Women's Local History Group,
1 Woodend St, Springhead, Oldham,
Lancs (061-652 2543). Very informal;
interested in researching into and
eventually publishing information
about the lives and activities of
women in the 19th and early 20th
centuries. No regular meetings, but
happy to make contact with other
women of similar interests

WOMEN AND PSYCHOLOGY,
c/o Janet Seed, Dept of Psychology,
University of Manchester,
Manchester M13 9PL

WOMEN'S RESEARCH AND RESOURCES
CENTRE, *The Richardson Institute,*
158 North Gower St, London NW1.
See p. 00. Collecting books,
pamphlets, conference papers,
leaflets and relevant newspaper
clippings, as a resource centre on the
contemporary women's movement.
Need help in making the collection
and welcome contributions of
literature. Index of research projects

WOMEN AND SCIENCE COLLECTIVE,
7b Chichele Mansions, Chichele Rd,
Cricklewood, London NW2
(01-452 6249). Women who have all
experienced science as a sexist-based
activity and who want to precipitate
greater awareness of social role of
science and technology within
women's movement and beyond it.
Have written introductory articles on
women and science in *Spare Rib*,
(no. 39) (p. 193). Produced a
women's issue of the magazine
Science for the People (no. 29)

WOMEN AND SOCIOLOGY,
British Sociological Association
Women's Caucus,
c/o Diana Barker and Deirdre Fraser,
London School of Economics,
Houghton St, London WC2. British
women sociologists who meet
together as a pressure group for
women's interests in the profession
and in higher education in general.
Involved in study groups and in
compiling lists of women doing
research; newsletter from the above
address

Jobs and training

CAREER ANALYSTS, *Career House,*
90 Gloucester Pl., London W1H 4BL
(01-935 5452)

CAREERS RESEARCH AND ADVISORY
CENTRE (CRAC) *Hobsons' Press,*
Bateman St, Cambridge CB2 1LZ
(0223-54445)

THE NATIONAL ADVISORY CENTRE ON
CAREERS FOR WOMEN, *251 Brompton Rd,*
London SW3 (01-589 9237)

NATIONAL EXTENSION COLLEGE,
8 Shaftesbury Rd, Cambridge CB2 2BP

THE NATIONAL INSTITUTE OF ADULT EDUCATION, *35 Queen Anne St, London W1M 0BL*

THE SOCIETY FOR PROMOTING THE TRAINING OF WOMEN, *Court Farm, Hedgerley, Slough, Bucks SL2 3UY*

TRAINING OPPORTUNITIES SCHEME (TOPS), (Head office Training Services Agency), *162–8 Regent St, London W1R 6DE.* Free booklet,

Training Opportunities for Women, available from Mrs S. Burn, Room 435 at the same address

VOCATIONAL GUIDANCE ASSOCIATION, *Upper Harley St, London NW1* (01-935 2600)

WORKERS' EDUCATIONAL ASSOCIATION, *Temple House, 9 Berkeley St, London W1H 8BY* (01-402 5608)

Working

Women's work is an important area of discussion and action within the women's movement. For women's professional organizations and union information see p. 118ff. Some unions now have women's groups and have adopted the WORKING WOMEN'S CHARTER (p. 116). Women's groups have campaigned against sex discrimination in jobs (p. 105), for better creche and nursery facilities (p. 80), better maternity leave conditions (p. 115), better pay and job opportunities (p. 116), more day release and in-service training (p. 123) and for full recognition of women's contribution as houseworkers (p. 106). Many women are involved in industrial action for better pay and conditions as women (*Women's Struggle Notes*, produced by BIG FLAME WOMEN'S GROUP, 13 *Tadmor St, London W6*, gives a regular account of women's strikes). See also AFTER SCHOOL p. 86; for films on the subject, p. 215ff.

OUTWORK, *13 Mansel Dr., Borstal, Rochester, Kent*

POWER OF WOMEN COLLECTIVE, *Wages for Housework Centre, 129 Drummond St, London NW1.* Organizes around the demand for wages for housework, seeing women's work in the home as centre of their role in society, and therefore worthy of social recognition in the form of wage. Journal, *Power of Women*, has information about campaign in Britain, North America, Spain, Sweden, other countries. Groups in London, Reading, Cambridge, Oxford and Bristol

WORKING WOMEN'S CHARTER CAMPAIGN, *Working Women's Charter Campaign Committee, London Co-ordinating Committee, 49 Lowther Hill, London SE23 1PZ.* For charter see p. 116. For more information and copies of the charter, contact the above address. They have a complete list of Charter Groups (send an SAE and 10p) and affiliated organizations, and a list of speakers. Bi-monthly newsletter. Posters, publicity booklet, badges, tee-shirts and set notes for speakers on the Charter. Organize conferences on relevant issues, e.g. on government spending cuts, Spring 1976

THE WOMEN'S CHARTER FOR NORTHERN IRELAND, *c/o E. Evason, Social Administration, new University of Ulster, Coleraine, Northern Ireland.* Similar charter of women's rights, taking into account special situation of women in Northern Ireland. Details and copies of charter from above address

WORKING MOTHERS ACTION GROUP, *25 Milton Rd, London N6*

Skill-sharing

SHE CAN DO IT, *c/o The Women's Liberation Workshop, 38 Earlham St, London WC2* (01-836 6081). A A woman's work register kept at WOMEN'S LIBERATION WORKSHOP. Lists women in London area with skills to offer: electricians, plumbers, decorators, gardeners, baby-sitters, translators, typists etc. If you would prefer to work for women, and have a skill to offer, or if you would rather hire a woman to work for you, register can put you in touch. An attempt to build up a women's work network

MOTHERTRUCKERS, *c/o The Women's Liberation Workshop, London* (address above). London women's removal team

Legal rights

Several groups are campaigning specifically for improvement in women's legal rights.

EQUAL PAY AND OPPORTUNITY CAMPAIGN, *20 Canonbury Sq., London N1.* Campaigning for women's rights in employment

RIGHTS FOR WOMEN, NCCL, *186 Kings Cross Rd, London WC1X 9DE* (01-278 4575). Women's officer appointed

SEX DISCRIMINATION ACT CAMPAIGN, *148 Bushey Mill La., Watford, Herts.* Has been campaigning on the Sex Discrimination Act (p. 123) for extension of its provisions

WOMEN'S RELEASE, *1 Elgin Av., London W9 3PR* (01-289 1123; 01-603 8654, emergency number outside office hours). Offers help and advice on women's legal and welfare rights. Can refer to reliable solicitor.

Offer pregnancy counselling and help with abortion, contraception and sterilization

WOMEN'S RIGHTS CENTRE, *c/o North Kensington Law Centre, 74 Golbourne Rd, London W10* (01-969 7473). Women giving legal advice to women and helping to find sympathetic solicitors and to get legal aid. Also concerned more generally with legal position of women in relation to welfare state, unions, employment, family and discrimination

EQUAL OPPORTUNITIES COMMISSION (EOC), *Quay St, Manchester 3 3HM* (061-833 9244). London office: *Commission House, 20 Grosvenor Hill, W1* (01-629 8233). See also pp. 194ff, Other Women's Organizations

Money – Our Rights

THE WOMEN'S LIBERATION CAMPAIGN FOR LEGAL AND FINANCIAL INDEPENDENCE, *7 Killieser Av., London SW2* (01-671 2779). Campaign fighting against laws which make women dependent on husbands or men they are living with, e.g. the Social Security co-habitation rule (p. 136). Explanatory pamphlet available from above address

CHILD POVERTY ACTION GROUP, *1 Macklin St, London WC2* (01-242 9149). Citizens' Rights Office provides advice and assistance to low-income families with or without children

AGE CONCERN, *Bernard Sunley House, 60 Pitcairn Rd, Mitcham* (01-640 5431). Campaigns for old people's welfare rights

CITIZENS' RIGHTS OFFICE, *1 Macklin St, London WC2*

COMPANY PENSIONS INFORMATION CENTRE, *7 Old Park La., London W1* (01-493 4757). Non-profit-making, draws attention to advantages of good occupational pension schemes. Free leaflet, *Pensions for Women*

OCCUPATIONAL PENSIONS BOARD, *16–19 Gresse St, London W1* (01-636 7584). Information on employers' pension schemes Also consult your local CAB or DHSS office

FEMALE FINANCIAL ADVISERS, *83 Cambridge St, London SW1V 4PS* (01-828 5923). Offers help and advice on all kinds of money problems, including mortgages. First interview and 2 leaflets (on managing money and getting a mortgage) are free

Claimants' unions

Groups of people receiving social security or unemployment benefit. Fight for claims at labour exchanges, social security offices, appeal tribunals and in courts; produce information about situation of claimants; organize playgroups, food co-ops, squatting, outings and other co-operative projects among claimants. Ten regional co-ordinating claimants' unions. Publish claimants' guidebook and newspaper, and *Women and Social Security* (p. 229).

London-south BATTERSEA AND WANDSWORTH CU, *172 Lavender Hill, London SE11*

London-north EAST LONDON CU, *Dame Colet House, Ben Johnson Rd, London E1*

North-west MANCHESTER CU, *Mosside People's Centre, St Mary's St, Manchester 15*

South-west BRISTOL CU, *54 Richmond Rd, Montpelier, Bristol 6*

North-east BUTTERSHORE CU, *2 Strensal Green, Buttershore, Bradford 6*

North EAST CUMBERLAND CU, *Low Broomhill, Low Row, Brampton, Cumberland*

Midlands MIDLANDS CU, *19 Carlyle Rd, Birmingham B16 9BH*

Wales SWANSEA CU, *18 Windsor St,*
Uplands, Swansea

Scotland EDINBURGH CU,
20 Stanley Rd, Edinburgh

Ireland DERRY CU, *87 Bishop St,*
Derry, N. Ireland

Victim and Criminal

WOMEN AND CRIME,
c/o Radical Alternatives to Prison,
Eastbourne House, Bullards Pl.,
London E2 (01-981 0041). Started
October 1975, with series of meetings
on crime, battered women, prisoners'
friends and families, and women in
prison. Plan to expand activities as
particular needs are discovered.
Meetings Tuesdays 7pm, Rm 321,
Polytechnic of Central London,
Marylebone Rd, London NW1

BIT (p. 196)

CITIZENS' ADVICE BUREAUX (CAB).
Look up address of local bureaux
in phone book

THE FAMILY FIRST TRUST, *The Croft,*
Alexandra Park, Nottingham, Notts.
MARY WARD CENTRE, *9 Tavistock Pl.,*
London WC1

NATIONAL COUNCIL FOR CIVIL
LIBERTIES, *186 Kings Cross Rd,*
London WC1 (01-278 9575)
NATIONAL SOCIETY FOR THE
PREVENTION OF CRUELTY TO

CHILDREN, *National Headquarters,*
1 Riding House St, London W1
(01-580 8812)

NEIGHBOURHOOD LAW CENTRE. Get the
address of your local centre or of
sympathetic solicitors from the LEGAL
ACTION GROUP, *28a Highgate Rd,*
London NW5 (01-485 1189)

PRISONERS' WIVES AND FAMILIES
SOCIETY, *14 Richmond Av., London N1*
(01-278 3981). Campaigning for
better conditions for prisoners and
their families; better visiting
facilities; better communications
between prisoners and families (e.g.
more letters and sending gifts to
prisoners be allowed; more parole
and home leave; setting up family
visiting centres); full rates of pay for
work done by prisoners. Offer
information, advice, practical help to
prisoners' wives and dependants

RELEASE, *1 Elgin Av., London W9*
(01-289 1123)

Battered women and rape

This section lists groups concerned with the protection of women
subject to or threatened with violence, either in the home or outside.

Women's aid

Name given to groups working to provide refuge for women driven
out of their homes by the violence of the men they live with. Phone
numbers of local centres are available from the London address,

and also from local women's centres and women's groups (p. 173ff). The WOMEN'S AID FEDERATION has regular national and regional meetings of women involved in battered women's refuges. They will also offer help and advice about grants, etc., to women setting up new centres. The WOMEN'S AID CENTRES which have grown out of women's liberation groups are committed to running the centres as far as possible according to the decisions of the women who seek refuge, avoiding rules and regulations. Others are organized more formally.

THE WOMEN'S AID FEDERATION,
51 Chalcot Rd, London NW1
(01-586 0104)

THE SCOTTISH WOMEN'S AID
FEDERATION, *c/o 4 Fleming Pl.,*
St Andrews, Fife

CHISWICK WOMEN'S AID, the first
centre to be opened in Britain by
Erin Pizzey (see p. 230 for her book)

Rape

A number of women's groups are starting RAPE CRISIS GROUPS. 'The purpose of a Rape Crisis Service would be to assist victims of rape and other sexual assaults by offering them legal advice, medical advice, psychological counselling, emergency accommodation if necessary, and above all the attention, sympathy, and understanding of other women' (from *Cambridge Women's Newsletter*, November 1975).

Groups meet to find out how rape cases are dealt with by doctors, the law, the police and the authorities, and to find a base for the service. Later they are ready to offer a phone service for women who have been raped, and to offer support, including someone to go with the victim to the police station if necessary. Groups are starting in Derby, Cambridge, London, Newcastle-upon-Tyne, Sheffield and other towns.

THE RAPE COUNSELLING AND RESEARCH PROJECT, has set up a Rape Crisis Centre in London: 01-340 6145. 24-hour service. P.O. Box 42, London N6 5BU.

Plans to publish pamphlets including setting up rape crisis service advice to counsellors, legal and medical information for victims and counsellors. Also hopes to extend the rape-counselling network and to train women to help others equip themselves emotionally to cope with rape and to defend themselves more effectively; to produce publicity to destroy current myths about rape (p. 144). Also doing research on pattern and incidence of rape

Other helpful organizations for this section are the NCCL, RELEASE, MARY WARD CENTRE, your local CAB and The LEGAL ACTION GROUP (who will find you a sympathetic solicitor). Addresses, p. 196.

Celebrations

These resources are largely from the women's movement. There's a good deal of material available, but it's often difficult to find.

Audio-visual

This section lists groups and organizations which produce and/or stock films, slides, video and tapes of interest to women and useful for showing to women's studies and other groups. It also lists some of the material women have produced. We haven't been able to include all the material, so write for futher information.

THE OTHER CINEMA, *12–13 Little Newport St, London WC2H 7JJ* (01-734 8508/9). 16 mm and black and white unless otherwise stated. The following made by the LONDON WOMEN'S FILM GROUP unless otherwise stated.

Women Against The Bill UK 1972 20 mins £4.50. Produced by ACCT Freeprop Films. Women shop stewards discussing the Industrial Relations Bill and what it means to them as women

Serve and Obey UK 1972 3 mins £2.50. Schoolgirls discuss their education, its irrelevance to them and how it differs from boys' education

Betteshanger, Kent 1972 UK 10 mins £3. About a woman involved in organizing women in a Kent mining community to support the 1972 miners' strike; also questions such as equal pay, housework, nursery facilities

Women of the Rhondda UK 20 mins £4.50. Based on interviews with four women about their memories of the General Strike and the role played in mining communities during the 20s and 30s. The women talk about their own job opportunities, education, trade union experience etc.

Fakenham Occupation UK 10 mins £3. About the take-over of a shoe factory by women workers threatened with redundancies

Miss/Mrs UK 6 mins £2.50. Explores and contrasts various images of women, from the strip dancer to the bride to the over-burdened housewife. Shows the difference between images women are supposed to conform to and what really happens.

The Amazing Equal Pay Show UK 1974 50 mins £12 colour. Fictional, music, dance, comedy. Deals with equal pay, legislation and problems facing women in male-dominated trade unions. Produced with LONDON WOMEN'S STREET THEATRE GROUP

The LONDON WOMEN'S FILM GROUP, 38 Earlham St, London WC2 will send someone to join in discussion after showing the films

LIBERATION FILMS, 6 Bramshill Gdns, London NW5 1JH (01-263 0163). Distribute the following, all 16 mm and black and white unless otherwise stated.

Co-habitation UK 1973 10 mins £2.50. Produced by Central London Polytechnic. Deals with the working of the cohabitation rules of the supplementary benefit scheme, using 2 case studies from HACKNEY CLAIMANTS' UNION

Janey's Jane US 1971 30 mins £3.50. Produced by Newsreel. A filmed interview with a mother of 5 children, separated from her husband, talking about her life and family

Woman, Are You Satisfied With Your Life? UK 1969 10 mins silent £1.25. Produced by TUFNELL PARK WOMEN'S LIBERATION GROUP. Silent film contrasting the real-life struggles of women with the mythical life image portrayed in the advertising media

A Woman's Place UK 1971 32 mins £3.50. Produced by Liberation Films. Film from the Women's Liberation conference in Oxford, February 1970 and the March 1971 women's demonstration on International Women's Day

Women Talking UK 1969–70 90 mins £6. Produced by Midge MacKenzie. A number of different women talking about themselves, their situations, and their growing political awareness as women, their need for liberation, and what can be done. The final scene is a discussion filmed after a showing of the film

One Two Three UK 1975 32 mins £5 colour. Produced by Sue Crockford. A film about the CHILDREN'S COMMUNITY CENTRE, Highgate New Town, London, showing the centre at work, the involvement of parents and other adults, and a discussion of the ideas which informed its development

CONCORD FILMS LTD, Nacton, Ipswich, Suffolk IP10 0JZ (0473-7602). Distributes the following; all 16mm and black and white unless otherwise stated. .

More Than Fair 1974 28 mins £2.60. Unesco television film showing aspects of women's position in society arguing for the recognition of women as equal partners with men in world development

Two Women 50 mins £4.40. Thames TV film comparing the lives of 2 women: a computer operator in Hungary and a housewife in England

The Important Thing Is Love 50 mins £4.40. Lesbians talking frankly about themselves and their lives

Women in Prison 70 mins £6. A BBC-TV Man Alive programme showing women in Holloway prison talking about their lives there

Women Alone 1973 27 mins £3. About the lives of a widow and a deserted wife in Australia, showing the emotional and financial hardships they experience and how they cope

Three Island Women 17 mins £3.60 colour. Three women (young, middle-aged and old) talk about life on a small Chinese island in Hong Kong waters

A Chinese Farm Wife 17 mins £3.60 colour. A Chinese woman farm-worker talks about her active life

SPARE RIB, 9 *Newburgh St, London W1A 4XS* (01-439 1674). Distributes the following:

The Big Chakra 13 mins price negotiable. 'A meditation on the human female vagina'

Schmeerguntz 15 mins £3.50 (Gunvor Nelson). A collage showing the daily life of a housewife: the images which television and films usually miss out

Take Off 12 mins £3 (Gunvor Nelson). A stripper at work

My Name is Oona 10 mins £3 (Gunvor Nelson). Images of a young girl becoming conscious of herself as she grows older

Moons Pool 15 mins £4 (Gunvor Nelson). An underwater fantasy

Kirsa Nicholina 16 mins £3.50 (Gunvor Nelson). Film of a child being born to a woman in her own home

Sylvia, Fran and Joy 30 mins price negotiable (Joan Churchill). Documentary of 3 women talking about their lives

I Change I am the Same 1 min price negotiable (Anne Severson). A series of fast role and clothes changes between woman and man on a balcony

CENTRAL FILM LIBRARY, *Government Buildings, Bromyard Av., London W3* (01-743 5555). Distributes the following:

Bridget McEwan – Engineer 10 mins. Shows how a woman becomes an engineering apprentice at Rolls-Royce and goes on to do an engineering degree

BBC FURTHER EDUCATION, *BBC Enterprises Film Hire, 25 The Burroughs, Hendon, London NW4 4AT* (01-202 5342). Distributes the following:

Women at Work 1975 5-part series 25 mins each £10 each (Suzanne Davies/BBC Further Education)

Other interesting films and audio-visual material include:

Women's Fight For Free Abortion on Demand UK 1975 25 mins b & w £5. Produced by Newsreel

The Nightcleaners 1974 2 parts 90 mins each part price neogiable. A documentary on the lives of nightcleaners and on their struggle for better pay and conditions of work, and unionization

Frames UK 5 mins £3 colour. Highlights the images and functions of women in our society as the outlines of a woman's face are gradually covered with a wide variety of masks

The BRITISH FILM INSTITUTE publishes a catalogue of films by women, about women or of interest to women, *Women and Film Resources Handbook*, EDUCATIONAL ADVISORY SERVICE, British Film Institute, *81 Dean St, London W1V 6AA* (01-437 4355). The films are available from the BFI Distribution Library, *42/3 Lower Marsh, London SE1* (01-928 2986). For further information on films relevant to women, contact the LONDON WOMEN'S FILM GROUP, the OTHER CINEMA, LIBERATION FILMS, the BFI, CONCORD FILMS, the BBC or SPARE RIB.

The following is material about the women's movement produced by groups within the movement.

How It Is. Videotape produced by Bolton Women's Liberation, *3 Lighthouse Av., Bolton, Lancs*. Dramatization of issues of the women's movement; intended for use in colleges of further education

Video of the Edinburgh Women's Conference 1974 Available through The Women's Centre, *218 Upper Brook St, Manchester 13*. Filmed on condition that it will be shown only to women

Bristol WL Gp 1974 60 mins price negotiable. Cassette sound-tape made for BBC Radio Bristol by members of Bristol Women's Liberation Group. Available from Helen Taylor, Lecturer in English and Communications, *Bristol Polytechnic, Ashley Down Rd, Bristol BS7 9BU*

Bristol Women's ACC 1974 30 mins ½″ National videotape b& w + Philips video cassette colour price negotiable. Available from WACC Women's Centre, *59 Lower Union St, Bristol BS1 2DU*. Women talking about their lives and their experiences of contraception and abortion; also demonstrates a pregnancy test as done by the WACC group

The Photography Workshop, 152 Upper St, London N1. Also 3 slide shows:
– Images of children from birth onwards, showing the clearly defined sex roles.
– A collection of ads about the other side of 'the perfect body' image – drugs, hair removal, piles, over-weight, 'breast developers'. Includes a section on sanitary towels, tampons, contraceptive ads. Useful introduction to discussing the body.
– Complete life cycle of women as depicted in adverts, including how to get your man, the pre-wedding period, preparing the home, the wedding, honeymoon, pre-motherhood, motherhood, family life. Good for showing with the contrasting images of the first two and HACKNEY FLASHERS' *Women and Work* show (p. 00). Hackney Flashers, *c/o 152 Upper St, London N1*.

Sheffield Radio Series
Tapes and a pamphlet from a feminist local radio series broadcast on Sheffield, *Not Just a Pretty Face;* six 20-minute programmes about the part played by women in society, relations between men and women in familiar contexts like education, domestic life, child-care and so on. Aimed at ages 14–17 but good general introduction. Available from Radio Sheffield

Bibliographies and catalogues:
An annotated bibliography of audio-visual materials on the subject of women's role in society, selected for particular use in further education, compiled by Helen Taylor, Lecturer in English and Communications, *Bristol Polytechnic, Ashley Down Rd, Bristol BS7 9BU*. Available with SAE from this address. This lists addresses of film-hire companies, and titles of films, price, length and short descriptions.

Theatre

LONDON WOMEN'S THEATRE GROUP, *22a Grosvenor Av., London N5* (01-226 4243). Interested mainly in performing in schools and youth clubs and following up performances with audience discussion. *My Mother Says I Never Should* is about 2 girls growing up; it raises issues of contraception and abortion and comments on women's traditional roles. Good starting-point for discussion. New play, *Work to Role*, follows up some of these issues while looking at the working lives of women and young girls

WOMEN'S STREET THEATRE, *73 Ridge Rd, London N8*. Has done play on Equal Pay (filmed as part of *The Amazing Equal Pay Show* by the London Women's Film Group, p. 00); is working on others

RED LADDER THEATRE, *c/o Marian Sedley, 20 Westminster Buildings,*

New York St, Leeds (0532-456 342). Both men and women actors; perform a play called *Women in the Trade Unions: Equal Pay*, an effective portrayal of women and work. Performed with minimum of props and can be put on in any hall or large room

BROADSIDE MOBILE WORKER'S THEATRE, *58 Holbein House, Holbein Pl., London SW1N BNJ* (01-730 5396 or 01-691 3702). Perform various plays, including one on women's issues. London based, but also tour

SISTERSHOW WOMEN'S THEATRE GROUP, *c/o Women's Centre, 59 Lower Union St, Bristol BS1 2DU* (0272-22760). Has produced several sister-shows, performed at conferences and at the Edinburgh Festival

WOMEN'S COMPANY, *Ann Mitchell, 17–18 Harrington Sq., London NW1* (01-387 3200)

Music

STEPNEY SISTERS, *c/o London Women's Liberation Workshop, 38 Earlham St, London WC2*. Group of women in London who play together as women's rock band

THE NORTHERN WOMEN'S LIBERATION ROCK BAND, *c/o 218 Upper Brook St, Manchester 13*. Has played at women's conferences, strike benefits, women's prisons etc.

Art

Women who produce creative work have set up groups where they can share their work with other women. Some of these are listed here. To find others and for news of exhibitions look at one of the newsletters (p. 191) or at *Spare Rib*.

FEMINIST ARTISTS, *c/o K. Walker, Women's Liberation Workshop, 38 Earlham St, London WC2*

WOMEN'S ART HISTORY COLLECTIVE, *65 Albert Palace Mansions, Lurline Gdns, London SW11* (01-622 8530)

WOMENS' ARTISTS GROUP, *20 Valentine Rd, Moseley, Birmingham 14*

WOMEN ARTISTS GROUP, *c/o The Women's Centre, 2nd floor, 59 Union St, Bristol BS1 2DU*

WOMEN ARTISTS' COLLECTIVE, *43 Blenheim Cres., London W11.* Working to encourage formation of small local groups and to start cultural centre

WOMEN'S FREE ARTS ALLIANCE, *Women's Art Centre, 10 Cambridge Terrace Mews, London NW1* (01-935 1841). Aims to encourage all forms of creativity in women. Workshops in theatre, dance, music, printing, photography, weaving, yoga, poetry, co-counselling, self-defence. Sponsors seminars, performances, exhibitions, lectures and film shows. Studio space for women artists and groups. An exchange programme being arranged with Women's Interart Center in New York

ART RESEARCH, *P.O. Box 6, Liverpool L8 1YG*. SAE with inquiries. Radical esoteric feminist art group. Free lessons in esoteric feminist meditation available for all feminists

HACKNEY FLASHERS COLLECTIVE, *c/o 152 Upper St, London N1.* Open group documenting the lives of women in Hackney. Produced exhibition *Women at Work in Hackney*. Slide show available for hire. Producing child-care exhibition

FACES COLLECTIVE, *c/o 152 Upper St, London N1.* Closed group, but holds occasional open workshops, including slide-shows and practical work

Communications

The communications media (television, radio, newspapers and advertisements) are among the most powerful opinion- and image-formers in society. The images they present of women are usually oversimplified and conventional and help to perpetuate existing roles for men and women. The groups listed below are working in this area.

WOMEN IN THE COMMUNICATIONS INDUSTRY, *170 Stroud Green Rd, London N4 3RS* (01-263 0410). Broad cross-union organization for all workers in communication industries; welcomes women in communications who do not belong to a trade union. Adopted the Working Women's Charter Working on producing guide-lines for a non-sexist code of practice in communications industry. Copies of code available from the above address

ALLIANCE FOR FAIR IMAGES AND REPRESENTATION IN THE MEDIA (AFFIRM), *Garden Flat, 11 North Rd, London N6*. Group of women campaigning against sexism and offensive stereotyping of women and of homosexuals in media, advertising, press

WOMEN IN MEDIA, *59 Drayton Gdns, London SW10*. Group of women working at every level in journalism, television, publishing, radio, cinema, theatre and publicity for improved situation and images for all women. Monthly meetings

Printing and publishing groups

There are a number of groups involved in printing and publishing feminist literature.

FEMINIST BOOKS, *PO Box HP5, Leeds LS6 1LN*. Non-commercial publishing group publishing feminist books, a number of pamphlets and feminist postcards

LEEDS WOMEN'S PRESS, *c/o Flat 2, 150 Woodsley Rd, Leeds LS2 9LZ*. Plan for a press owned and run by women, to print feminist literature

VIRAGO, *3 Cheyne Pl., London SW3 4HH* (01-352 0524). A feminist imprint. Has published a number of books, including this directory

WOMEN IN PRINT, *139 Hemingford Rd, London N1* (01-607 1724). Group of women learning to print and planning to acquire their own press for use in printing feminist literature. Already have a good deal of equipment

WOMEN'S PRESS GROUP, *c/o Lilian Mohin, 89 Ladbroke Gr., London W11*

Distribution

FEDERATION OF ALTERNATIVE BOOKSHOPS, c/o Grass Roots (p. 00). Setting up distribution network

THE FEMINIST LITERATURE DISTRIBUTION NETWORK, *c/o Feminist Books,*

PO Box HP5, Leeds LS6 1LN. Aims to make feminist literature of all kinds widely available. Publishes regular literature list, and supplies at discount to women's groups and bookshops

Bookshops

It's likely that you'll know the major bookshops in your town, W. H. Smith and so on. This list therefore concentrates on the smaller sometimes more specialist bookshops likely to stock books and pamphlets which might otherwise be difficult to find. Many sell books by direct mail and have catalogues. Telephone numbers, where they apply, can be found in the phone book or obtained from directory enquiries.

Banner Books, 90 Camden High St, NW1

Bellman Books, 155 Fortress Rd, NW5

Bethnal Rouge, 248 Bethnal Green Rd, E2

Bogle l'Ouverture, 141 Coldershaw Rd, W13

Book Addict, 186 Wandsworth Bridge Rd, SW6

Central Books, 37 Gray's Inn Rd, WC1

Centreprise, 136 Kingland High St, E8

Colletts, 66 Charing Cross Rd, WC2

Compendium, 240 Camden High St, NW1

Freedom Bookshop, 84b Whitechapel High St, E1

Grass Roots Storefront, 61 Golborne Rd, W11

Hammersmith Books, Barnes High St, SW13

High Hill Bookshop, 6–7 Hampstead High St, NW3

Houseman's, 5 Caledonian Rd, N1

IS Books, 265 Seven Sisters Rd, N4

Moonfleet, 39 Clapham Park Rd, SW4

Muswell Hill Bookshop, 29 Fortis Green Rd, N10

New Beacon Books, 76 Stroud Green Rd, N4

Paperback Centre, 28 Charlotte St, W1

Pathfinder Press, 47 The Cut, SE1

Progressive Books, 569 Old Kent Rd, SE14

Red Books, 24 Boundary Rd, NW8

Rising Free Bookshop, 142 Drummond St, NW1

Sisterhood Books, c/o 22 Windmill St, W1

Spark Bookshop, 18 Cecile Pk, N8

Sterling Bookstore, 57 St Martin's La., WC2

Village Books, 7 Shrubbery Rd, SW16

Village Bookshop, 69 Regent St, W1

World Books, 375 Cambridge Heath Rd, E2

BATH, Avon
University Bookshop, Claverton Down

BIRMINGHAM
Action Centre, 40 Hall Rd, Handsworth
Key Books, 25 Essex St
Peace Centre, 18 Moor St, Ringway

BRIGHTON, Sussex
Public House Bookstore, 21 Little Preston St
The Unicorn, Gloucester Rd

BRISTOL
Chapter and Verse, 86 Park St
Women's Books, The Women's Centre, 59 Lower Union St
Falling Wall Press, 79 Richmond Rd, Montpelier

CAMBRIDGE
Last Exit, 54 Mill Rd
Bowes and Bowes, 1 Trinity St
Heffers, Trinity St

CANTERBURY, Kent
Albion Bookshop, 13 Mercery La.
Dillons Canterbury Bookshop, The Library Building, University of Canterbury

CARDIFF, Wales
Communist Bookshop, 108 Salisbury Rd, Cathays

CHELTENHAM, Glos.
General Store Basement
11 Grosvenor Pl., South

COLCHESTER, Essex
John Drury, 11 East Stockwell St

COVENTRY, Warks.
The Left Centre, 65 Queen Victoria Rd

DONCASTER
Proletaria, 289 Station Rd,
Dunscroft

DURHAM
Ivan Corbett, 89 Elvet Bridge

EDINBURGH
Shirlee's Stall, Greyfriars Market,
14 Forrest Rd
H. Rutovitz, Hendricks House,
31 Royal Ter.

EXETER Devon
University Bookshop,
Devonshire House, Stocher Rd

HUDDERSFIELD, Yorkshire
Greenhead Books, Carlton House,
Whitestone La.

HULL
John Sheridan, 19 Anlanby Rd
Bogus, 21 Prince's Av.
Martin Shaw, IS Books,
67 Salisbury St

IPSWICH
Orwell Books, 4 Upper Orwell St

KEELE, Staffordshire
Students Bookshop, University of
Keele

LANCASTER
University Bookshop, Alexandra Sq.,
Bailrigg
Single Step, 86 King St

LEAMINGTON SPA, Warks
The Other Branch, 7 Regent Pl.

LEEDS
Books, 84 Woodhouse La.
Subterraneum, 66a New Briggate

LEICESTER
Black Flag, 1 Wine St

LIVERPOOL
October Books, 99 Mount Pleasant
News from Nowhere, 9 Sefton Dr.
Atticus Bookshop, 38 Clarence St

LUTON, Bedfordshire
Partisan Books, 34 Dallow Rd

MANCHESTER
Grass Roots, 109 Oxford Rd

NEWCASTLE
People's Bookshop, 189 Westgate Rd

NOTTINGHAM
Pathfinder Book Centre,
93 Goldsmith St
Mushroom, 15 Heathcote St

OXFORD
Blackwell's, Broad St
Parker's, Broad St
Thornton's, Broad St

PLYMOUTH, Devon
Narnia, 8a Camden St, North Hill

ST ALBANS, Herts
Index Books, 101a St Peter's St

SHEFFIELD
Sheffield Bookshop, 93 Wicker St

SOUTHSEA
Spice Island, 30 Osborne Rd

SOUTHAMPTON
Red Light Books, 202 Derby Rd
The Bookshop, 35 St Mary's Rd

WINCHESTER
Tara Books, Shortacre Park Rd

Select Bibliography

This section lists a selection of books and pamphlets you will find useful and interesting. Many of them are by women. All are about women or subjects of interest to them. Books which are good introductions to the issues are marked with an asterisk. Prices of pamphlets are included; '(pb)' indicates that the publication is a paperback. You will find more literature by following up references in the books listed here, and by using other bibliographies, p.232. The section is subdivided as follows:

1. General handbooks
2. Women and history
3. Women and society
4. Books and pamphlets by section
   - Our bodies, our minds
   - Living together, living alone
   - Children
   - After school
   - Working
   - Sex discrimination
   - Money
   - Women: victim and criminal
   - Celebrations: film, theatre, literature, music, visual arts
   - Other bibliographies

General handbooks

* BOSTON WOMEN'S HEALTH COLLECTIVE, *Our Bodies Ourselves*, Simon & Schuster 1976 – guide for women, covering reproduction, sexuality, homosexuality, nutrition, birth control, abortion, having children, rape, exercise, the menopause and health
* A. COOTE & T. GILL, *Women's Rights – A Practical Guide*, Penguin 1974 (pb) – guide to the laws, tradition and regulations which affect women, covering equal pay, welfare benefits, birth control, marriage, divorce, maintenance, custody, education, housing, immigration and prison
  S. RENNIE & K. GRIMSTAD, *The New Women's Survival Catalog*, Coward McCann and Geoghan 1973; and *The New Woman's Survival Sourcebook*, Random House 1975 – guides to groups, books and other resources from the women's movement in the United States and elsewhere
  N. SAUNDERS, *Alternative London, Alternative England and Wales*; and

B. WRIGHT & C. WORSLEY, *Alternative Scotland*, Wildwood House/Saunders 1975 – guides to housing, communications, drugs, homemaking, eating, liberation, crafts, self-development, sex, getting around, surviving in London and all over the country

History

V. BULLOUGH, *The Subordinate Sex*, University of Illinois Press, 1973

M. CHAMBERLAIN, *Fenwomen*, Virago 1975

E. GOULD DAVIS, *The First Sex*, Penguin 1975 (pb)

B. EHRENREICH & D. ENGLISH, *Witches, Midwives and Nurses – Complaints and Disorders – The Sexual Politics of Sickness*, Compendium 1975

E. GOLDMAN, *Living My Life*, Dover 1971, 2 vols, (pb)

P. LASLETT, *The World We Have Lost*, Methuen 1971 (pb)

* M. MEAD, *Male and Female*, Penguin 1971 (pb)

M. MEAD, *Sex and Temperament in Three Primitive Societies*, Dell 1967

* J. S. MILL, *The Subjection of Women*, Dent 1972

E. MORGAN, *The Descent of Woman*, Corgi 1974 (pb)

* J. O'FAOLAIN & L. MARTINES (eds), *Not in God's Image – A History of Women in Europe from the Greeks to the Nineteenth Century*, Fontana 1975 (pb)

C. PORTER, *Fathers and Daughters – Russian Women in Revolution*, Virago 1976

A. RAEBURN, *The Militant Suffragettes*, Michael Joseph 1973 (pb)

E. REED, *Women's Evolution*, Pathfinder 1975 (pb)

M. ROSALDO & L. LAMPHERE, *Women, Culture and Society*, Stanford University Press 1974 (pb)

A. ROSEN, *Rise Up Women*, Routledge 1974

C. ROVER, *Love, Morals and the Feminists*, Routledge 1970

* S. ROWBOTHAM, *Hidden from History*, Pluto 1973 (pb)

S. ROWBOTHAM, *Women, Resistance and Revolution*, Penguin 1974 (pb)

M. STONE, *The Paradise Papers*, Virago 1976

W. THONNERSON, *The Emancipation of Women – the rise and decline of the women's movement in german social democracy 1863-1933*, Pluto 1969

C. TOMALIN, *The Life and Death of Mary Wollstonecraft*, Weidenfeld & Nicolson 1974

E. WILSON, *Women and the Welfare State*, Red Rag pamphlet no. 2 1974

* M. WOLLSTONECRAFT, *A Vindication of the Rights of Women*, Penguin 1975 (pb)

C. WOODHAM SMITH, *Florence Nightingale*, Fontana 1969 (pb)

see S. Rowbotham, *Women's Liberation and Revolution* (p. 232) for a fuller list

Women and society

R. ADAM, *A Woman's Place 1910–1975*, Chatto & Windus 1975

P. ALLEN, *Free Space – a perspective on the small group in women's liberation*, Times Change 1970 (pb)

* S. ALLEN, L. SANDER & J. WALLIS, *Conditions of Illusion – papers from the women's movement*, Feminist 1975 (pb)

E. H. ALTBACH (ed.), *From Feminism to Liberation*, Schenkman 1974 (pb)

T. G. ATKINSON, *Amazon Odyssey*, Links 1974 (pb)

* S. DE BEAUVOIR, *The Second Sex*, Penguin 1972 (pb)

B. C. BLUH, *Woman to Woman – European Feminists*, Starogubski Press 1974

M. BRADLEY and others, *Unbecoming Men*, Times Change 1971 (pb)

M. DALY, *Beyond God The Father*, Beacon Press 1973 (pb)

F. ENGELS, *The Origin of the Family*, Pathfinder 1972 (pb)

* E. FIGES, *Patriarchal Attitudes*, Panther 1972 (pb)

S. FIRESTONE, *The Dialectic of Sex*, Paladin 1972 (pb)

* B. FRIEDAN, *The Feminine Mystique*, Penguin 1965 (pb)

V. GIRNICK & B. MORAN, *Woman in Sexist Society – Studies in Power and Powerlessness*, Signet 1971 (pb)

E. GOLDMAN, *The Traffic in Women and other essays on Feminism*, Times Change 1970 (pb)

R. GRAVES, *The White Goddess*, Faber 1961 (pb)

* G. GREER, *The Female Eunuch*, Paladin 1971 (pb)

J. HOLE & E. LEVINE, *Rebirth of Feminism*, Quadrangle 1971 (pb)

E. JANEWAY, *Man's World Women's Place*, Michael Joseph 1972

J. KING & M. STOTT (eds), *Is this your Life?*, Virago 1977

V. I. LENIN, *On the Emancipation of Women*, International Publishing Co. 1970

J. MITCHELL, *Women's Estate*, Penguin 1973

* R. MORGAN (ed.), *Sisterhood is Powerful*, Vintage 1970 (pb)

A. OAKLEY, *Sex, Gender and Society*, Temple Smith 1972

S. ROWBOTHAM, *Women's Consciousness, Man's World*, Penguin 1974 (pb)

E. SULLEROT, *Woman, Society and Change*, Weidenfeld & Nicolson 1970 (pb)

L. TANNER, *Voices from Women's Liberation*, Signet 1970 (pb)

E. ZARETSKY, *Capitalism, The Family and Personal Life*, Pluto 1975 (pb)

We have not had space to include the vast literature on women in other countries.

Books and pamphlets by section

Our bodies, our minds

* S. ABBOTT & B. LOVE, *Sappho was a Right-on Woman*, Stein & Day 1973

ABORTION LAW REFORM ASSOCIATION, *A Woman's Right to Choose*, 1975

* L. BARBACH, *For Yourself – a Guide to Orgasmic Response*, Doubleday 1975

M. BARNES, *Two Accounts of a Journey through Madness*, Penguin 1973 (pb)

I. BENGIS, *Combat in the Erogenous Zone*, Quartet 1974 (pb)

H. BENJAMIN, *The Transexual Phenomenon*, Julian Press 1966

H. BENNETT & M. SAMUELS, *The Well Body Book*, Wildwood House/Bookworks 1974 (pb)

* BOSTON WOMEN'S HEALTH COLLECTIVE, *Our Bodies Ourselves*, Simon & Schuster, 1976

J. BROWN, E. BURYN, E. LESSER & S. MINES, *Two Births*, Random House/ Bookworks 1972 (pb)

* P. CHESLER, *Women and Madness*, Avon 1972 (pb)
  CONSUMERS ASSOCIATION HANDBOOKS, *Pregnancy*, 1974; *New Born Baby*, 1974;
  Sex with Health (contraception), 1972; *Infertility*, 1972
  W. COOPER, *No Change – a biological revolution for women*, Hutchinson 1975
  K. DALTON, *The Menstrual Cycle*, Penguin 1969 (pb)
  GAY LIBERATION FRONT, *Psychiatry and the Homosexual*, GLF pamphlet no. 1
  C. P. GILMAN, *The Yellow Wallpaper*, Feminist Press 1973
  Issues in Radical Therapy, IRT Collective, PO Box 23544, Oakland, California
  94623, USA
  W. GREENGROSS, *Entitled to Love*, Malaby Press 1976
* A. KILMARTIN, *Understanding Cystitis*, Heinemann 1973 (pb)
  A. C. KINSEY, *Sexual Behaviour in the Human Female*, W. B. Saunders 1953
  S. KITZINGER, *The Experience of Childbirth*, Penguin 1970 (pb)
  R. D. LAING & A. E. ESTERSON, *Sanity, Madness and the Family*, Penguin 1970 (pb)
  The Lane Report, HMSO 1974, 3 vols (report on the Lane Committee's
  investigation into abortion facilities in Britain)
* F. LEBOYER, *Birth Without Violence*, Wildwood House 1975
  D. MARTIN & P. LYON, *Lesbian Woman*, Glide Publications 1972
  T. MCGUIRE, *The Tooth Trip*, Wildwood House/Bookworks 1975 (pb)
* N. MCKEITH (ed.), *British Women's Health Handbook*, Feminist 1976 (pb)
* J. B. MILLER (ed.), *Psychoanalysis and Women*, Penguin 1974 (pb)
  K. MILLETT, *Flying*, Ballantine 1974 (pb)
  J. MITCHELL, *Psychoanalysis and Feminism*, Penguin 1975 (pb)
  MONTREAL HEALTH GROUP, *Birth Control Handbook*, 1975; *VD Handbook*, 1972
  J. PEEL & M. POTTS, *Textbook of Contraceptive Practice*, Cambridge
  University Press 1969
  E. PHILLIPP, *Childlessness – its causes and what to do about them*, Arrow 1975
  (pb)
  A. K. RUSH, *Getting Clear: Body Work for Women*, Random House/Bookworks
  1972 (pb)
  M. SCHOFIELD, *Promiscuity*, Gollancz 1976
  M. J. SHERFEY, *The Evolution and Nature of Female Sexuality*, Vintage 1972
  SWANSEA WOMEN'S HEALTH GROUP, *Having Your Baby*, Feminist 1976 (pb)
  C. WOOD, *Vasectomy and Sterilization – a guide for men and women*, Temple
  Smith 1974

Living together living alone

* P. ASHDOWN-SHARP, *Single Woman's Guide to Pregnancy and Parenthood*,
  Penguin 1975 (pb)
  J. BERNARD, *The Future of Marriage*, Souvenir Press 1973
* L. CAINE, *Widow*, Houghton Mifflin 1974
* L. COMER, *Wedlocked Women*, Feminist 1975 (pb)
  D. COOPER, *Death of the Family*, Penguin 1972 (pb)
  G. FRIEDMAN, *How to Conduct Your own Divorce in England and Wales*,
  Wildwood House 1975 (pb)
  H. GAVRON, *The Captive Wife – conflicts of housebound mothers*, Penguin 1975
  (pb)
  GINGERBREAD, *One Parent Families – a Finer Future*, Gingerbread 1975 (pb)

C. GORMAN, *People Together*, Paladin 1975 (pb)

ISLINGTON SQUATTERS, *Squatters Handbook*, Islington Squatters, 2 St Pauls Road, London N1 (pb)

P. LASLETT (ed.), *Household and Family in Past Time*, Cambridge University Press 1975 (pb)

M. MEADE, *Bitching*, Garnstone Press 1973

NATIONAL COUNCIL FOR ONE PARENT FAMILIES, *Guide to the Finer Report*, 1975

A. OAKLEY, *Housewife*, Allen Lane 1974

A. OAKLEY, *The Sociology of Housework*, Martin Robertson 1974

A. RIGBY, *Communes in Britain*, Routledge & Kegan Paul 1974 (pb)

* E. RUDINGER, *Getting a Divorce*, Consumers Association, 1972

R. SIMON, *Breaking Up*, Arrow 1974 (pb)

M. TORRIE, *Begin Again*, Aldine 1974 (pb)

P. WILMOTT & M. YOUNG, *Family and Kinship in East London*, Penguin 1969 (pb)

Children

* C. ADAMS & R. LAURIKIETIS, *The Gender Trap*, Virago 1976, 3 vols, (pb)

* P. ARIES, *Centuries of Childhood*, Penguin 1975

* E. G. BELOTTI, *Little Girls*, Readers and Writers Publishing Co-op 1975 (pb)

B. BETTELHEIM, *The Children of the Dream*, Paladin 1971 (pb)

* U. BRONFENBRENNER, *The Two Worlds of Childhood – USA & USSR*, Allen & Unwin 1972

* CALTHORPE PARK PLAYGROUP, *Out of the Pumpkin Shell*, 1976 (pb) (available from Birmingham Women's Centre)

CONSUMERS ASSOCIATION HANDBOOK, *How to Adopt*, 1973

R. DINNAGE & M. K. PRINGLE, *Foster Home Care – Facts and Fallacies*, Longman 1967 (pb)

S. HANSEN & J. JENSEN, *The Little Red Schoolbook*, Stage One 1971 (pb)

I. ILLICH, *Deschooling Society*, Readers and Writers Publishing Co-op 1975 (pb)

M. KELLMER PRINGLE, *The Needs of Children*, Hutchinson 1974

D. KLINE & H. OVERSTREET, *Foster Care of Children*, Columbia University Press 1974 (pb)

J. LUCAS & V. MCKENNELL, *The Penguin Book of Playgroups*, Penguin 1974 (pb)

L. DE MAESE (ed.), *A History of Childhood*, Souvenir 1976

NOTTINGHAM WOMEN'S CENTRE, *Sexism in Education Conference*, 1975 (available from Nottingham Women's Centre)

J. ROWE, *Yours by Choice: A Guide for Adoptive Parents*, Routledge 1968 (pb)

M. RUTTER, *Maternal Deprivation Reassessed*, Penguin 1972 (pb)

D. GERSONI STAVN, *Sexism and Youth*, Bowker 1974

J. STONE & F. TAYLOR, *Handbook for Parents with a Handicapped Child*, CASE Publications, 17 Jacksons Lane, Billericay, Essex (15p)

WHITE LION FREE SCHOOL, *How to Set Up a Free School*, White Lion Free School, 57 White Lion Street, London N1

After school

Details of publications are contained in the section AFTER SCHOOL.

Working

M. BENET, *The Secretary: An Enquiry into the Female Ghetto*, Sidgwick & Jackson 1972 (pb)

* S. BENTON, *Patterns of Discrimination Against Women in the Film and TV Industry: report*, Association of Cinematographic and Television Technicians, 1975

B. BOLTON, *An End to Homeworking*, Fabian Society 1975

A. COOTE, *Women Factory Workers*, NCCL 1974
Danger! Women at Work, NCCL 1974 (50p)

W. EDMOND AND S. FLEMING (eds), *All Work and No Pay: Women, Housework and the Wages Due*, Falling Wall Press 1975 (70p)

M. FOGARTY and others, *Sex Career and Family*, Allen & Unwin 1971

D. GREGORY & J. MCCARTY, *The Shop Steward's Guide to Workplace Health and Safety*, Spokesman Books (60p)

* P. HEWITT, *Rights for Women*, NCCL 1976 (65p)

M. HOBBS, *Born to Struggle*, Quartet 1974 (pb)

J. HUNT, *Organising Women Workers*, WEA

P. KINNERSLEY, *The Hazards of Work and How to Fight Them*, Pluto Press 1974 (pb)

R. LISTER & M. LOWE, *Equal Pay and How to Get It*, NCCL 1975 (20p)

L. LLOYD, *Women Workers in Britain: A Handbook*, Socialist Women Publications 1972

A. MYRDAL & V. KLEIN, *Women's Two Roles: Home and Work*, Routledge 1968 (pb)

R. & R. RAPAPORT, *Dual Career Families*, Penguin 1971 (pb)

A. WISE, *Women and the Struggle for Worker's Control*, Spokesman no. 33

Department of Employment, Manpower Papers:
    no. 9 *Women and Work: A Statistical Survey*, HMSO 1974
    no. 10 *Sex Differences in Society*, HMSO 1974
    no. 11 *Women and Work: A Review*, HSMO 1975
    no. 12 *Women and Work: Overseas Practice*, HMSO 1975

Sex discrimination

* P. HEWITT, *Rights for Women*, NCCL 1976
Sex Discrimination – a guide to the Sex Discrimination Act, HMSO 1975

Money

* CHILD POVERTY ACTION GROUP, *The Co-habitation Rule*, Guide to Supplementary Benefit Appeals Tribunals, National Welfare Benefits Handbook

CLAIMANTS UNION MOVEMENT, *Women and Social Security*

CONSUMERS ASSOCIATION, *Money Which*; *Which Tax Guide*

* A. COOTE & T. GILL, *Women's Rights – a Practical Guide*, Penguin 1974 (pb)

R. LISTER, *Supplementary Benefit Rights*, Arrow 1974 (pb)

T. LYNES, *Penguin Guide to Supplementary Benefits*, Penguin 1972 (pb)

E. WILSON (ed.), *The Woman's Handbook*, New English Library 1975 (pb)

Women: victim and criminal

* S. BROWNMILLER, *Against Our Will – men, women and rape*, Secker & Warburg 1975
  N. CONNELL & C. WILSON, *Rape – a sourcebook for women*, New American Library 1974
* A. COOTE & T. GILL, *Battered Women – how to use the law*, Cobden Trust 1975 (pb)
  A. COOTE & T. GILL, *The Rape Controversy*, NCCL 1975
  A. COOTE & L. GRANT, *Civil Liberty, the NCCL Guide*, NCCL 1972
  J. DAVIES & N. GOODMAN, *Girl Offenders aged 17–20 years*, HMSO 1972
  S. DELL, *Silent in Court*, LSE Occasional Papers, Bell 1967
  R. GIALLOMBARDO, *Society of Women – a study of a woman's prison*, Wiley 1970 (pb)
  K. MILLETT, *The Prostitution Papers*, Paladin 1975 (pb)
* E. PIZZEY, *Scream Quietly or the Neighbours will Hear*, Penguin 1974 (pb)
* J. RENVOIZE, *Children in Danger – causes and prevention of baby battering*, Routledge 1974

Celebrations

Film

M. HASKELL, *From Reverence to Rape: the treatment of women in the movies*, Penquin 1974 (pb)
C. JOHNSTON (ed.), *The Work of Dorothy Arzner: towards a feminist cinema*, British Film Institute 1975
M. ROSEN, *Popcorn Venus*, Peter Owen 1975
J. MELLEN, *Women and their Sexuality in the New Film*, Davis-Poynter 1974

Theatre

I. DUNCAN, *Love Letters to Gordon Craig*, Random House 1971
J. ELFORM, *Erotic Theatre*, Secker and Warburg 1973
R. FINDLATER, *Lillian Baylis: The Lady of the Old Vic*, Allen Lane 1975
Z. HALLS, *Women's Costumes 1750–1800*, HMSO 1972
E. JOHNS, *Dames of the Theatre*, W. H. Allen 1974
I. SHUBIK, *Play for Today: the evolution of TV drama*, Davis-Poynter 1974
I. TURGENEV, *Letters to an Actress*, Allison & Busby 1973

Literature

There are a number of important women writers whose novels are well worth reading. Most of them are available in paperback or at your local library. We recommend Jane Austen, Simone de Beauvoir, Anne, Charlotte and Emily Bronte, Colette, George Eliot, Mrs Gaskell, Nadine Gordimer, Ursula Le Guin, Doris Lessing, Anais Nin, Jean Rhys, Olive Schreiner, Virginia Woolf. We also recommend the following female poets: Emily Dickinson, Maureen Duffy, Elizabeth Jennings, Erica Jong, Sylvia Plath, Anne Sexton, Rosemary Tonks.

There are also some major male authors who have written particularly sensitive novels and plays about women. We recommend Arnold Bennett's *Anna of the Five Towns* and *The Old Wives' Tale*; Joseph Conrad's *Chance*; Gustave Flaubert's *Madame Bovary*; George Gissing's *Odd Women*; Thomas Hardy's *Tess of the D'Urbervilles*; Nathaniel Hawthorne's *The Scarlet Letter*; Henrik Ibsen's *A Doll's House*; D. H. Lawrence's *Sons and Lovers*; George Meredith's *Diana of the Crossways*; G. B. Shaw's *Mrs Warren's Profession* and Leo Tolstoy's *Anna Karenina*.

We should also like to mention particular novels by some contemporary writers:

DJUNA BARNES, *Nightwood*, Faber 1950 (pb)
M. BARRENO, *The Three Marias – The New Portuguese Letters*, Paladin 1975 (pb)
R. M. BROWN, *Rubyfruit Jungle*, Daughters Inc. 1974 (pb)
M. DUFFY, *That's How it Was*, Hutchinson 1969
NELL DUNN, *Poor Cow*, Pan 1973 (pb)
—, *Up the Junction*, Pan 1973 (pb)
I. MILLER, *Patience and Sarah*, Hart-Davies 1972 (pb)
E. NACHMAN, *Riverfinger Women*, Daughters Inc. 1974 (pb)
MARGE PIERCY, *Small Changes*, Doubleday 1973
CHRISTINA STEAD, *The Man Who Loved Children*, Penguin 1970 (pb)
FAY WELDON, *Down Among the Women*, Penguin 1973 (pb)
—, *Female Friends*, Heinemann 1975
M. WITTIG, *Les Guerillères*, Picador 1971
—, *The Lesbian Body*, Peter Owen 1975

Criticism

F. BASCH, *Relative Creatures: Victorian Women in society and the novel, 1837–67*, Allen Lane 1974.
A. DWORKIN, *Woman Hating*, E. P. Dutton 1974
E. HARDWICK, *Seduction and Betrayal – Women and Literature*, Weidenfeld & Nicolson 1974
C. HEILBRUN, *Towards a Recognition of Androgyny*, Knopf 1973
LONDON WOMEN WRITERS GROUP, *Collection of Poetry and Prose*, Feminist Books 1975 (pb)
K. MILLETT, *Sexual Politics*, Abacus 1971 (pb)
G. B. SHAW, *The Quintessence of Ibsenism*, Constable 1922

Collections

L. BERNIKOW (ed.), *The World Split Open – Four Centuries of Women Poets in England and America 1552–1950*, Vintage 1974 (pb)
J. GOULIANOS (ed.), *By a Woman Writt*, New English Library 1974
F. HOEW & E. BOSS (eds), *No More Masks*, Anchor 1973 (pb)
R. MORGAN, *Monster*, Vintage 1972
MUNDUS ARTIUM, *International Women's Issues – poems from all around the world*.
A. STANFORD (ed.), *The Women Poets in English*, McGraw-Hill 1973

Music

S. DRINKER, *Music and Women*, Coward-McCann 1948
A. ELSON & E. E. TRUETTE, *Woman's Work in Music*, L. C. Page 1931
W. LANDOWSKA, *Landowska on Music*, ed. D. Restout, Stein & Day 1964
E. LUTYENS, *A Goldfish Bowl*, Cassell 1972
E. SMYTHE, *Female Pipings in Eden*, Peter Davies 1933

Art

J. BERGER, *Ways of Seeing*, Penguin 1972 (pb)
T. H. HESS & E. C. BAKER, *Art and Sexual Politics*, Collier-Macmillan 1973 (pb)
E. TUFTS, *Our Hidden Heritage: Five Centuries of Women Artists*, Paddington Press 1974

Other bibliographies

Many books and pamphlets in this bibliography include their own list of literature relevant to the subject of the book, and further reading can be found through them. This section lists more comprehensive bibliographies of literature on women. Some (marked *) are stockists or bookshops with a mail-order service. Send an SAE for these.

* *Bristol Women's Booklist*, 59 Lower Union St, Bristol BS1 2DU
* *Compendium Sexual Politics Catalogue*, 240 Camden High St, London NW1
* *Grassroots Women's Booklist*, 109 Oxford Road, Manchester
  Z. FAIRBAIRNS (ed.), *Women's Studies in the UK*, London Seminars 1975
  LIBRARIANS FOR SOCIAL CHANGE, *Sexual Politics – a basic reading list*, Release 1975 (pb)
  S. RENNIE & K. GRIMSTAD, *The New Women's Survival Catalog*, Coward McCann & Geoghan 1973 (pb)
  —, *The New Women's Survival Sourcebook*, Knopf 1975 (pb)
  S. ROWBOTHAM, *Women's Liberation and Revolution – a bibliography*, Falling Wall Press 1972 (pb)
* *Sisterhood Booklist*, 22 Great Windmill Street, London W1
* *Women's Books and Pamphlets List*, H. Rutovitz, 31 Royal Terrace, Edinburgh 7
* *Women's Liberation Workshop List*, 38 Earlham Street, London WC2
  Women's Work and Women's Studies, The Women's Centre, Barnard College, New York City, NY 10027, 1971, 1972, Know Inc. (over 2500 entries)

Index

abortion, 22, 42–3, 68, 117, 168, 169, 170, 171, 172; right to, 24, 39–40; and anti-abortion backlash, 40–41; addresses, 197–8
Abortion Act (1967), 39–40, 42
Abortion (Amendment) Bill, 41
Abortion Law Reform Association (ALRA), 41
Action for the Disabled Association, 207
acting, women in, 156–8
Adams, Carol, 88
adoption, 82–4; addresses, 207
Adoption Resource Exchange, 83, 207
Adult Education, 97
Advisory Centre for Education (ACE), 72, 89, 90, 93, 96, 204
Advisory, Conciliation and Arbitration Service, 114
Age Concern, 212
agoraphobia, 53, 56
AIM, 190
Al-Anon Family Groups, 202
alcoholism, 53
Alliance for Fair Images and Representation in the Media (AFFIRM), 221
Alternative London, 152
Alternative Prospects of Universities and Polytechnics, 94
Anorexics Aid, 202
anorexia nervosa, 53
ante-natal care, 22, 26, 31; classes, 27–8
Anxieties Anonymous, 202
apprenticeships, 91–2
Argyle, Judge Michael, 151
Art Research, 220
arts, women and the, 154–67, 169, 170; creative groups' addresses, 215–20
Ashley, Jack, 145

Association of British Adoption Agencies, 83, 84
Association of Cinematograph and Television Technicians, 105
Association for Deserted and Alone Parents, 206
Association for Relatives of the Mentally, Emotionally and Nervously Disturbed, 202
Association of British Adoption Agencies, 207
Aware, 172–3, 183
Aware Health Collective, 197

battered children, social problem of, 150–52
battered wives, social problem of, 139–44; addresses, 206–7
BBC Further Education, 217
Beaumont Society, 207
Benton, Sarah, 105
BIT, 152, 196 213, 217
Birkbeck College, 96
birth control, *see* contraception
Birth Without Violence, 31
Black Women's Group, 189
bookshops of specialist literature, addresses, 221–3
Booth, Judith, 100
Boston Women's Health Collective, 23
Bread and Roses, 192
Breaking Up: A Practical Guide to Separation and Divorce, 64
breast, self-examination of, 22; and breast cancer, 47–8
Breast Cancer Self-Examination, 48
breast-feeding *v.* bottle-feeding, 31–3 .

British Association for Early Childhood Education, 205
British Film Institute, 218
British Pregnancy Advisory Service (BPAS), 26, 40
Broadside Mobile Worker's Theatre, 219
Brook Advisory Centre, 26, 33, 48, 198
Brothers/Men Against Sexism, 191
BUPA, 48, 200

Calthorpe Park Playgroup, 78, 205
Cambridge Women's Newsletter, 214
Campaign for Homosexual Equality (CHE), 207
Campaign to Impede Sex Stereotyping in the Young (CISSY), 71, 203
cancer, in women, 47–9
careers, for school-leavers, 86–9; advisory organizations, 89; vocational guidance, 90; training, 91–2; addresses, 209–10; *see also* further education; higher education
Careers Advisory Office, 98–99
Careers Analysts, 90, 209
Careers Encyclopaedia, 88
Careers for Girls, 88
Careers Guide, 88
Careers Intelligence Service, 89
Careers Research and Advisory Centre (CRAC), 89, 209
Careers Services Agency, 89
Central Film Library, 217
cervical examination, 22; cancer, 48–9
Cherish, 206
Chesler, Phyllis, 54
Child Care Outside School Hours, 205

234

236